The Unity of the Trinity

Listening to the Tradition of Israel in the Church

Pierre Lenhardt nds

The Unity of the Trinity

Listening to the Tradition of Israel in the Church

Pierre Lenhardt nds

Translation by Katherine Wolff nds

ATF THEOLOGY

Adelaide
2019

Front Cover: 'Synagoga and Ecclesia in Our Time' by artist Joshua Koffman was commissioned by Saint Joseph's University in Philadelphia to mark the fiftieth anniversary of the 1965 Second Vatican Council declaration Nostra Aetate and the 1967 founding of the university's Institute for Jewish-Catholic Relations.

978-1-925612-84-4 soft
978-1-925612-85-1 hard
978-1-925612-86-8 epub
978-1-925612-87-5 pdf

Cover design by Myf Cadwallader
Layout by Extel Solutions
Text: Minion Pro size 10 &11

Published by:

An imprint of the ATF Press Publishing
Group owned by ATF (Australia) Ltd.
PO Box 504
Hindmarsh, SA 5007
ABN 90 116 359 963
www.atfpress.com
Making a lasting impact

Table of Contents

A Tribute to Pierre Lenhardt, nds

As Superior General of the Religious of Zion and as such it is my pleasure to write to you this tribute to our confrere Pierre Lenhardt, religious of Sion, who made his Passover on 1 July 2019, after a long and happy life in Notre-Dame de Sion.[1]

His Master's thesis, *Conditions for the Legitimacy of a Christian Testimony to the Jews*, under the direction of Professor Pierre Grelot, was never published in French, but translated and published in German under the title, *Auftrag und Unmöglichkeit eines legitimen christlichen Zeugnisses gegenüber den Juden.*[2]

Brother Pierre, in this first exercise of academic research, already raises existential and fundamentally theological question: what would be the conditions of legitimacy of a Christian witness to the Jews. Here there are two things that marked Pierre's entire life: the *sine qua non* condition for a Christian witness, but also a search for legitimacy for a credible listening to Israel, as a Christian.

Thirty-five years after this Master's thesis, laid down as a fundamental stone, life program and research path, Pierre made his major

1. Father Donizeti Luiz Ribiero, nds, Doctor in Theology from the Catholic Institute of Paris, is currently the Superior General of the Congregation of the Religious of Our Lady of Zion (mandate: 2011-2021). The brothers or priests of Zion are a religious congregation born in Paris in 1852 where their Mother House is located. They are present in Brazil, where the General House is located, France and Israel. Their founders, brothers Marie Alphonse and Théodore Ratisbonne, also founded the Congregation of the Religious of Notre-Dame de Sion in Paris.
2. *Auftrag und Unmöglichkeit eines legitimen christlichen Zeugnisses gegenüber den Juden. Eine Untersuchung zum theologischen Stand des Verhältnisses von kirche und jüdischem Volk* (Studien zu jüdischem Volk und christlicher Gemeinde 1), Berlin, 1980.

contributions in two volumes called, *Listening to Israel in the Church*, Essays from the Cathedral School, edited Word and Silence, Paris, 2006 and 2009.[3]

In his first volume of the book, *Listening to Israel in the Church,*[4] Pierre begins by taking up the notion of 'Talmud-Torah' as the leitmotiv (red thread) of his study and teaching. Here is what he wrote in a chapter entitled 'Talmud Torah of the Jews and Jewish Studies of Christians'. 'It is first and foremost the Talmud Torah of the Jews, the study and teaching of the Torah, of the Word of God, which makes it possible to know God and to make him known. It is this Talmud Torah, listened to and studied by Christians, listened to for itself but also and inseparably in its resonance with Jesus Christ, who must and can enlighten the faith, hope and practice of Christians.'[5]

Listening to the Word, both Oral and Written Torah, transmitting it through teaching, especially to Christians, and living as a Christian in this listening to and sharing of the Word, are elements of Brother Pierre life and thought and the invitation which he still addresses us today, to us.and to any Christian who would like to listen to Israel, the root on which we stand.

Pierre Lenhardt was a Religious of Our Lady of Zion and since he entered the 'order', as he liked to say, he had constantly urged his confreres to renew their lives with the charism of Our Lady of Zion. The contribution of Brother Pierre to the formation and charism of Zion is quite central and undeniable. In addition to his many teachings, he wrote notes for the formation of Zion and took part in many general chapters, including the chapter of *aggiornamento*, of updates of our Constitutions.[6]

His most important book is without doubt *The Unity of the Trinity: Listening to the Tradition of Israel*, Collège des Bernardins (Paris:

3. These two books are currently being translated and will be published in Brazil, in the series 'Judaísmo e Cristianismo', CCDEJ/Fons Sapientiae, São Paulo.
4. P Lenhardt, À l'écoute *d'Israël, en Eglise,* Essais de l'Ecole Cathédrale (Paris : Parole et Silence, Paris, 2006).
5. À l'écoute d'*Israël, en Eglise,* volume I, 13.
6. The Constitutions of the Religious of Our Lady of Zion, updated and approved by the Church in 1996, are divided into three parts: 1st: life and mission of the congregation of the religious of Our Lady of Zion; 2nd: formation of its members; and 3rd: organisation and government of Our Lady of Zion.

Parole et Silence, Paris, 2011), ehich we now have here in English translation.[7]

Always faithful to his principle of 'Listening to the Tradition of Israel', Pierre makes a great effort here to think of the fundamental question, as in 1970, of the unity of the Trinity, but this time by articulating it with the great texts of the Tradition of Israel. A fundamental work, difficult to read and surely the crowning achievement of his thought, Pierre Lenhardt makes two dyads resound, as a Christian who listens to Israel, to reach the triad: GOD, TORAH AND THE PEOPLE:

- The first: the unity of God and the Shekinah.
- The second: the unity of the Shekinah and the Holy Spirit.

Pierre heard the triad: God, the Torah and the People in resonance with the Trinity, since the One and Only God is confessed as Father, Son and Holy Spirit.

In a nutshell, I remind you of the coherence of Brother Pierre's journey of life and research: from the Master's thesis in 1970 to the unity of the Trinity, he does not stop listening to Israel and setting the conditions for this listening as a Christian; and then, this which he listens, he does not stop transmitting, from Zion to Zion, working with his brothers and sisters so that the family of Zion does not give up listening to Israel in the Church.

Finally, thanking our dear Pierre and in the joy of seeing his major work translated into English, I leave, to those who are courageous and love research, a beautiful doctoral subject: The conditions for legitimacy of the Listening to the Tradition of Israel, according to the work of Pierre Lenhardt. He who has ears, let him hear.

Thank you very much, dear Brother Pierre. From now on, in the Yerushalayim from above, with the other brothers and sisters of Zion, you listen and live fully in the Presence—Shekinah—of God who is One and Unique.

P Dr Donizeti Luiz Ribeiro, nds
Zion General House, São Paulo, 05 July 2019

7. This book by Pierre Lenhardt is available in Italian, Portuguese, Spanish and now here in English.

Listening to the Tradition of Israel

Note of appreciation by Pierre Lenhart nds for the Translation by Sister Katherine Wolff

Sister Katherine Wolff has done an excellent job translating my book. She assumed the difficulty of the book and respected its imperfections. She wrote a very good translation of the preface by Msgr. Maurice Gardès, which is important to me for several reasons. First of all, this preface gives me a kind of imprimatur which justifies the legitimacy and usefulness of my work in listening to the Tradition of Israel. It is also good that the preface says that the book is difficult. It is, in fact, difficult to read, as it was difficult to write. Msgr. Gardès did not want to say that the book is imperfect. I shall do so. It is imperfect first of all because, of the errors that are more or less inevitable and for which I am responsible. One can also say that it is imperfect because it is incomplete. But there, I shall defend it by saying that its incompleteness corresponds with the study undertaken. The book is incomplete. If I were to claim equality with Michelangelo, one might see it as a torso. However, my claim is of a different kind. I want to make it possible to hear that the Word of God to which Israel's Tradition listens is more powerful than the genius of a human artist. The Tradition regarding the Unity and the Trinity gives more than a torso; it starts out from an unfathomable beginning and goes towards an end that cannot be grasped.

I would like the book to give people the possibility of visiting a building site on which work is still in process. The repetitions, the awkwardness of certain expressions, the chaos in certain explanations testify to the building site's reality. Imperfection, incompleteness - should the book be re-written? I would not be able to do so, and I do not want to do so. The further considerations and the appendices offered at the end of the book sufficiently indicate my wish to see my possible readers setting out in their turn in their search for God, for the meaning of God's Word, of God's Unity which is Trinity.

Pierre Lenhart nds
Paris
June 2019

Preface

Rabbi Eleazar ben 'Azariah said: If there is no Torah, there is no knowledge-of-how-to-live; if there is no knowledge-of-how-to-live, there is no Torah. If there is no wisdom, there is no fear; if there is no fear, there is no wisdom. If there is no discernment, there is no knowledge; if there is no knowledge, there is no discernment. If there is no flour, there is no Torah; if there is no Torah, there is no flour.

(Pirke Avot 3, 17)

This statement by a Father serves as an introduction to Brother Pierre Lenhardt's new book on the Unity of the Trinity. We know that for Christians, the trinitarian mystery was the topic of countless discussions, debates, even theological conflicts before arriving at the words of the Nicean Creed. It is true that God's identity transcends all our attempts at human formulations and that we must nevertheless express our faith.

The importance of this difficult—let's not conceal that fact!—yet gripping book is that it reminds us of our Jewish roots. The author, nourished by rabbinic traditions, leads us on a beautiful journey to the heart of this treasure, of this wealth that we do not know enough, but which enlightens our thinking and our faith.

The author begins in the first part by letting us hear that the Lord is One and thus the Only. For this, he offers beautiful texts from the prayer of the synagogue and from midrash. Then, always based on texts, he speaks of the Ones in the Torah, which can be perceived by accepting the paradoxes of Creation, of Revelation and of Redemption. This first part is a magnificent introduction to the second part of the book, which looks at the numbers one, two, and three and their place in the Unity. The texts bring out two dyads: God and God's *Shekhinah* (the divine presence in the world), the *Shekhinah* and the Holy Spirit, as well as several triads that come close to the Trinity. The work ends in a third part on the Christian expression of the Trinity as it resonates with the message of Israel's Tradition. All these pages help us better to take on the expression of our Christian faith.

The undertaking is audacious and courageous. It is in no way a mystical short-circuit or an unfortunate mixture. Each identity is totally respected. But this magnificent book encourages us to discover more the extent to which we are heirs to this beautiful Jewish Tradition. Too often we abstain from receiving such rich teaching from our brothers and sisters. May the author help us to perceive better all that we owe to our Jewish brothers and sisters! It has to do with our identity. It has to do with our relationship with all our human brothers and sisters.

A big thank you to the author for having undertaken such a work, the fruit of many years of study and teaching. Before passing the word on to him, let us remember Rabbi Eleazar's saying: *Without knowledge, no intelligence; without intelligence, no knowledge!*

+ Maurice Gardès
Archbishop of Auch

Foreword

Pierre Lenhardt has been a leading voice for inter-religious reconciliation in Jerusalem for many decades. I had the privilege of engaging with him fifty years ago on a subset of his current volume, that is the question of Christology.

In the present book he widens the scope of his inquiry to include the totality of the Trinity. He does so following a principle that has been central to his perspective throughout his academic career, namely, that Christians and Jews cannot properly understand the teachings of Jesus and the subsequent theology developed by the Church about his person apart from their roots in Judaism. As a result of the move away from a Jewish context to a philosophical basis of Christian self-expression which is grounded in Greek thought and its categories at large, which would be seemingly impenetrable, a wall was created between Judaism and Christianity in the articulation of fundamental Christian beliefs regarding Christology and the Trinity.

A remarkable transformation has occurred in our understanding of the relationship between Christians and Jews in the first several centuries of the Common Era. This transformation has come about largely through the research and writings of biblical scholars, both Jewish and Christian. They have shown that their eventual separation was lengthy and complex. They also validated one of the fundamental emphases in Vatican II's historic declaration *Nostra Aetate,* namely, that Jesus was a faithful Jew whose preaching and ministry were positively impacted by the variegated Jewish tradition of his day, and that he did not project wholesale opposition to first century Common Era Judaism as Christian theologians and homilists often argued in the pre-Vatican II years. Rather he embraced most of its core teaching while critiquing certain interpretations of the Jewish tradition advocated within certain circles, interpretations that often resulted in serious injustices.

As Lenhardt sees it, reintegrating fundamental Christian teachings into their original Hebrew/Aramaic context will not eliminate some of the significant differences between Jewish and Christian faith perspectives. But by study of the Torah and its interpretations the Christian community can recognise certain similarities and also enhance its understanding of the meaning of key texts that form the basis for core beliefs in the Church on such questions as the Trinity. We have often depicted some of these beliefs solely within Greek philosophical categories and sometimes as unique to Jesus. This latter type of interpretation can be seen in the way certain biblical scholars under the sway of noted exegete Rudolf Bultmann explained Jesus' parables as completely innovative without any parallels in the thought developed in post biblical Judaism, yet the pioneering scholar in Christian-Jewish relations Clemens Thoma, SVD, clearly demonstrated that many parabolic stories told by Jesus in the Gospels closely resemble parables found in first century CE Jewish texts.

Lenhardt also demonstrates how placing New Testament perspectives in the glow of Torah texts often gives them a power and richness which their rendition in Greek does not fully duplicate. Lenhardt has pursued this interpretive tract for decades with this new volume serving as a central culmination of his lifetime commitment to this effort.

Recently Pope Francis has given important recognition to the Torah based exegesis that Lenhardt has championed throughout his academic career. In a preface to a new volume in Italian *La Bibbla dell'Amicizia* (*The Bible of Friendship*), the Pope strongly affirms Lenhardt's basic perspective that it is crucial for Christian believers to discover and promote an understanding of the Jewish tradition in the process of developing an authentic self-understanding. Torah study stands at the heart of this process. 'That is why', says Pope Francis to the co-authors 'I want to entrust your research to the words of the invocation that every Jewish believer recites daily at the end of the Amidah prayer (according to the Italian rite): "Let the doors of the Torah of wisdom, intelligence and knowledge of nourishment and sustenance, of grace, of love and of mercy and gratitude be open before You"'.

Pope Francis' Foreword and Lenhardt's book also respond to a major challenge in the on-going effort to speak theologically about the Catholic Church's relationship with Judaism in light of *Nostra Aetate.* In a number of his writings Saint John Paul II emphasised that the Church has a relationship with Jews and Judaism unlike anything it has with other religious traditions. This theme was also picked up by Cardinal Kasper in his capacity as the head of the Holy See's Commission for Religious Relations with Jews and by Pope Benedict XVI in remarks he made during his visit to the Jewish Synagogue in Rome. The thrust of this argument has been rooted in the view that Judaism is the only non-Christian tradition to possess 'authentic revelation' (through the Old Testament) from the standpoint of Catholic theology. But Judaism throughout the Common Era up until today has not relied for its faith outlook and its moral principles solely on its scriptural tradition. Torah interpretation is central for contemporary Jewish belief. Hence we in the Christian community need to ask how we regard the post-biblical Torah interpretation that is part of Judaism's sacred literature alongside the Hebrew Bible. Is it any sense 'revelatory' and, as a result, a necessary feature of Christian theological hermeneutics? While he never stated this in print, Cardinal Kasper, in private conversation, insisted that Pope Benedict's inclusion of a quotation from post-biblical literature in his synagogue address in Rome constituted an affirmation of the continuing vitality of the Jewish covenant after the Christ event and hence retains hermeneutical relevance for Christian interpretation as well. Such an understanding would definitely strengthen the argument Lenhardt posits in this volume as well as Pope Francis' endorsement of *La Bibbia dell'Amicizia.*

Overall Lendhart's book makes an important contribution to the process of altering Catholicism's historic template to its relationship with Jews and Judaism. Lenhardt has established that the teachings of Jesus and his early followers and the theological affirmations they sourced cannot be properly understood apart from a familiarity with Torah commentaries. The Trinity, one of Christianity's defining beliefs, is certainly a case in point. His contribution will need to be integrated with studies by Jewish scholars such as Daniel Boyarin who has argued that 'Christology' was a job description already present in post-biblical Judaism prior to its application to the life and work of Jesus and Shaul Magid who has shown how a certain understanding of 'incarnationalism' permeated parts of the Hasidic literature.

There will also be need to mine the wider body of Jewish mystical literature for additional examples of possible 'incarnational' themes. Likewise, Lenhardt's work raises the necessity of probating how this emphasis on the centrality of Torah interpretation for a proper understanding of key elements of the Christian dogmatic tradition generally is stated, at least in the Western church, in Greek philosophical categories that are likely to remain the setting for official descriptions of Christian dogmatics.

Lendardt's book thus offers us an invaluable start on a major hermeneutical shift mandated by *Nostra Aetate,* so that hopefully others will join him in this indispensable effort.

John Pawlikowski osm
Catholic Theological Union
Chicago
President of the National Council for the Unity of Christians and for Relations with Judaism

Introduction

The specific and irreducible newness of the Christian Tradition in relation to the Jewish Tradition (Pharisaic-rabbinic) that it takes on, is to announce that the One and Only God of Israel is Triune, Father, Son and Holy Spirit.[1] For a Christian, the mystery of the divine Trinity is that of its Unity. The Christian testimony concerning the Trinity is rejected by Jewish and by Muslim orthodoxy as contrary to monotheism. On the other hand, both Western and Eastern, Catholic and Protestant Christian orthodoxy declares that it is monotheistic. It affirms its faith in *only one God* who is the One and Only God. God is the Only because God is One, the One God of Israel and of Jesus Christ (Deut 6:4; Mk 12:29, 32), the One God, Father, Son and Holy Spirit. The Christian affirmation of the divine Trinity rests on the Jewish affirmation of the divine Unity. The Christian affirmation of the God's being the Only rests on the affirmation of God's Unity.

In what is to follow, I will assume that the dogmatic landmarks offered by the Church in order to guide and sustain the faith of its faithful in the Blessed Trinity are known.[2] I shall not enter into specu-

1. Tradition of Israel, Jewish Tradition: I write these with a capital 'T' in order to show that for the Pharisees, for the rabbis and for the great majority of believing and practicing Jews who follow their teachings, these are Word of God, oral Torah just as Scripture is called the written Torah. As for Christian Tradition, it is also, at least for Catholics, Word of God, One, made up of Scripture and of Israel's Tradition that it assumes in the One and Only Covenant, which has become New and Eternal in and through Jesus Christ. On the distinction that is to be made between Tradition and traditions, I refer to Yves Congar OP, *La Tradition et les traditions* (Paris: Fayard, Volume I, 1960; Volume II, 1963).
2. These dogmatic landmarks are the Apostles' Creed and the Nicene Creed, as well as other texts of the Latin liturgy, such as the Gloria, the preface for Trinity

lation on the mystery of the Trinity. This speculation, which takes place in countless works, certainly helps Christians to assume the Church's trinitarian doctrine, but it does not succeed in bringing this doctrine out of a certain isolation in dogmatic theology.[3] My aim is to show that the teachings of Israel's Tradition on the Unity of God can shed light on the Christian faith that is nourished by the mystery of the Trinity.

As a Catholic, I start from the Christian faith, upon which my Church sheds light through its relationship with the Jewish people.[4] From the Christian point of view, this relationship, which has

---

Sunday and the eighth preface for Sundays. I would add to these landmarks the Creed Quicumque of Pseudo-Athanasius (Dentzinger 75–76), the authority of which is recognised both by the liturgy of the Eastern Church and by those of the Roman Catholic Church (*Roman Breviary, the Office for Prime on Sundays*) and the Anglican Church (*Common Prayer Book*).

3. I am taking this judgment as to the isolation of the trinitarian dogma from Karl Rahner (*Dieu Trinité*, [Paris, Cerf, 1999], 17–22). He writes: 'I have the feeling that Christians, in spite of the perfect orthodoxy of their profession of faith in the Trinity, are practically 'monotheistic' in their concrete religious life. I would go so far as to say that if one dared to rid the religious writings of everything that has to do with the doctrine of the Trinity (supposing that this doctrine was wrong) the vast majority of these writings would remain practically unchanged.' 'Remarques sur le Traité dogmatique "De Trinitate"', in *Ecrits Théologiques* VIII (Paris, DDB, 1967), 109. See also what Bruno Forte has written: The 'isolation of the trinitarian doctrine from the rest of dogma and ethics has not yet been resolved, not even in the many present-day theological studies. Whether we are dealing with new expressions of old treatises, with renovating intuitions or explorations, with the hermeneutics in narrative theology, with the politics of the theology of liberation, it does not seem that the "trinitarian gospel" plays a really decisive role. It is not exaggerated to say that we are still faced with the Trinity's exile from Christian theory and practice. Perhaps it is precisely this exile that motivates the rediscovery of the "trinitarian homeland" in theology and life.' (B Forte, *La Trinité comme Histoire. Essai sur le Dieu Chrétien* [Paris: Nouvelle Cité, 1989]). From Bruno Forte I receive the confirmation that we must shed light on Christian theology and life based on the Jewish sources. The idea is not to minimize the immense wealth of ancient teachings, of Saint Augustine and Saint Thomas, etc, or of the new teaching of Karl Barth (*Church Dogmatics*), Karl Rahner, Michel Corbin, etc. However, to the extent to which these teachings are not based on the Tradition of Israel or, if they do refer to it, do not know it well, in the spirit of the Second Vatican Council, it is today right to enlighten Christian faith more by basing it on the Jewish faith in the Unity of God.
4. My Catholic position is the same as that of the large Churches, which agree in seeing Christianity's Jewish origin and sources as that which enables us to know God and Jesus Christ better and thus to support the ecumenical movement.

been profoundly renewed since the Second Vatican Council (*Nostra Aetate,* No 4, of October 28, 1965), is based on God's one and only covenant with God's people Israel, an eternal covenant which was never revoked and which became New through and in Jesus Christ. Certainly, there are still here and there in the Church some battles coming from the rearguard; plenty of sermons can still be heard in which the new covenant replaces the old. Thus we must remain vigilant. But it is above all appropriate to be enriched by the fact that the Church invites us to know the covenant by listening to Judaism.

Starting with Christianity, in my study of the New Testament, of the Church's Tradition, and of Christian life, I seek for what comes from the Old Testament and from the Tradition of Israel.

My *first (analytical) step* will thus be to *seek the roots of my Christian faith.*

But I do not want to limit my listening to Judaism to what corresponds exactly with my Christian, perhaps too narrow understanding of the Word of God. I am convinced that the Word of God is one, perfect, coherent, and that what it says to the Jews also speaks to Christians.

In a *second (synthetical) step*, I will offer *as broad a listening as possible to what the Tradition of Israel says about God's Unity* as it makes itself known in various contexts.

The two steps (analytical and synthetical) must be distinguished, but they cannot be in opposition to one another or separated. My exposition will begin with the Christian faith and it will not depart from it at any time, while listening to Israel. Throughout this exposition, it is the Christian faith that will enable us to hear resonances, which the Christian reader will perceive of his or her own accord or which I shall invite him and her to discover.

After some preliminary remarks on the presuppositions and the method of my presentation, I will deal in the *first part,* entitled *Unity,* with the Unity of God as taught by the Tradition of Israel.

I shall begin with Mark's Gospel (12:28–34). Since this text teaches that God is One and Only, I shall seek what the Tradition of Israel says about this One and Only God, of which the gospel speaks.

In the *second part* entitled *Unity-Trinity*, I shall deal first with what Scripture can teach about the Trinity, about the numbers one and two, about the number three, about the things that are third, about the triads. I will then show what the Tradition of Israel says about the Unity of God and about God's presence in the world (which is called

Shekhinah), then about the Unity of the *Shekhinah* and the Holy Spirit (and/or the heavenly voice, which is called *Bat Kol*).

I shall begin with Luke's Gospel (3:21–22; 9:28–36) and then seek for what immediately sheds light on these texts in the Tradition of Israel (analytical step). I will then suggest a listening to the Tradition of Israel that sheds light more broadly on the Christian faith (synthetical step).

In the *third part* entitled *Trinity*, I will recall some teachings of Christian Tradition about the Trinity by taking up certain resonances that will already have been heard in the Tradition of Israel. This conclusion will open up some possible broadening of Christian reflection that is supported through contact with Israel.

The Unity of God, the divine Trinity, cannot be proven. These realities are unfathomable. They can be felt when the believer, Jewish or Christian, receives the intelligence of Tradition and of Scripture from God through the Holy Spirit, a free gift of the knowledge of God (*daat elohim,* Hos 6:6).

In its teaching, the Tradition of Israel favours the language of the people and popular wisdom. Listening to it, a Christian is invited to question and to argue much more than to speculate. Through contact with this Tradition, the Christian learns to value the diversity of opinions and the unlimited openness of debates on the God of Israel who is revealed and hidden, and who saves (Isa 45:15).

My exposition will be based above all on rabbinic texts, which I shall present in English translation. Among them, I shall give priority to those which, whether anonymous or not, are closest to the period in which the New Testament was written. I shall also offer other texts from the Tradition of Israel that stem from later masters or schools. Among these, I give first place to the Hassidic masters; these recent masters give profound interpretations to the teachings of the ancient masters. The spiritual pertinence of their messages is more important to us than their chronological dependence.

Most of the texts will be introduced before giving their translations. I shall explain them afterwards and indicate their pertinence for our subject.

In this written exposition, I had to give up the study of many texts. Explaining them would have been difficult and unnecessarily tedious. Nevertheless, I believe it is necessary to indicate in appendices (I, II, III, IV and V at the end of the book) the texts that should be studied.

For all the texts studied in this book or indicated in the appendices, it should be possible to return to an oral exposition. Nothing can replace the Pharisaic and rabbinic oral tradition, which remains the vital center (*hiyyut*) of studying-teaching (*talmud*) the Word of God.

In order to correspond with this fundamental oral tradition, I shall imitate the oral Tradition, which takes pleasure in repeating things for fear of forgetting what has already been heard. The result is a certain heaviness which risks tiring the reader, but which in reality can help him or her to hear the message better.

Finally, I must clarify what makes up the background of the texts that I shall offer for our study. They all belong to the Tradition of Israel, which for the Pharisaic masters and their successors even to our day is the Word of God, the oral Torah that precedes, engenders, passes on and interprets Scripture, the written Torah. This value of Tradition, which is clearly recognised by the Catholic Church, does not allow us to speak of Judaism or of Christianity as religions of the book.[5]

The rabbinic texts presented in this book are written notations of oral traditions. The only aim of the scribes who took up these traditions was to support the memory of the communities and to facilitate their access to the oral tradition. They did not have to write in a perfect or complete way, and they did not always succeed in arranging the elements available to them in the best way possible.

I have used various translations, some of which are inexact and often antiquated. I corrected the obvious errors and indicated in parentheses what will help us to understand the scribe's notations. I believe it to have been better to follow the original Hebrew or Aramaic written notations closely in order to let something be heard of what was originally said orally. Through too great a concern with the style, one risks missing that which makes up the charm of an oral text, a charm that can often be sensed through the written notation. At times I have indicated in brackets the transcription of the Hebrew or Aramaic word used in the text; this transcription, which has been kept as simple as possible, maintains the international customs, for example *amidah* instead of *'amidah*.

5. As regards Judaism, cf. P. Lenhardt, M. Collin, La Torah orale des Pharisiens; Supplément au Cahier Evangile 73, Paris, Cerf, 1990. Regarding Christianity, see the Catechism of the Catholic Church, Christianity, 108 (after 107: the inspired books teach the truth): "Still, the Christian faith is not a 'religion of the book.' Christianity is the religion of the 'Word' of God, 'not a written and mute word, but incarnate and living.'"

1
The Lord (YHWH), The God (Elohim) of Israel, Is the One and the Only (1st Paragraph of the Shema)

The pedagogical structure of Israel's Tradition in teaching that the One God is the author of 1) Creation, 2) Israel's Election in view of Revelation, and 3) Redemption, can form a useful backdrop to our study. This teaching is given through the community's established (*keba*) and obligatory (*hovah*) prayer, which is the most authoritative instance of Tradition (oral Torah).[1]

I am not using this ternary structure as a basis for an interpretation of the Trinity, but rather as the basis for the study of the paradoxical nature of God's ineffable Unity, to which Israel can only witness by covering its face at the beginning of the *Reading of the Shema*.

In this first part of the study, I shall suggest three fundamental paradoxes that correspond with this structure: the paradox of Creation, the paradox of Revelation, the paradox of Redemption.

1. On the status and authority of established (*keba'*) and obligatory (*hovah*) prayer, *cf* what two great Jewish masters taught in their time, S Schechter (1847–1915), *Aspects of Rabbinic Theology* (New York: Schocken Books (1909), 1961), 1–20; J Heinemann (1915–1978), *Prayer in the Talmud* (Berlin/New York: De Gruyter, 1977), 1–36. Contrary to the cliché that can still be heard today, according to which Judaism has no dogmas, S Schechter discussed the 'dogmas of Judaism', which he saw as taught by Jewish prayer [*cf* S Schechter, *Aspects of Rabbinic Theology* and 'The Dogmas of Judaism', in *Studies in Judaism* (Philadelphia: The Jewish Publication Society of America, 1896), 147–181]. The Christian saying, *lex orandi lex credendi*, which is quoted above all in the Catholic Church, has its roots in the Tradition of Israel (pharisaic and rabbinic). Established prayer is obligatory. When it is incumbent on the community, it is considered to be the service (*abodah*) owed to God, and it is simply called prayer (*tefillah*). The service of prayer, which is considered to be service of the heart (Deut 11:13) is connected to the service of the altar, the Temple sacrifices. It holds this place so long as the Temple, destroyed in the year 70 CE, is not rebuilt.

The structure of Israel's established and obligatory prayer (Shema, Shabbat)

Let us call to mind the structure of Israel's prayer:

I. The first blessing before the *Shema*: CREATION
[the central blessing of the prayer (*Amidah*) on the eve of Shabbat]

II. The second blessing before the *Shema*: REVELATION-ELECTION
[the central blessing of the prayer (*Amidah*) the morning of Shabbat]

The first paragraph of the *Shema*: Deuteronomy 6:4–9 (the yoke of the Kingdom of Heaven)
GOD'S Unity
LOVE OF GOD
The second paragraph of the *Shema*: Deuteronomy 11:13–21 (the yoke of the commandments)
COMMANDMENTS
RETRIBUTION
The third paragraph of the *Shema*: Numbers 15:37–41
CONSECRATION
EXODUS FROM EGYPT

III. The third blessing after the *Shema*: REDEMPTION
[the central blessing of the prayer (*Amidah*) the afternoon of Shabbat]

The Lord, our God, the Lord is One (Deut 6:4; Mk 12:28)

We shall start with the New Testament, and we shall look for the Jewish context in the rabbinic sources that best sheds light on the Gospel passage in Mark, which interests us here.

In chapters 11 and 12 of Mark's Gospel, several teachings are introduced that were probably given in the Temple (Mk 11:27).[2] This frame enables us to understand why, in response to a pharisaic scribe's question (Mt 22:34–35), Jesus quotes the first verse of the *Reading of*

2. I am taking the Gospel text as it is offered to the Christian in Greek, Latin or modern translations in the usual editions. The specialists can probably make interesting comments on the text's composition. Until proven otherwise, the text as offered by the Church has sufficient authority for our study.

the Shema, which is an obligatory prayer for every Jew in the evening and the morning (Deut 6:4): *Hear, O Israel (shema Israel), the Lord (YHWH), our God (eloheinu, elohim), the Lord (YHWH) is One*. This verse comes in response to the question: Which is the first of all the commandments? And the answer given by Jesus is appropriate if one knows the context of Jewish prayer.

In fact, Jewish prayer establishes the reading of Scripture within a clearly visible pedagogical frame, according to which a person first prays to God as to the one who creates the world, then as the one who reveals himself there, and finally as the one who redeems the world. According to this pedagogy, the proclamation of the One God (Deut 6:4) is preceded and prepared for by the blessing *Ahavah Rabbah* (or *Ahavat Olam*). We shall study this prayer, in which Israel asks God to unify the heart, to make one the fear and the love of God, which enables the person to proclaim the ineffable Unity (text 2).

Mark 12:28–34 (Text 1)

> A scribe asked him: Which is the first of all the commandments? Jesus answered him [Deut 6:4–5]: '*Hear, O Israel, the Lord, our God, the Lord is One* [*eis, unus*], and *you shall love the Lord your God . . .*'
> The scribe said to him; Good Master, you have said according to the truth that he is One [*eis, unus*] and that there is no other than He [he is the Only], and that to love him with all one's heart . . .

In this Gospel passage, we hear Jesus proclaiming together with Israel that the Lord is One; we then hear the scribe approving of Jesus and teaching the Unity of God as the foundation for God's being the Only (Mk 12:32).

Thus we already know that God's Unity cannot be compared to anything and is ineffable. It is the Only. Thus it is right to reject the translations and the interpretations flowing from them, according to which Jesus says: 'The Lord our God is the only Lord', and the scribe: 'He is the only and there is no other.' Neither the literal text (*eis* and not *monos*) nor the ancient Jewish context, contemporary with the New Testament, that we shall study, allows for errors that deprive the Christians of what is essential to the message and on which the scribe's approval leaves no doubt: first comes the Unity, and being the Only flows from it.[3] It is true that some Christians confuse Unity and being the Only. It must be said that many presentations, at times written by recognised and renowned theologians, reveal surprising imprecisions.[4] The battle against idolatry demands that the fact of God being the Only must always be taught. But God's Unity precedes this and gives it its foundation. It goes without saying that in the history of thought this precedence and priority have not always been clearly expressed. Human understanding first grasps numerical Unity and only later comes to grasp ontological Unity.[5]

Moreover, we must leave to the specialists in the Hebrew language and Bible the question, what, in its final redaction, Deuteronomy understood by the word *ehad* (one, alone, or only?) in the context of the verse in Deuteronomy 4:6.[6] As for the New Testament, according to Jesus and the scribe, the Greek word *eis*, which translates the word

---

3. Bad translations, which have the scribe say: 'He is the only and there is no other', are unacceptable: a scribe would be incapable of suggesting a pleonasm.
4. Such imprecisions are also surprising when different translations and interpretations of the beginning of the Surah 112 (*ikhlas*, the purity of faith) are consulted. Two Muslim commentaries that are considered by specialists to be the best, justify their interpretation of the word ahadun in the proclamation: 'Say: He, God, is One [*ahadun: ehad*]; God is the impenetrable [*al-tstsamadu*].' According to these commentators, *ahadun* with the *tanwin* of indetermination points towards the ineffable Unity of God. This *Surah* resonates perfectly with the fundamental text of Mk 12. Can we assume that in his contacts with certain Christians, Mohammed received the good interpretation of Deut 6:4: *Ehad, Ahadun*, One? From this interpretation flows the interpretation of the word *tsamad*, an enigmatic hapax meaning: impenetrable, compact, whole, not divided, perfect. Moreover, *tsamad*, a hapax in the Qur'an and in Arabic, resounds with the root *tsamad*, to bind, to attach, to join, linked with *tsemed*, yoke, in biblical and rabbinic Hebrew. Based on Hebrew, which Mohammed perhaps heard from Jewish speakers, *tsamad* could mean: attached, joined, linked.
5. *Cf* Thomas Aquinas, *Summa Theologica*, 1a q. XI, 2 – 4.
6. It is surprising that certain translations of the Septuagint translate Deut 6:4 (*eis* and not *monos*) as only. Let us also note the recent translation of the Jewish Publication Society, Oxford University Press, New York, 1985: 'Hear, O Israel! The Lord is our God, the Lord alone.' The editors also mention the other possible translation: 'The Lord our God, the Lord is one.' They consider it to be influenced by the polemic against Christianity. This translation does not seem to us to be influenced by polemic; it is the result of becoming aware of the main message that ancient Jewish established prayer wants to teach: God is One in God's own self, One, perfect, not divided, the principle of unification.

ehad (Mk 12:29; Deut 6:4), means *One*.[7] God is One, and only God is One, only God is not divided, God is the Only.[8]

The process that we have undertaken begins with the Gospel. It situates the teaching of Jesus within the frame of the *Reading of the Shema*, the fundamental prayer of the Jewish people, which gives the foundation for the commandment to love God and one's neighbour (texts 2 to 7). This prayer, established by the oral Torah and made obligatory, is the expression and the school of Israel's faith in its One and Only God. The blessing *Ahavah Rabbah* (text 2), which precedes the *Reading* and prepares the proclamation of God's Unity (Deut 6:4), is pertinent to our study. We shall study this first of all.

After the blessing, we shall study five passages from the *midrash*: on Deuteronomy 6:4–5; Leviticus 19:18; Genesis 5:1 and Leviticus 25:35 (texts 5 to 8). The *midrash* is a search for God and a search for the meaning of God's Word in Scripture. This search is demanded by God, who is himself the first to search.[9]

---

7. We will have to say clearly what we understand by the word One. This will be done based on the rabbinic texts cited later.
8. It is possible to criticise my presentation of the Gospel. Does anyone have the right to say that Jesus teaches the One and Only God because the Gospel says so and because I interpret this literally and in a naïve and fundamentalist way? I have a triple answer to such a reproach. First of all, the pharisaic-rabbinic context that we shall study shows that the Gospel teaches exactly the same as what Jewish prayer and the midrash of the Sages of Israel teach. Second, I do not see any passage in the New Testament that contradicts the message of the Gospel according to Mark. And finally, if this were the case, I would call upon the Church's teaching concerning the Old Covenant that was never revoked. This Covenant with the One and Only God is assumed by the Church. It is good that the Gospel according to Mark furnishes excellent support for the Church's teaching. Support and not proof, since the New Testament, as Scripture, does not give proofs. The Church's reading is not fundamentalist.
9. The oral Torah extends its authority over the two large domains of the Word of God, that of the *halakhah*, which discusses works, and that of the *haggadah*, which discusses faith. In the two domains, Israel's activity is commanded by the obligation to search for God; this search is demanded by God in response to the search, which is first of all that of God. I am deliberately using the vocabulary of the Letter of James, chapter 2. Its expression of the relationship between faith and works corresponds with the balanced position of the pharisaic and rabbinic masters of the past and present. The distinction between faith and works can be found in Scripture, which mentions the Torah and the commandments (Ex 24:12). Scripture and Tradition also offer the Torah and the commandments, in the plural (2 Kings 17:34; Mishnah Makkot 3, 16). In these expressions, the

The Unification of the Love of God, the Love of Neighbor, and the Love of Self

The blessing *Ahavah Rabbah* precedes the *Reading of the Shema*, which is established and obligatory. Every Jew is obliged to say it twice a day, in the evening and the morning. This prayer is said by the individual, but it is said in the first-person plural in reference to the community of Israel.

The *Reading* itself is made up of Deuteronomy 6:4–9, Deuteronomy 11:13–21, and Numbers 15:37–41. It is preceded and followed by blessings. These blessings were established by oral Tradition in order to prepare and enlighten the reading of Scripture.

The blessing *Ahavah Rabbah* comes from an ancient oral tradition to which the beginning of the Letter to the Ephesians testifies.[10] It has no overture or proem (*petihah*). It does not begin with a liturgical formula: *Blessed are You, Lord (YHWH) . . .* because it rests on the first blessing, which precedes the *Reading of the Shema*, the blessing *Yotser* (text 30). However, in its conclusion it includes the liturgical formula without which it would not be a blessing. It presents from the beginning that which makes up the body of its teaching and which we are going to make explicit, and it ends with a conclusion (*hatimah*), using the liturgical formula and the terms of the blessing's main message: Israel's election.

---

commandment, the commandments signifies that which has to do with practice (the works), which is to say the *halakhah*; the Torah signifies the *Haggadah*, which is to say everything that is not *halakhah*, in particular that which has to do with the knowledge of God, faith and hope, spiritual life.

Scripture does not say that God seeks the people of Israel. What is said is that God seeks the Land of Israel (Deut 11:12), which gives the foundation to the demand that the Land be sought (*derishah*) (*Sifre on Deuteronomy* 11, 12, pp. 80–81). The same is true for Jerusalem; the search is demanded in response to the Lord's complaint (Jer 30:17): No one is seeking Zion (BT Sukkah 41a). As for the people of Israel, the prayer for the feast of Sukkot teaches that God is seeking it. This is said in the people's *Hosha'not* entreaty: 'Our God . . . our Creator . . . our Redeemer . . . our Seeker (*dorshenu*) . . . save us (*hoshana*)!' As for seeking the meaning of the Word of God in Scripture, which is called midrash in the strict sense, it is clear that this happens in response to God. Rashi in his interpretation of Scripture (Gen 1:1) has God say through Scripture: Seek me! (*dorsheni*).

10. *Cf* S Lyonnet, 'La bénédiction d'Ephésiens 1, 3–14 et son arrière-fond judaïque', *A la rencontre de Dieu*, Mémorial Albert Gélin (Lyon: Editions Xavier Mappus, 1961).

The Blessing Ahavah Rabbah (Text 2)
(We have numbered the paragraphs so as to facilitate the commentary).

1. With great love you have loved us, Lord (YHWH), our God. With great and immense mercy you have had mercy on us.
2. Our Father, our King, because of our Fathers who trusted you and to whom you taught laws of life, be gracious to us and teach us. Our Father, merciful Father, you who have mercy, have mercy on us.
3. Make our heart to discern and to understand, to hear, to learn and to teach, to observe, to do and to accomplish all the Words of the Talmud of your Torah with love.
4. Enlighten our eyes through your Torah, attach our heart to your commandments and unify our heart so that it might love and fear your Name. May we never be ashamed. For we have trusted your holy, great and fearsome Name. We shall be jubilant and joyful because of your salvation.
5. Bring us back in peace from the four corners of the earth and lead us with heads held high to our Land.
6. For you are a God who works salvation, and you have chosen us from among all the peoples and all the languages, and you have brought us close to your great Name, Selah, in truth, in order to give you thanks and to unify you with love.
7. Blessed are you, Lord, who chooses his [your] people Israel through love.[11]

§ 1. With great love . . .

This beginning, which announces the conclusion: 'Blessed are you, Lord, who elects [chooses] your [his] people Israel through love', teaches that God is the first to love Israel (*cf* 1 Jn 4:10). It is a preparation for reading the verse that follows the proclamation of the One and Only God (Deut 6:5): *and you shall love the Lord your God.*

This message on the reciprocity of love between God and Israel is in its rightful place within the pedagogical framework, which situ-

11. The anomaly that uses the third person in a phrase addressed to the second person is maintained in order to teach that God is immanent, present to prayer, but that God is absent in his impenetrable transcendence.

ates the election of Israel through love after the creation of the world through mercy (texts 10 and 11). Because the blessing celebrating God as the author of creation describes God as the one 'who enlightens the earth and those who dwell on it through mercy'. This resonates with the Gospel's heavenly Father who *causes his sun to rise over the evil and over the good* (Mt 5:45). Mercy is unilateral, whereas love requires reciprocity. That is the role of the blessing *Ahavah Rabbah*: 'With great love you have loved us' prepares for the teaching about the reciprocity of this love. It is God who first loves, it is God who asks for Israel's response (Deut 6:5): *and you shall love the Lord your God.*

§ 2. *Our Father . . .*

This invocation of *Our Father* and the call to the *Merciful Father* (*cf* 2 Cor 1:3) do not seem to be in the right place in a prayer that celebrates the love and the relationship of love that presupposes and demands reciprocity. Mercy is unilateral. According to the teaching of the first blessing that precedes the *Reading of the Shema* (text 10), this is God's attribute as creator. We shall leave to the specialists the question as to when this passage was introduced into the blessing. For the believer, whether Jewish or Christian, the call for mercy has its place in a prayer that teaches the election of Israel. For from the beginning, Israel as the chosen people is threatened with death and exposed to persecution, as the *Pesach Haggadah* and history teach.[12]

§ 3. *To accomplish . . .*

The blessing asks God to cause Israel's heart 'to accomplish all the Words of the Talmud of your Torah with love.' This shows the link between *Talmud Torah* (the study-teaching of the Torah) and love of God, a link that is specific and characteristic of Israel, based on its election through love. This love of God is nevertheless inseparable from the fear of God, as the prayer teaches in what follows: 'unify our heart so that it might love and fear your Name.'

---

12. Concerning the *Pesach Haggadah*, *cf* below the main *midrash* on Deut 26:5, which is interpreted as follows: *An Aramean* (Laban) *wanted to kill my Father* (Jacob). As to history, it speaks for itself.

§ 4. Enlighten our eyes . . . and unify our heart

This request is a direct preparation for the proclamation of the One God, the principle of unification through love, and that of the Only, the only one who merits exclusive love.

The unification that is requested is that of the love and fear of God. Unity of the heart is required in order to proclaim the Unity of God. It will also be the consequence of proclaiming the Unity of God and of putting into practice the unification that is required by God and made possible through the fulfilment of the commandment to love God.

§ 5. Bring us back in peace . . .

This passage corresponds with Israel's situation after the destruction of the Temple in the year 70 CE and after the suppression of the Bar Kokhba revolt in the year 135 CE.

§ 6. For you are a God who works salvation . . .

This passage is close to the conclusion and proclaims Israel's election, which is the theme of the conclusion. For established prayer usually announces the conclusion in terms that are similar to its overall theme.

Thanks to this election, Israel receives the task of unifying God, which has to be implemented at two levels, the liturgical level: proclaiming that God is One; and a second level that has to do with Israel's role in the history of the world; at this level, Israel not only proclaims that God is One, but must teach and advance the unification of all of reality.

§ 7. The conclusion with its liturgical formula: Blessed are You, Lord . . .

It sums up all the praises and all the requests expressed in the body of the blessing. Thus, in faith, God, who is touched by the liturgical formula, hears the prayer and answers it. God maintains Israel's election through love.

Thus the prayer enlightens from within the message of Jesus on the love of God. The study of this first text from oral Tradition gives rise to two comments:

In the first place, oral Tradition teaches what it must teach without having to base it on Scripture through a citation formula. Scripture teaches Israel's election (Deut 7:6; Ps 105:6), but Tradition knows that all interpretation of Scripture is controversial. Thus it must affirm in the present, without citing Scripture, that God chooses his people Israel through love, today and always.[13] This election has to be seen as an element of Christian faith that cannot be uprooted.[14] It flows from the coherence of Christian faith, which sees Jesus as the chosen one *par excellence* (Eph 1:4; Lk 9:38; text 4).

Secondly, we must underline the pertinence of the blessing as it sheds light on the teaching of Jesus in Mark's Gospel concerning God's Unity. The blessing is pertinent for two reasons: it is contemporary with the compiling of the New Testament, and it is part of the established and obligatory prayer that has the greatest authority in the oral Torah. It constitutes the most sure anchorage for understanding what Jesus said about the One God.

The light flowing from this prayer is sufficient to affirm that a consequence of God's Unity is the fact that God is the Only.

A text by Maimonides and two liturgical hymns drawn from his teaching confirm what has become the common teaching of religious Judaism.

Maimonides (1135–1204), *Hilkhot yesodey ha-torah* 1, 7 (Text 3)

---

13. Oral Torah fulfils Scripture. It confirms Scripture. Of course Scripture enlightens and supports Tradition, but it cannot teach directly without passing by way of Tradition's interpretation. We shall return to Israel's election in the second part of this study, because for a Christian, this election is inseparable from the election of Jesus, of which Ephesians 1:4 and Luke 9:35 speak.

14. *Cf* what P von der Osten-Sacken wrote; he is a Lutheran exegete and theologian who cannot be suspected of not knowing Saint Paul or the many and various ways of interpreting him: 'One must become theologically aware of one single fundamental proposition, which must then be put into practice: the certainty that God upholds Israel's election and his preferential choice of his people, even when this people says no to Jesus Christ, is part of the Christian faith. This certainty thus belongs both to the Credo and to the Christian catechism.' (*Katechismus und Siddur* [Berlin: Selbstverlag Institut Kirche und Judentum, 1994], 18). It is interesting to see a Protestant exegete recognising the value of Tradition in defining an element of Christian faith.

> This God is One. He is neither two nor more than two, but One, and his Unity cannot be compared to any of the unities that exist in the universe . . . And since God does not have a bodily reality, he cannot be affected by any bodily accident in such a way as to be divisible or separable from another being. Also, he can only be One, and the knowledge of this truth constitutes a positive commandment, for it is said (Deut 6:4): *The Lord is our God, the Lord is One.*

The liturgical hymns derived from Maimonides say respectively:

Adon Olam (Text 4a)

> He is One and there is no second one who can be compared to him.

And *Yigdal Elohim* (Text 4b)

> He is One, no unity is comparable to his.

Maimonides' teaching gives rise to two comments:

The affirmation, 'He is neither two nor more than two', by which Maimonides perhaps has in view the Christian faith in the Trinity, does not say anything that is in contradiction to that faith. For according to the Christian faith, the three divine persons do not add up numerically.

The affirmation concerning the necessity to conceive the One God as not being in any way divisible is obviously fundamental. In fact, God's Unity, which is positively affirmed by Scripture and by the Tradition of Israel and of the Church, is joined to the negative affirmation of God's indivisibility. This indivisibility can in turn be joined to the positive affirmation of perfection. This will be shown further on.

Since the established and obligatory liturgical prayer is the privileged place where the faith and hope of Israel are expressed and taught, it is right to listen to it first of all. Nevertheless, as was mentioned above, we must complete our process by listening to the results of the exegetical search (*midrash*), which is applied to the first two verses of the *Reading of the Shema*: Deuteronomy 6:4–5. For like the prayer, this search is an essential activity of the oral Torah.[15]

---

15. Let us complete what we said above on *midrash*.

For Scripture, a distinction is made between commentary (*perush*, separation, explanation) and search (*midrash*, scrutinising, interpretation). To the extent

We shall see below how, in a debate between Rabbi Akiba and Ben Azzai, recourse to Leviticus 19:18 and Genesis 5:1 can give support to the commandment to love one's neighbour. Finally, based on an interpretation of Lev 25:35, we shall learn how and why Hillel loved himself and could therefore love his neighbour.

Sifre Deuteronomy 6:4, pp. 53–54 (Text 5)

Midrash Sifre gathers together the most ancient rabbinic traditions on the verses of Deuteronomy. These anonymous traditions represent the authorised opinions of a majority of masters. They are probably at least contemporary with traditions about Jesus collected in the Gospels. Every word of Scripture is scrutinized, *sought*, in order *to find* the meaning that enlightens faith and supports deeds. *Midrash Sifre* is a *midrash halakhah*. There we find the interpretations that support

---

that it is possible, the commentary determines the exposed, simple, literal meaning (*pashut, peshat*) of Scripture. The search wants to find God who speaks in Scripture. It lets one hear the present-day meaning or meanings (*midrash, derash*), which engage the reader to live, to hope and to act. The search (*midrash*), which occurs within the search for God, is, like prayer, an essential task of the oral Torah. The results of this search, also called *midrash* (plural *midrashot* and *midrashim*), are considered to be authorized references so long as they have not been explicitly rejected by the community. The *midrashim* of the various words from Scripture are gathered together in collections, which are also called *midrashim*.

Starting with the literal meaning of Scripture, which is clarified as far as possible and respected as the fundamental reference, the *midrash* seeks the meaning that engages the believer in practice or that enlightens his and her faith and hope. The *midrash halakhah* seeks to show the Torah's coherence by basing the *halakhah*, the norm for practice, on Scripture. The *midrash Haggadah* (*aggadah*) uses Scripture as a support for what one must know of God and what one hopes of God. During the Yavne period after the destruction of the Temple, between 70 and 219 CE (the year 219 is the *terminus ad quem* for the oral publication of the *Mishnah* by Rabbi Yehudah ha-Nassi), the *Tannaim* (the masters who teach) gathered together the *halakhic midrashim* that deal above all with *halakhah*, but that include much *haggadah*. Between the years 219 and 400, which is the probable date of the Jerusalem Talmud's incomplete collection, the *Amoraim* (the masters who say) returned to the older *Haggadah*, the *Haggadah* of the *Tannaim*, which was not included in the *halakhic midrashim*. They collected this *Haggadah* and completed it with their own *Haggadah*. The most important *haggadic midrashim* (*midrashei aggadah*, *cf* Rashi on Gen 3:8), which are contemporary with the *Jerusalem Talmud, are Genesis Rabbah, Leviticus Rabbah, Lamentations Rabbah, and Pesikta de-Rav Kahana.*

the commandments to love God and to love the neighbour. The priority given by *halakhah* to doing does not exclude *haggadah*. On the contrary! The latter reveals the reasons for loving God and the neighbour.

> Deut 6:4: *the Lord, our God, the Lord is One.*
> Why is this said? Is it not said, the Lord is One? What does the Talmud tell us: the Lord, our God? It is to us that his Name applies the most strongly. Analogously (Ex 34:23): Three times a year every male among you will show himself before the face of the Lord YHWH, the God of Israel. Why do I need this? Is it not said: before the face of the Lord YHWH? What does the God of Israel come to tell us? It is to Israel that his Name applies the most strongly . . . Another interpretation. Deut 6:4: The Lord, our God: to us; the Lord is One: to all who come into the world [*cf* Jn 1:9]; the Lord, our God in this world; the Lord is One for the coming world; that is what Scripture says (Zech 14:9): And the Lord will be king over all the earth. On that day, the Lord will be One and his Name One.

The *midrash* clarifies (*medayyek*) and actualises the *our* of 'our God' and the *One* of the 'One God'. The fact that God is *our* God requires that Israel commit itself to God according to what Scripture then says and what Tradition interprets. The *midrash* makes clear that Israel's commitment to its God must lead to all human beings recognizing the One God.[16]

Sifre on Deuteronomy 6:4, pp. 53–54 (Text 5, continued)

> Deut 6:5: *and you shall love the Lord your God.*
> Act out of love. Scripture distinguished between the person who acts out of love and the one who acts out of fear. The reward of the one who acts out of love is doubled and doubled again. From the fact that it is said (Deut 10:20): *It is the Lord your God whom you shall fear and whom you shall serve* [if Deut 6:5 did not exist, this verse could lead to misunderstanding]. For in the reality that you know, there is a person who fears the one who is like him when the latter has power over him. But when the oppressor lets go of him, the

16. This understanding resonates for Christians in the fact that Christians must commit themselves so as one day to make known to all the One and Only God, the One and Triune God.

> oppressed goes away and leaves his oppressor. But in reality [in the relationship with the Lord, which the two verses Deut 6:5 and 10:20 have in mind], you, act out of love, for you never have love with fear and fear with love except in the quality [of the relationship felt in contact] with the Place [God].

The midrash brings out the absence of fear in the main verse of the *Reading of the Shema*. This makes clear that love is the first and main foundation for Israel's deeds. But immediately afterwards, the fear of God must be taught, and this must be supported by Scripture, by showing that in the relationship with God, fear and love are inseparable.

The above blessing *Ahavah Rabbah* requested: 'unify our heart so that it might love and fear your Name.' Midrash and prayer teach the same thing, thus showing that *the Torah of the Lord is perfect* (Ps 19:8).

Sifre Deuteronomy on Deut 6:5, 53–54 (Text 5 continued)

> Another interpretation (Deut 6:5): *and you shall love the Lord, your God.*
> Love Him in creatures, like Abraham our Father, according to what is said (Gen 12:2): *and all the personnel that they made [that they acquired] in Haran.* But if everyone comes together in the world in order to create a mosquito and to breathe a soul into it, are they capable of this? In reality, the verse teaches that Abraham our Father [and Sarah and Lot] made proselytes and let them enter under the wings of the *Shekhinah.*

The message helps to see the link that exists between the love of God and the love of the neighbour (the creature). This love of neighbour is translated into deeds, which bring the neighbour close to God and to God's love.

Sifra on Leviticus 19:18, p. 89b (Text 6)

Midrash Sifra, which is also called *Torat Cohanim*,[17] is a *midrash halakhah* that aims at connecting the norm for practice that is taught by Tradition regarding practice (*halakhah*) and Scripture. It wants to show which text of Scripture supports the commandment to love

17. Tradition gives the same name to *Torat Cohanim* (the Torah of the Priests), the Book of Leviticus, and the midrashic collection that interprets it.

one's neighbor prescribed by Tradition. The verse Lev 19:18 obviously offers a good support, but it is perhaps not the best. The *midrash* transmits the debate on this question. From within, the chosen people risks arrogance and hypocrisy, as criticisms both from within and from the outside show.

> (Lev 19:18): *And you shall love your neighbor as yourself.*
> Rabbi Akiba said: "This is a great principle in the Torah." Ben Azzai said: (Gen 5:1): This is the book of generations of Adam. The day God created Adam, he made him in the likeness of God. This is a greater principle than the other.

Ben Azzai, a colleague and disciple of Rabbi Akiba, thinks that Gen 5:1 on the creation of the human being in the likeness of God is a better support than Lev 19:18, for it offers an objective foundation for the love of the neighbour. The following text, which attaches the debate to Genesis 5:1, explains the reason for this preference.

Genesis Rabbah on Gen 5:1, Par. 24, 7 (Text 7)

As we have seen, *Genesis Rabbah* is a *midrash haggadah (aggada)* from the period of the *Amoraim.* It transmits ancient interpretations from the period of the *Tannaim*, the aim of which is not to support or justify practice. The *Book of Genesis*, which deals with the creation of the world and the story of the patriarchs, speaks of what preceded the history of Israel and the gift of the Torah with its commandments. However, certain verses, such as Gen 1:26 on the obligation to be fertile and Genesis 5:1 on the love of the neighbour, are pertinent to *halakhah.*

> Gen 5:1: *This is the book of generations of Adam. The day God created Adam, he made him in the likeness of God.*
> Ben Azzai said: 'This is a great principle in the Torah.' Rabbi Akiba said (Lev 19:18): *And you shall love your neighbour as yourself.* This is a great principle in the Torah. So that you say not: 'Since I was denigrated, may my neighbour be denigrated with me; since I was cursed, may my neighbour be cursed with me.' Rabbi Tanhuma said: 'If you behave in this way, know that you are denigrating, for "*he made him in the likeness of God*".'

The midrash concludes the debate between Ben Azzai and Rabbi Akiba by first giving the anonymous opinion of the *Amoraim*, according to which love of the neighbor has an objective foundation if it is based on the likeness to God. Rabbi Tanhuma justifies this opinion, which goes in the sense of Ben Azzai. *Genesis Rabbah* says nothing that might support Rabbi Akiba's opinion. Did it not know the ancient tradition about how Hillel took care of himself in order to honor the divine likeness in himself? This tradition, received from the *Tannaim*, is reported in the midrash *Leviticus Rabbah*, a homiletical *midrash haggadah* of the *Amoraim* that comes from the same circles as *Genesis Rabbah* and the *Jerusalem Talmud*.

Leviticus Rabbah on Lev 25:35, Par. 34 & 35 (Text 8)

Leviticus Rabbah is a *midrash haggadah* that gathers together homilies on the first verses of the pericopes in the *Book of Leviticus*. In contrast to *Genesis Rabbah*, which explains (*parshani*), *Leviticus Rabbah* is homiletical (*darsham*). It makes abundant use of the proem (*petihah*) at the beginning of the homily in order *to open the mind to understanding the Scriptures* (Lk 24:45).[18]

> Lev 25:35: *If your brother who lives with you falls into difficulty*. This is what is written (Prov 11:17): *The merciful man does good to himself, but an uncompromising man afflicts his own flesh*. When Hillel the Elder separated from his disciples, he went and walked with them. His disciples said to him: 'Rabbi, where are you going?' He told them: 'To do a commandment.' They said to him: 'Which commandment is that?' He told them: 'To wash myself in the bath house.' They said to him: 'But is that a commandment?' He told them: 'Yes! If the persons in charge of the statues of kings that are set up in the theaters and circuses clean them and wash them, they are payed for that; and more than that, they are considered to be great among the great in the kingdom. So how much more I, who was created in the image and likeness, as it is written (Gen 9:6): *For in the image of God he made man*!'
>
> Another interpretation: '*The merciful man does good to himself*, that is Hillel the Elder. At the hour when he separated from his disciples, he went and walked with them. His disciples said to him: 'Rabbi, where are you going?' He told them: 'I am going to do good to this guest who is in the house.' They said

18. The reproach of hypocrisy is attested in the New Testament and is often taken up in Christian sermons. The criticism by the Pharisees is less known. It is at least as harsch as that of Jesus (*cf* T.B. Sotah 22a-b)

> to him: 'You have a guest every day?' He told them: 'Is not this poor soul a guest in the body? Today it is here, tomorrow it is no longer here.'
> Another interpretation: '*The merciful man does good to himself.*' That is the one who distributes alms. '*But an uncompromising man afflicts his own flesh.*' Rabbi Alexandri said: 'That is the one who comes to the joy [of a celebration] and who does not join his relatives to himself because of their poverty.' Rabbi Nahman said: It is written (Deut 15:10): *Because (biglal) of that* [of charity] . . . [fortune] is a wheel [*galgal*] that turns in the world. That is why Moses warns Israel: *If your brother who lives with you.*

The text suggests understanding the meaning of Leviticus 25:35 by means of the verse from Proverbs 11:17, which is taken up again several times in order to enrich the message about love of one's neighbour. The last time this is taken up returns the reader to Leviticus 25:35 and concludes the proem.

The text transmits a tradition of the *Tannaim* about Hillel the Elder, which leaves no doubt as to the interpretation of Leviticus 19:18 suggested by Hillel in order to justify the commandment to love the neighbour. Love of the neighbour as oneself presupposes that one loves oneself, because one must love the likeness to God in oneself. That is what *Genesis Rabbah* added as a complement to the debate between Rabbi Akiba and Ben Azzai. Since the Torah is coherent and perfect, it is reasonable to believe that Rabbi Akiba thought along the same lines as Hillel and that Jesus thought along the same lines as Hillel who preceded him and as Rabbi Akiba who came after him, which is to say, that he based his thinking on Leviticus 19:18, seeing the likeness to God in the *neighbour* and in *himself*. This suggests that one must prefer the pharisaic-rabbinic asceticism of sobriety (1 Pet 1:13–16) to that of the mortification and destruction of self.

According to all New Testament traditions, the teaching of Jesus on love of the neighbour linked with the love of God is very important. It is worth underlining this teaching's rootedness in the pharisaic tradition. This rootedness enables us to grasp the coherence of the oral Torah, according to which, as we have seen, one must love God in God's creatures, following Abraham. The radical newness of Jesus on the background of continuity is that Jesus is not only created in the likeness of God. He is the Son, *the brilliance of God's glory, the image of God's substance* (Heb 1:2–3).[19] According to the line of thinking of Hillel, Jesus, and Rabbi Akiba, the neighbour is not only the Jew, but every human being created in the likeness of God, destined for unification through love, of which the One God is the principle. According to Jesus' line of thought, every human being is called to be one and united with the other human beings, as Jesus is One with the Father (Jn 17:20–22).

The pharisaic message concerning love of God and love of the neighbour created in the likeness of God and called to unification, sheds light from within on the mystery of the Incarnation and the paradox of the Revelation that manifested itself in the Incarnation. This teaches that for the believer, the love which acts for other human beings is the path of the love of God.

For a Christian, love of God and love of the neighbour, united by Jesus and the scribe in Mark's Gospel [Mk 12 (text 1)], can resonate as the basis for witnessing to the Unity-Trinity. The testimony concerning God can only be heard if it is borne out by deeds at the service of *creatures.*

Based on Leviticus 19:18, Jesus teaches love of neighbour, which cannot be separated from love of God: *And you shall love your neighbour as yourself.* This reference to Scripture is not fundamentalist. It is probably possible to use this verse as a basis for teaching love of the neighbour, but the value of such a recourse has to be discussed. That is what the debate between Rabbi Akiba and his disciple Ben Azzai mentioned in the midrashim *Sifra Leviticus* and *Genesis Rabbah* showed. Moreover, the midrash *Leviticus Rabbah* informed us of the way in which Hillel loved himself by taking care of his body.

The One and Only God was the first to love; God offered his program of unification out of love. Through its teaching, through its practice, Israel implements this program. A beautiful tradition reveals how God and Israel express their reciprocity.

19. The newness that Jesus brought is radical. It fulfils and confirms by anticipation the message of love that Rabbi Akiba would bring, according to Mishnah Avot 3, 14: 'Beloved (by God) is the man who was created in His image—a love that is even greater because he was informed of the fact of having been created in God's image, as it is said (Gen 9:6): For God created man in his image.'

Reciprocal Unification

B.T. [Babylonian Talmud] Berakhot 6a (Text 9)

The *Babylonian Talmud*, which extends the teaching in the *Mishnah* from the period of the *Amoraim*, collected what they taught between about the year 219 (*terminus ad quem* of the *Mishnah*'s oral publication) and 250 until about the year 500. The treatise *Berakhot* (Blessings) transmits very many halakhic and haggadic traditions on prayer.

> Rav Nahman bar Itshak said to Rav Hiyya Bar Abin: 'Does the Holy One, blessed be He!, praise [glorify] himself with the praise [with the glory] of Israel?' [He answered him]: Yes! It is written (Deut 26:17): *You proclaimed the Lord today*, and it is written (Deut 26:18): *And the Lord proclaimed you today*. The Holy One, Blessed be He!, said to Israel: 'You have made of me One Unity [*hativah ahat*] in the world, and I will make of you one unity in the world. You have made of me One Unity in the world, for it is said (Deut 6:4): *Hear, O Israel, the Lord our God, the Lord is One*. And I shall make of you One Unity in the world, for it is said (2 Sam 7:23; 1 Chr 17:21): *Who is like your people, Israel, One people [goy] on the earth?*'

The interpretation of the identical verse in 2 Samuel and 1 Chronicles might seem forced. The immediate context of the verse legitimises this interpretation. The verses preceding the cited verses say of the Lord: *There is no one like you, and there is no other God than you alone.*[20]

This tells us that God is first One and then the Only. The explicit message can be transferred to Israel, of which the text speaks immediately afterwards: Israel is also one and only.

God is One and Israel is one. This will be taken up again forcefully and with the authority of prayer in the central blessing of the *Shabbat Amidah* (text 62), in which the *Jewish Trinity* appears, of which we shall speak again later.

Here, we shall end our analytical search into the Christian faith by listening to Israel so as to shed light on the teaching of Jesus in Mark 12 (text 1).

---

20. God is One and Only. Scripture, like the scribe in Mk 12, does not fall into redundancy of language.

In the synthesising process that I shall now begin, we shall see how, by its teaching, its word and its deeds, Israel attempts to put unification into practice through love. As we have seen, proclaiming the One God is to commit oneself to implement God's program of unification through love. The Unity of God must be approached by the negative way of knowledge of God's indivisibility. On this background, God's ineffable perfection can be revealed. In order to join the Unity of God, God must be imitated in God's non-division, in his perfection.[21]

Some reference points:

> The Lord, Creator God, Heavenly Father, is perfect [*Tam-Tamim*: "not divided"]. The Lord is perfect (Mt 5:48).
> By his mercy, the Lord enlightens [all] the inhabitants of the earth.
> The Lord causes rain to fall on the righteous and on the unrighteous (Mt 5:44–45).
>
> *The Yotser Blessing, the first blessing before the morning* Reading of the Shema (Text 10)

The opening (*petihah*) of this first blessing consists in the complete liturgical formula: 'Blessed are You, Lord, our God, King of the universe'. It concludes (*hatimah*) with the brief formula: 'Blessed are you, Lord.' This blessing is said to be the 'long model', whereas the blessing 'With great love', studied above (text 2) only has the brief conclusion, and because of this it is the so-called 'short model'.

As always, the conclusion (*hatimah*) indicates the blessing's theme. The prayer blesses the Lord who formed (*yotser*) the luminaries. 'To form' (*yotser*) is one of the verbs used for the act of creating (*bara*).

The body (*guf*) of the blessing addresses the God who forms, the creator, whose specific attribute is mercy. It includes a *kedushah*, a proclamation of God's sanctity by quoting Isaiah 6:3 and Ezekiel 3:12.

(We have numbered the paragraphs in order to facilitate the commentary.)

---

21. When Jesus gives the command to imitate the perfect God, he situates himself within the immense program of the imitation of God as taught by Israel's Tradition based on Deut 11:22.

1. Blessed are You, Lord our God, King of the world,
2. Who forms [*yotser*] light, Creator [*bore*] of darkness, who makes [*'osseh*] peace and who creates everything [cf. Isa 45:7, which is used in part but not quoted].
3. Who through mercy enlightens the earth and those who dwell there,
4. Who by his [your] kindness every day, constantly, renews the act of the beginning.
   How numerous are your works, Lord! You have made them all with Wisdom. The earth is full of the things that you produce (cf. Ps 104:24).
5. Be blessed, our Rock, our King and our Redeemer, Creator of saints . . . Former of servants . . . All beloved, all chosen . . . all do the will of their creator [*konam*, their producer] with fear and trembling . . . All open their mouth . . . All together, they start to sing the *Kedushah* and to say with fear (Isa 6:3): *Holy, Holy, Holy, the Lord of Hosts, all the earth is filled with his Glory*! And the Wheels and the holy Living ones raise themselves with great noise before the Seraphim and say (Ezek 3:12): *Blessed is the Glory of the Lord from his Place*![22]
   They address their songs to the blessed God . . .
6. God causes salvation to sprout, he creates healings . . . Through his kindness, he renews every day, constantly the act of the beginning, as it is said (Ps 136:7): [*Praise*] *Him who made the great luminaries, for his Kindness is eternal*!
7. You shall cause a new light to shine upon Zion; may we all soon merit its brightness!
8. Blessed are You, Lord, who forms [*yotser*] the luminaries.

§ 1 and § 8: As we have already said, the blessing is called long because it begins and ends with the liturgical formula, 'Blessed are you'.

§ 2 uses Isaiah 45:7, *I form* [*yotser*] *light* [the former, *yotser*, of light], without quoting Scripture.[23] As we already said in connection with

22. This must be translated as 'from his Place' *(mi-mekomo)* and not 'in the place of his abiding' (Jerusalem Bible). The latter misses the point and eliminates the paradox. *Cf* the explanation of § 5.
23. Whenever possible, the prayer uses the present participle, which can have the meaning of a noun: *yotser*, former, formator, or of the present tense when the phrase is in the present: 'I form' (*yotser*) the light (Isa 45:7).

Israel's election, in doing this, the oral Torah confirms in prayer the teaching of Scripture. The creator God is the one who forms (*yotser*) his creation. God does not abandon it after 'the initial flicker'. According to the age-old tradition of Israel and of the Church, the creation of the world is a continuous or continued creation.[24] Thus God remains present in the world, as is affirmed by the text in what follows.

§ 3 attributes to the creator God the unilateral mercy that gives light to all the inhabitants of the earth. Mercy is the specific attribute of God as Creator, as heavenly Father who sheds light on the good and the evil, *who causes his sun to rise on the evil and on the good, and the rain to fall on the righteous and the unrighteous* (Mt 5:45). This heavenly Father is perfect (*tam, tamim*, 'non-divided'); we must imitate him and love the enemies as well as the friends (Mt 5:44–45, 48).

§ 4 teaches two things:

- Isaiah 45:7 is used, but not entirely. For in reality, the prophet said: *He who makes peace and creates evil; I am the Lord who makes all these things*. The *Talmud* (*B.T. Berakhot* 11ab) justifies the suppression of 'creates evil', which it is impossible to say in prayer, but the *Talmud* does not reject what the prophet said and which one may not water down through demagogy by replacing *evil* with *misfortune*. What follows in the verse and which is maintained with a slight modification in the prayer, 'who creates everything' instead of 'who makes all these things', teaches that the Lord is responsible for all of his creation; evil cannot be outside of creation. We again find the fundamental conviction that God is One and that God's creation is one. The existence of evil is a fundamental but paradoxical element in creation: How can God in his kindness create evil, or at least, a world in which evil exists?

- This way of using Isaiah without quoting him, shows the power of the oral *Torah* to confirm Scripture. Isaiah, used by Scripture, even becomes a new Scripture. For the midrash *Sifra* on Leviticus 26:6 uses the text of the prayer cited as Scripture as the basis for its teaching, according to which peace weighs as heavily as everything

24. *Cf* the commentary by H de Lubac on the Second Vatican Council's Declaration *Dei Verbum*, *La Révélation divine* (Paris: Cerf, 1983), 63–69.

(all good things), since Scripture says: 'Who makes peace and creates everything.'[25]

§ 5 gives the *kedushah*, the quotation from Isaiah linked with that of Ezekiel, and continues in a way that, in contrast to what we shall see in the text of the additional prayer for Shabbat and feasts, is not very developed. The blessing does not mention Israel. It does so only at the end through a later addition (§ 7). For the blessing *yotser* does not want to talk about anything except the Creator God and God's creation. The heavenly liturgy revealed to Israel by Isaiah and Ezekiel has entered into Israel's prayer based on the prayer of a group that spoke of contemplation and meditation on the mystery of creation.[26]

The prayer receives from Isaiah the vision of the Glory of the Holy God in his Temple. This Glory appears in the world. As Israel's Tradition says later, the Glory is the reality of God's presence in the world. It is the *Shekhinah*, the particular 'real presence' of God in the Temple and in the world. The Seraphim in Isaiah acclaim this presence of the One who is seated on a raised throne, and Isaiah, who shares this vision, is sent to communicate it to Israel. Now the heavenly liturgy has come down to earth, but because of its origin, it remains in contact with the Holy God, whose Place remains unknown. That is what Ezekiel's Living Creatures give to understand when they communicate their experience to the prophet: the Glory of God's *Shekhinah* manifests itself in the world, in the *known Place* in the Temple, but it proceeds from *its Place*, which remains *unkown*.

The paradox of the *known Place*, which reveals the *unknown Place* is so fundamental that it will justify one of the names given to God by Tradition. God is called *the Place* (*ha-makom*) because God is the *Place par excellence*, the *Place of the world*, which does away with the cosmic illusion, according to which the world is the real *place*, the *place* that counts (*cf Genesis Rabbah on Gen* 28:11, 16–17. Par. 6, 9). This *kedushah* does not say that God and God's *Shekhinah* are *One* single and same reality. Israel is not yet there to say it. Israel will say this in the Great *Kedushah* of the additional prayer for Shabbat and feasts, which we shall study.

25. *Sifra* on Lev 26:6 p. 111.
26. *Cf* J Heinemann, *Prayer*, 232–233.

§ 6 takes up the formula of § 4, which teaches the ongoing creation. It is interesting to see that the formula is based on Psalm 136:7: *You who* form *the luminaries*, in the present tense.

§ 7: In mentioning Israel, this paragraph is not part of the original text, which probably dates from before the destruction of the Temple. Neither Zion nor Israel must appear in this blessing, which celebrates God as the universal Creator of all of creation.

§ 8 gives the conclusion with the liturgical formula and sums up the entire blessing. This blessing speaks of Creation and not of Revelation. The explanation for the insertion of the *kedushah* could be the circumstances imposed by history, but the insertion's result makes possible the teaching of the paradox of creation and openness to the question that never ceases to arise: how can God, who creates the world out of kindness and who remains present in it in order to maintain its existence, remain in God's transcendent sanctity, in silence and absence, abandoning the world to misfortune, to evil, to the suffering of innocent people?

In order to enter better into the debate on God's paradoxical Unity, it is good to see how Tradition teaches the obligation to imitate God and God's mercy, based on Scripture. God *suffers with* those who suffer (*cf* Ps 91:15: *He calls me and I answer him; I am with him in distress*).

Let us return to the midrash *Sifre*, a midrash halakhah that bases the commandment to imitate God on Deuteronomy 11:22.

Sifre on Deuteronomy 11:22, pp. 114–115 (Text 11)

> Deuteronomy 11:22: *For if you really keep and put into practice all these commandment that I command you, loving YHWH your God, walking in all his ways and attaching yourselves to him. 'Walking in all his ways'.* These are the ways of the Place [God] (Ex 34:6): *YHWH, God [El] who is merciful and gracious*; and Scripture says (Joel 3:5 /NRSV Joel 2:32): *And every person who will be called by the name of YHWH will be saved.* But is it possible for the human being to be called by the name of God? Yes indeed! The *Place* is called merciful; you too be merciful.

Here, we hear the most explicit midrash on the obligation to imitate God, *to walk according to all his ways*, according to God's mercy, according to God's justice . . . The list is not a closed one. In addition, it is taught that God must also be imitated according to God's sanctity, God's humility and God's perfection. The way of perfection, which is not as clearly taught as one would wish, is fundamental, because it joins the human person to God's Unity. Joining God in his Unity is to enter eternal life. That is the teaching for which the midrash aims, and it becomes *midrash haggadah* by basing itself on Joel 3:5.

To imitate God is to unify oneself with God (*to be called by God's name*, Joel 3:5). Imitation in the way of mercy is the way of 'non-division', which leads to perfection. The imitation of the perfection to which Jesus invites (Mt 5:47) leads to 'non-division', to the union with God that Jesus lives fully (Jn 10:20) and to which he leads his disciples (Jn 17:21–22).

The Lord asks that a person attach him- or herself to him in the perfection ('non-division') of love.

Rabbi Akiba died not divided, speaking the words of the *Shema Israel*, uniting the love and the fear of God in his heart (texts 12 and 13).

The Lord asks that a person attach him- or herself to him in the perfection ('non-division') of love.

Some reference points:

The Torah of the Lord is perfect (Ps 19:8).

The Lord God is the Rock, God's activity is perfect (Deut 32:4). The Lord asks to be imitated (Deut 11:22; Lk 6:27–40; Eph 5:1–2).

Scripture (the Hebrew Bible) does not say that God is perfect. However, this does flow from what Scripture does affirm (Ps 19:8): *The Torah of the Lord is perfect*, and (Deut 32:4): *He is the Rock, his action is perfect*. It is thus clear that God is perfect. The oral Torah can say this, as does Jesus in Matthew's Gospel (5:47): *You therefore be perfect as your heavenly Father is perfect*. This message resonates entirely with the *Gospel according to Luke*, which teaches imitation of God along the lines of mercy and of 'non-division' (6:35). Saint Paul for his part exhorts to the forgiveness and love *which bring about unity in perfection* (in 'non-division', Col 3:15).

We shall now read the texts.

Tradition includes several versions of the martyrdom of Rabbi Akiba. The two main versions offered here, that of the *Babylonian Talmud* and that of the *Jerusalem Talmud*, converge to give the full message of Rabbi Akiba: that of *Unity* in the *Babylonian Talmud*, that of *non-division* in the *Jerusalem Talmud*.

Before recounting Rabbi Akiba's death, the *Babylonian Talmud* transmits the exegesis of Deuteronomy 6:5, which Akiba proposed along the lines of his teacher Rabbi Eliezer. The *Talmud* underlines how the life and death of Rabbi Akiba manifest the unification practiced in imitating the One God.

I have added an extract from the *Letter on Ecstasy* by R Dov Baer of Lubavitch, which magnificently extends Rabbi Akiba's teaching.

B.T. Berakhot 61b. Dov Baer of Lubavitch, Letter on Ecstasy (Text 12)

> It has been taught: Rabbi Eliezer said: If it says (Deut 6:5) *with all your soul*, why does it say *with all your strength*, and if it is says *with all your strength*, why does it say *with all your soul*? But in reality [*ella*], you can find one man who prefers his body to his money; that is why it says *with all your soul*; and you can find one man who prefers his money to his body; that is why it says *with all your strength*. Rabbi Akiba said: *with all your soul*, even if he takes your soul.
>
> Our masters taught: It happened once that the perverse kingdom [Rome] decreed that Israel would no longer be occupied with the Torah. Pappos ben Yehudah went to see Rabbi Akiba and found him bringing together public assemblies and being occupied with the Torah. He said to him: 'Akiba! Are you not afraid of the kingdom?' Akiba answered him: 'I shall show you by means of a parable what our situation is like. It is like a fox who was walking along a river and who saw fish gathering together and fleeing from one place to another. He said to them: "Why are you fleeing?" They told him: "We are fleeing from the nets that the children of Adam put out for us." He said to them: "If you want, you can come up on the dry land and we will live together, you and I, like my fathers lived with your fathers." They said to him: "Are you the one of whom it is said that you are the most cunning of the animals? You are not cunning, you are stupid! For if we

> are afraid in our vital element [*'hiyyut*], how much more must we fear to go to a place that is our death!" It is the same for us. If now we are afraid while we are seated and occupied with the Torah, of which Scripture says (Deut 30:20): *For this* [*hu*: *this* or *it*] *is your life and the length of your days*, how much more must we fear if we would abandon and leave it!' It is recounted that a short time afterwards, R Akiba was arrested and put in prison in chains. Pappos ben Yehudah was also arrested and put in chains next to him. R Akiba said to him: 'Pappos, who brought you here?' He answered him: 'Happy are you, R Akiba, who were arrested because of the words of the Torah! Unhappy Pappos who was arrested for vain things!'
>
> When R Akiba was brought out to be put to death, it was the hour for *Reading the Shema*. His skin was torn with iron combs, and he 'received the yoke of the Kingdom of Heaven'. His disciples said to him: 'O our master! Even to this point!' He said to them: 'Every day of my life I was preoccupied by this verse "*with all your soul*", which means: even if he takes your soul. I asked myself: "When will I be able to accomplish it [*akayyemnu*]?" And now that this is given me, should I not accomplish it?' He prolonged the word *One* [*ehad*] until he gave up his soul. A heavenly voice was heard saying: 'Happy are you, Akiba, whose soul went out saying "*One*"! The Angels of Service said before the Holy One, blessed be He!: This Torah and this reward (Ps 17:14): *deaths by your hand, Lord, deaths*!' He said to them, 'their part is in life'. A heavenly voice came out and said: 'Happy are you, Rabbi Akiba, for you are invited to the life of the world to come!'

R Dov Bear of Lubavitch 1773–1827, Letter on Ecstasy, Likutey Beurim, 1868, 5a

> Why does Scripture say (Deut 30:20): *For He* [*hu*] *is your life*? The literal meaning of Scripture which is certainly understandable for everyone, is that *He is your life*. That is why you shall love him. Why must you love him? Because He is your life.

The fable about the fish and the fox shows the value of water as the vital milieu (*hiyyut*) for the fish. Just as the water is the vital milieu for the fish, the Torah is the vital milieu for Israel.

With *Rav Dov Baer of Lubavitch*, we go further along the lines of Rabbi Akiba in understanding that the text of Deuteronomy 30:19–20 means: 'Choose therefore life . . . loving God . . . attaching yourself to him, for He [*hu*, he and not that] is your life.' This interpretation hints at *the triad: God, the Torah, Israel,* which we shall encounter again.[27] The way this triad resonates for Christians is: God, Jesus (Torah: incarnate Word), Israel-Church. Because for the Christian who has received the Holy Spirit in baptism, Jesus is the Torah *par excellence*; he is One with God the Father, as the Torah is One with God.

J.T. Berakhot 7, 67b (Text 13)

> Rabbi Akiba was tried before Tineius Rufus the Impious. The time came to read the *Shema*. He began to read the *Shema* and he was filled with joy. [Rufus] said to him: 'Old man, are you a sorcerer or do you despise suffering?' He answered him: 'May the spirit of this man go out! I am not a sorcerer and I do not despise suffering. But every day I read this verse *and you shall love the Lord your God with all your heart, with all your soul and with all your strength.* I was preoccupied and I said to myself: So when will these three things come into my hand? I have loved him with all my heart, I have loved him with all my money, but *with all your soul*–this had not yet been proven. Now that the time has come to prove *with all your soul*, now that the time for *Reading the Shema* has come, I have not turned aside from it.'

We can also understand: '*My soul did not become divided* (in my relationship with God)' [*cf Sifre Deuteronomy on Deut* 6:4 (text 5)].

Rabbi Hananiah ben Teradion, like his contemporary Rabbi Akiba, died as a martyr under the Romans around the year 185 CE for having defied the Romans' prohibition of being occupied with the Torah. His wife and his daughter were condemned with him. Like him, they found verses in Scripture which *justified the judgment* of God. They all accepted the condemnation allowed by God in his unfathomable justice. They all remained 'non-divided', attached to the perfect God, to the One and indivisible Rock. God's justice is One with God's mercy. Deuteronomy 32:4: *The Rock, his doing is perfect.*

Sifre on Deuteronomy 32:4, p. 346 (Text 14)

---

27. See the summing up of the triads at the end of this chapter.

> When they seized Rabbi Hananiah ben Teradion, it was decided that he would be burnt together with his book. He read [*kara*] this Scripture [*mikra*]: *The Rock, his doing is perfect*. They said to his wife: 'It has been decided that your husband will be burnt and that you will be killed.' She read this Scripture (Deut 32:4): *Faithful God and without iniquity*. They said to his daughter: 'It has been decided that your father will be burnt, your mother killed and that you will have to work [in a house of tolerance].' She read this Scripture (Jer 32:19): *Great in your plans, powerful in your exalted deeds, you whose eyes are open on all the ways of human beings*. Rabbi said: 'How great are these righteous who in the hour of their distress have called upon three verses concerning the Justification of Judgment [*tsidduk hadin*], which have no equal in all the Scriptures!' While they were directing [*kivvenu*] their heart and they were justifying the judgment upon them, a philosopher arose against the governor of his province and said to him: 'Lord, may your spirit not pride itself on having burnt the Torah, for from the place whence she came out, she has returned to the house of her father.' He said to him [the governor to the philosopher]: 'Tomorrow you will also be judged like them.' He said to him [the philosopher to the governor]: 'You have just announced good news [*besorah*, gospel] to me. May my part tomorrow be with them in the world to come!'

Jesus died while crying out the Psalm (Ps 22:2; *cf* Mt 27:46) whose cry *my God, my God* is addressed to the God of Mercy, as Israel's Tradition lets us understand (text 22). In his most profound abandonment, Jesus remained 'non-divided', perfect. His trust in divine Mercy, which he maintained in his suffering even unto death, *made him perfect* (Heb 4:8–9; 7:28).

Midrash Tehillim (a late rabbinic compilation of ancient interpretations of the Psalms) helps us to hear how Psalm 31:5–6: *Into your hands I place my spirit*, which according to the Gospel of Luke (23:46), Jesus cries at his death, completes Psalm 22, which he cries according to Matthew (27:46) and Mark's (15:34) Gospels.

Midrash Tehillim on Psalm 25:1 (Text 15)

> Psalm 25:1: *To you, Lord, I lift up my soul*. That is what Scripture says (Ps 31:6): *Into your hands I place my spirit*.

> According to the custom of the world [*nohag she-ba-olam*], you give someone objects as a pledge, and he replaces this with that, that with this, because the objects are not known. But the Holy One, blessed be He, is not like that, for (Ps 31:6): *Lord [YHWH] God [El] of truth.* For fear that someone will get up in the morning, will ask for his soul and won't find it, or for fear that he will find his soul in the hand of another, or the soul of another in his hand, that is why it says (Ps 31:6): *It is you who redeem me, Lord, God of truth.*
>
> Rabbi Alexandri said: 'To flesh and blood [*basar vedam*] you give new objects [as a pledge]; they remain in his house, and he returns them used and aged. But to the Holy One, blessed be He!, you give used and deteriorated objects and he returns them new. Know that it really is like this, for look: Here is a worker who does his work all day and his soul weighs on him from fatigue and use, but when he sleeps in the state of fatigue, he builds up his soul again and places it into the hand of the Holy One, blessed be He! In the morning, his soul returns to his body as a new creature, as it is said (Lam 3:22–23): *The Lord's favors are not finished, nor is his mercy exhausted; they are renewed each morning; great is his fidelity.*'
>
> Rabbi Shimeon in the name of Rabbi Simon said: 'Because of the fact that you restore us [every] morning, we know and we believe that you return our souls for the resurrection of the dead.'
>
> Rabbi Alexandri said: 'Because of the fact that you renew us every morning in the diaspora, we know that your fidelity is great for redeeming us.'

Psalm 22 (Matthew and Mark) expresses the *suffering of abandonment by God*; Psalm 31 (Luke) expresses the *trust of abandonment to God.* The trust takes on the suffering. The 'non-division' in suffering is the fulfilment of human imitation of God's Unity. The imitation of God by the human person and by the God-Man (Jesus Christ) is for the Christian the great testimony given to the Trinity. The Holy Spirit makes it possible to express this testimony by inspiring the Psalms and those who cry them at the moment of death.

The Unity of the Torah as the Basis for its Diversity

Imitation of the One God enables one to attain the perfection of love—of love of the neighbour even when he or she is the enemy. The Torah of the One God is One by its origin, but it is plural and diverse for the human beings for whom it is meant. Plurality and diversity are the two necessary developments of the Torah as revealed to human beings according to their multitude and diversity. The texts that we shall study now manifest the conviction that the Unity of the Torah and of God underlies and legitimises the multiplicity, diversity, even divergence that unfold in the world, in view of bringing everything to Unity. Unity is reached by means of conformity, not conformism. The texts do not answer the question as to how the plural and the diverse can come from the unfathomable, ineffable, transcendent Unity proclaimed by the *Shema Israel* (Deut 6:4: *The Lord is One).*[28] They transmit the inspired, paradoxical experience of the God who is revealed and hidden, present and absent (immanent and transcendent), just and merciful.

Based on God's perfection (non-division), we have seen how the Unity of God is proclaimed and joined in a negative way. Let us now see how God's Unity is proclaimed in a positive way. This shall be done in two stages:

1. proclaiming God's Unity based on the Unity of God's Word;
2. proclaiming God's Unity based on those who witness to God.

Proclaiming God's Unity based on the Unity of God's Word

The text of the *midrash Sifre Deuteronomy* transmits an ancient anonymous tradition on the Canticle of Moses (Deut 32:2), in which the

28. We shall see further on, with text 33, how the One Torah is 'the beginning of his way'; the beginning, 'begotten, not made', come forth from the One Creator God. Israel's Tradition as shown by Ben Sirach (Sir 24:23) identifies Wisdom with the Torah. For Christians, Jesus, the incarnate Word, is the Torah. He is begotten, not made. As the Father is One, he is One, non-divided; he is also ineffably One with the Father. The Church, in teaching the mystery of the Trinity, does not teach how to go out of the One. That would mean resolving Parmenides' *aporia*. Following Israel, the Church teaches that the One begets the One and Only, through whom the world is created and can know the Creator.

teaching of Moses, who speaks in the first person, is presented as the teaching of God.[29]

Sifre on Deuteronomy 32:2, p. 339 (Text 16)

> *Deuteronomy* 32:2: *May my teaching stream like rain!*
> Just as rain falls onto the trees and gives each of them the taste that suits it, the one that suits the vine, the one that suits the olive tree, the one that suits the fig tree, even so the words of the whole Torah are One [Unity], and in it there is *mikra* [what one reads, Scripture] and *mishnah* [what is transmitted through repetition, oral Tradition], Talmud [what one learns and teaches, especially exegesis], *halakhot* [normative traditions for putting into practice] and *haggadot* [narrative, homiletic traditions].

The use of the link between teaching and rain is particularly appropriate for showing the divine origin of the Torah and its ability to unite all its developments. The different categories and disciplines are detailed clearly based on the Torah's two great expressions: *Mikra*: Scripture, written Torah, and *Mishnah*: Tradition, oral Torah. Mentioning the *Talmud* (the oral Torah that makes the link between Scripture and Tradition) as well as the *Haggadah* and the *Halakhah* (the two great genres in both the written and the oral Torah) means that the list includes the words of *the whole Torah,* where all the words of the Torah are One (*ahat*). This One is feminine because the Torah is feminine. The feminine form of *One* probably refers back to the *One* (*ehad*, masculine) in the *Shema Israel*: *The Lord is One* (in the masculine). The Torah of the One God (masculine, ehad) is thus One (feminine, ahat) in all its developments. This was the conviction of the pharisaic masters and is that of religious Judaism, which ensures its living continuity in our day. In opposition to the Sadducees and their successors, who do not recognise Tradition as the Word of God, the Pharisees and their successors believe that the interpretation of Scripture (which the *Talmud* does through *midrash*) is as much the Word of God as Scripture itself.

---

29. Deuteronomy speaks with the authority of Moses, who speaks in the first person, in order to transmit the Word of God. However, this does not prevent problems arising. *Cf* for example the case of Deuteronomy 11:14 (I shall give rain in its time . . .), which the Septuagint has in the third person.

By referring to the fruits of the trees that are made fertile through rain, the text suggests that each of the Torah's disciplines has its own flavor. This is quite evident in the *Mishnah* of Rabbi Yehudah ha-Nassi within the *mishnah* (*oral Torah*). The Torah that comes from heaven (*Torah min ha-shamaim*) gives the editors of the *Mishnah* of R Yehudah ha-Nassi (the Jews say *Our Mishnah*) what is necessary for their oral text to have the flavor that characterizes it: lapidary conciseness, stylistic elegance, etc. Of course, it is not possible to go so far as to say what the Muslims say about the Qur'an: 'miraculously inimitable' (*'i'jlaz 'al-qur'an*), uncreated (*'al-qur'an ghayru makhluq*). Nevertheless, it remains difficult not to taste the oral nature of the *Mishnah*. One can equally savor the musical dialectic of many passages from the *halakhic midrashim* and the Talmudic discussions. As for the roar in the *yeshivah*, which is as great as the sea (Debussy), it is the specific expression of Jewish music. This said, the aim and merit of our text is above all that it teaches the *Unity of the whole Torah,* and at the root of that Unity, the Unity of the oral and of the written Torah. We owe to the pharisaic masters that they confirmed and developed what Judaism was already, according to the *Second Book of Maccabees*: the Unity of Jewish life based on the Torah (*Scripture and Tradition*).[30] The Torah is One (ahat) because it is given by the One (ehad) God. It is dual, Scripture and Tradition, because it needs to develop in reference to authorised reference points. For the Christians, Jesus Christ unites in his person the original, age-old, ancient (Mosaic and written) Torah and the historical, oral Torah, of which, as the incarnate Word and *abridged Word,* he is the summit.[31]

Our text as heard by a Christian brings out the need to be based on the duality of the Torah and on its diversity, which manifests its Unity when witnessing to the Trinity. The Unity of *Halakhah* and

30. According to the *Talmud (B.T. Menahot 65a-b)*, Rabban Yohanan ben Zakkai opposed the complete Torah (*torah shelemah,* Scripture and Tradition) of the Pharisees to the vain conversation (*sihah betelah*) of the Bethusians (Sadducees). The complete Torah of the Pharisees and their successors unites Tradition and Scripture. The Church receives this reality from the Synagogue. It is to be regretted that Luther did not recognize the value of this heritage and reproached the Jews with not seeing the Trinity as taught by Scripture. It is Tradition that interprets Scripture and teaches the Trinity. It is not Scripture (alone).

31. On the abridged Word, *cf* H de Lubac, *Exégèse Médiévale II* (Paris: Aubier, 1961), 181–197; *L'Ecriture dans la Tradition* (Paris: Aubier-Montaigne, 1966), 232–246.

Haggadah must also be underlined; in many rabbinic texts, they support and enlighten one another.[32]

After seeing the diversity of disciplines and genres in the Torah, it is appropriate to look at the tension between Unity and multiplicity at the level of the Torah's addressees.

Proclaiming God's Unity based on those who Witness to God

The *Mekhilta de-Rabbi Ishmael* is a *midrash halakhah*, the aim of which is to recall the practice (the *halakhah* taught by Tradition) in the text (of Scripture) of the *Book of Exodus*. The *Mekhilta* thus begins with the interpretations of the first commandment given to Israel even before the gift of the Torah at Sinai, the commandment to establish the calendar (Ex 12:1–2). The priority given to *halakhah* does not prevent Tradition from giving the meaning of the Exodus and of Passover by means of the *haggadah*. The text sheds light on the meaning of the gift of the Torah at Sinai as well as on the meaning of the theophany that is the prelude to this gift and that illuminates it.

The following text introduces two masters of rabbinic exegesis, *Rabbi Ishmael* and *Rabbi Akiba*, who clarified and developed the methods and teachings of their masters in Yavne at the beginning of the second century CE.

The verse Exodus 20:18 presents an anomaly, for can one see voices? Rabbi Ishmael eliminates the difficulty along the lines of the principle that is characteristic for him: 'The Torah spoke according to the language of human beings.' Thus it suffices to complete the phrase and to say: 'And when the people saw the lights and heard the voices.' In general, the Sages of Israel prefer this rational and reasonable exegesis. Nevertheless, one cannot ignore Rabbi Akiba's interpretation, which is along the lines of his master (Nahum Ish Gamzo), and which has its origin in the same way of understanding as that of Jesus in Matthews' Gospel (5:18). For Jesus and for R. Akiba, the Torah was no doubt said and written in human language. However, the written text keeps the indelible trace of its divine origin. Every detail, every anomaly must be respected and if possible interpreted. For R Akiba,

32. *Cf* Y Fraenkel, 'La relation entre la halakah et la aggadah (in Hebrew: ha-yahas bein halakah la aggadah)', in Darkey ha-aggadah we-ha-midrash, hotsa'at yad ha-talmud, giv'atayyim, 1991.

contact with the One God at Sinai enables the people to see and to hear the manifestations of God in a single act of perception.

What follows in the text is along the lines of Rabbi Akiba. For the multiplicity of voices and lights in the theophany is not the result of literary emphasis at the service of the event's greatness, as Rabbi Ishmael could say. The multiplicity is given in order to correspond with the multiplicity and diversity of revelation's addressees. Each person in Israel, man and woman, receives his or her voice and light from Sinai, his or her limited and particularized, authenticated Torah as '*Torah coming from heaven*'. This conviction can find support in the interpretation of Psalm 29:4: *Voice of the Lord in strength.*

Mekhilta de-Rabbi Ishmael on Exodus 20:18, 235 (Text 17)[33]

> Ex 20:18: *And when all the people saw the voices* [and the lights and the voice of the shofar and the smoking mountain . . .]. "They saw the visible and heard the audible", words of Rabbi Ishmael. Rabbi Akiba said: "They saw and heard the visible. They saw a word of fire that came out of the mouth of the All-Power [*gevurah*] and that engraved itself on the tablets, as it is said (*Ps* 29:7): *Voice of the Lord that engraves flames of fire*".
>
> *And when all the people saw the voices* [and the lights]: voice [singular], voices [*casus constructus*], voices [plural]; light [singular], lights [*casus constructus*], lights [plural]. But how many voices were there and how many lights were there? In reality, each person was made to hear according to his and her strength, as it is said (Ps 29:4): *Voice of the Lord in strength* [according to the strength of each listener]. Rabbi said: 'This comes to proclaim the praise of Israel. For when they all stood before Mount Sinai to receive the Torah, they heard the Word and they explained it. As it is said (Deut 32:10): either "He [the Lord] *surrounded* [Israel] and made it understand", or "He went around it, he understood it". For as soon as they heard the Word, they began to explain it.'

33. The de in the title is the Aramaic equivalent to the Hebrew shel. The Mekhilta is attributed to Rabbi Ishmael because he is the first master to appear in the collection, which in its original form begins with the interpretation of Exodus 12:2.

Psalm 29 exalts the glory and power of the Lord, king of the universe, the strength of his voice which produces thunder and lightning. This praise has its place in a tradition that interprets the theophany at Sinai. In the context of the theophany, verse 4 of Psalm 29 means literally (*pashut*) that the voice of the Lord spreads out in the strength that dominates the measurements and the elements of the created world. This is true, but it remains banal. It goes without saying that the thunder and lightning of the Creator of the world go beyond those of Zeus, the most powerful of Greece's gods. The search (*midrash*) for the deep meaning of Scripture finds God and recognizes God as the one who paradoxically manifests his power by limiting it.[34] The interpretation offered here, along the lines of Rabbi Akiba, is a perfect example of how excellent the rabbinic principle is, according to which "Scripture does not leave its simple meaning." (*B.T. Shabbat* 63a) The principle means that exegesis (*midrash*) cannot ignore the literal sense (*pashut*), and even less can it contradict it. Our text offers an interpretation (*midrash*) which not only respects the literal sense (*pashut*), but fulfills it by deepening it: God is strong in his creation and in his revelation; in revealing himself, God limits himself to the strength of the one person, the individual men and women, to whom God gives his Torah.

Each person in Israel receives from the One (from the One God) the ability to be One with God, to be, through God and with God, One and Only. Each person receives God's voice and God's light from Sinai, his or her Torah which is One with the One Torah of the One God. The *Jewish Trinity*, a formula used by J.Z. Lauterbach which we shall see further on, corresponds with this primordial experience of Israel's at Sinai, an experience according to which "God, the Torah and Israel are One (Unity)."

Each person in Israel can and must be a living Torah.[35] The master is a living Torah for his disciples.[36] All the more so and in a radical way, Jesus Christ is for Christians the living and lived Torah.

---

34. E Urbach, *The Sages. Their Concepts and Beliefs* (Jurusalem: Magnes Press, The Hebrew University), 95, mentions 'the paradoxical statement of Abba Hanan that God's silence is His might.'
35. *Cf* Rashi on B.T. Shabbat 105b.
36. B.T. Sanhedrin 101 a b; Sanhedrin 68a. Rabbi Nahman of Bratslav, Likutey Moharan I 207 112d.

Through midrash and its precedents, especially through the necklace (*harizah*) and the prelude or proem (*petihah*), the oral Torah manifests the Unity and the Divinity of the Whole Torah.

Chapter 2 of the Mishnah's treatise *Hagigah* notes Tradition's reservations regarding the uncontrolled way of studying and interpreting the biblical accounts of Creation as well as the visions of Isaiah and Ezekiel. In the development of the mishnah, the Jerusalem Talmud recounts experiences of certain masters in these domains that are more or less recommended.

The best-known experience is that of Rabbi Akiba, Ben Azzai, Ben Zoma and Elisha, who entered Paradise and who came out in very different ways: Rabbi Akiba was safe and sound, Ben Azzai died, Ben Zoma lost his mind, and Elisha became a heretic. The Talmud continues to speak of Elisha and of his disciple Rabbi Meir who sought to bring his master back to God. The question arises whether Elisha, the son of Abuyah, wasn't under a bad influence right from the start. One tradition that is placed into Elisha's mouth recounts what was told him on the day of his circumcision. The account is extended by a conclusion that makes the bad influence explicit.

The text interests us for a different reason. It shows us how traditional exegesis can manifest the Unity and the Holiness of the whole Torah.

J.T. Hagigah 2 77b (Text 18)

> My father Abuyah was one of Jerusalem's great personalities. When the day came on which I was to be circumcised, he invited all the great personalities of Jerusalem and installed them in a house. As for Rabbi Eliezer and Rabbi Yehoshua, he put them in another house. When those invited had finished eating and drinking, they began to clap their hands and to dance. Rabbi Eliezer said to Rabbi Yehoshua: 'While those are spending their time in their way, let us occupy ourselves in our way.' So they began to be occupied with the words of the Torah, going from the Torah to the Prophets and from the Prophets to the holy Writings. A fire came down from heaven and surrounded them. My father Abuyah said to them: 'My Masters! Did you come to set my house on fire?' They answered him: 'God forbid! But we were sitting and making a necklace [*horzim*] with the words of the Torah. We went from the Torah to the Prophets and from the Prophets to the holy Writings, and behold, these words became joyful as they were

> when they were given at Sinai, and the fire began to lick them like it licked them at Sinai.'
>
> And in fact, when these words were given the first time at Sinai, they were given in fire, as it is said (Deut 4:11): *And the mountain burned in the fire even to the heart of heaven.*
>
> Then my father Abuyah told them: 'My masters! Since such is the strength of the Torah, if this son remains alive, I shall separate him for the Torah.'
>
> Since his intention [that of Abuyah] was not in the name of Heaven, his words were not fulfilled for this man [for Elisha].

The feast of circumcision, concerning which Elisha received the story, occurred at a time of peace, which preceded the Jewish revolt and the destruction of the Temple in the year 70. Rabbi Eliezer and Rabbi Yehoshua were already considered to be important pharisaic masters and were honored as such. Abuyah was rich and influential, which resulted in many invited guests surrounding and feasting him by dancing. The masters were not required to clap their hands and to dance as they would have been if their host had been poor and without visitors.

The fire that falls is the fire of Sinai made present through the masters' exegesis. The experience of fire is not limited to the masters' subjectivity. It is experienced around them by those who hear and see and go to warn Abuyah. The masters explain that they were making a necklace (*harizah*) out of verses drawn from the three parts of Scripture.

The conclusion given by the Talmud deduces Abuyah's bad intention from his words: to separate his son (to consecrate him) for the Torah (because the Torah gives power).

This is the most ancient manifestation of the power of exegesis and of the *harizah* resulting from it that we know in rabbinic tradition. It clearly resonates with the two applications of the *harizah* by Jesus at the end of the Gospel of Luke (24:27, 44). In these contexts, the mind opens to understanding the Scriptures and the fire of Sinai causes the hearts to burn in joy.[37]

37. *Cf* P Lenhardt, 'Trois chemins: Emmaüs; Gaza et Damas'; *Cahiers Ratisbonne*, 4 (June 1998): 13–34, reprinted in: *A l'écoute d'Israël, en Eglise, Volume II* (Paris: Parole et Silence 2009), 147ff.

The experience that is described is not a mystical experience. This is said clearly after the destruction of the Temple as regards Ben Azzai. *Midrash Shir ha-Shirim Rabba* relates his experience and connects it to the necklaces (*haruzim*) that increase the beauty of the Beloved woman in the Song of Songs (1:10). The necklace symbolism is very enlightening if one uses it well. According to the spiritual interpretation of the Song of Songs, the Beloved woman is the Assembly of Israel. The male Beloved, God, sees above all the beauty of his Beloved, Israel, who puts into practice the oral Torah and decorates herself with the pearls of Scripture (written Torah). The main beauty is that of Israel and the oral Torah. The relative, secondary beauty of the necklace, of Scripture, increases the beauty of the beloved woman and becomes one with her.

Israel's midrash puts into practice the One Torah, oral and written; it manifests God's Sanctity and God's Unity, which are perceived by means of the diversity of the Word that is entrusted to Israel.

Let us underline once more that the experience of the necklace's fire, like that of hearing the heavenly voice, of which we shall speak (text 20) and to which we shall return in Part II,[38] are not subjective, mystical experiences but manifestations that are addressed to the listeners or spectators chosen by God in order to be visual or auditory witnesses for their successors in faith (*cf* Jn 12:30 and 20:29: *Happy are those who have not seen and who have believed*).

Since the Torah is one and divine, it is not only capable of expressing itself in the diversity of its expressions. It can also dominate the differences in its expressions. In order to be implemented by those who receive it, the One Word must be at least dual and at times contradictory.

Let us see how the *Mekhilta de-Rabbi Ishmael* interprets the double Word of the Decalogue concerning the manner of practicing the Sabbath.

Mekhilta de-Rabbi Ishmael on Exodus 20:8, 229 (Text 19)

> (Ex 20:8): *Remember* and (Deut 5:12) *Observe* . . . the two were said in one single statement.
>
> (Ex 32:14): *The one who defiles it shall be put to death* and (Num 28:9): *and on the day of Shabbat you will offer two lambs* . . . the two were said in one and the same statement.

38. *Cf* the notes and texts 94 and 95 in Part II.

> (Lev 18:16): *You will not uncover the nakedness of your brother's wife* and (Deut 25:5): *Her husband's brother will come upon her* . . . the two were said in one and the same statement.
>
> (*Deut* 22:11): *You shall not wear a hybrid cloth* and (Deut 22:12): *You shall make tassels* . . ., the two were said in one single statement.
>
> It is not possible for human beings to say this in that way, as it is said (Ps 62:12): *God said one thing, I heard two* and Scripture says (Jer 23:29): *Is my word not thus: like a fire, word of the Lord* [like a hammer that pulverizes the rock]?

The ancient, authorised anonymous Tradition gives an enlightening answer to the question that arises concerning the Decalogue. Why do we have two versions for a teaching that is as fundamental as this one, two versions with differences, the most important of which is that of *Remember* and *Observe*? Everyone in Israel knows the laconic answer, everyone who sings the *Lekhah Dodi* (Come, my Beloved [male]!) at the conclusion of the *Shabbat Welcome* on Friday evening: 'The two were said in one single statement.' One can easily understand that the practice of Shabbat responds to two demands: that of *remembering* (the creation of the world, the exodus from Egypt, the sanctity of Shabbat which in a real way anticipates that of the world to come) and that of *observing* (the rest and the commandments that protect it). These two demands are joined: one must attach oneself to God and live God's ineffable Unity. When well understood and lived, these demands let one feel the Unity from which they proceed. Then one understands that the two words which prescribe remembering and observing were in truth said by God in one single statement. The text gives several deliberately heterogeneous examples of implementations for which the diversity is legitimate from the beginning. The text's conclusion in two stages teaches something fundamental.

First of all, the reference to Psalm 62:12 lets us understand that what comes from the Unity emerges as a primordial duality through which, according to what follows in the Psalm (62:12–13), God manifests the strength of his love (mercy) and works retribution on the deeds of human beings (justice). Thus one manifestation of God's

Unity is fundamentally that of the Unity of God's mercy and of God's justice.[39]

We then learn that such a duality enables one to express the ineffable Unity and at the same time, so to speak, to 'go out of' that Unity.[40] Let us note in this connection that the value of the number *two* is that it opens up plurality. Israel's Tradition emphasises this when it has to interpret an undetermined plurality. It brings that plural back to *two* according to the principle: 'you have seized what is numerous, you have not seized; you have seized what is few in number, you have seized' (*tafasta merubbeh lo tafasta, tafasta mu'at tafasta*) In other words: If you take on too much, you don't do any of it well (or if you prefer, "Who grabs all loses all"). Once one has gone out of the One by means of the Two, Tradition, based on the Two, can develop into infinity the rich multiplicity of manifestations of the original Unity.[41] Let us underline the importance of what the Decalogue's duality regarding the Sabbath makes possible to teach. In addition to memory's two motivations, the two complementary aspects of remembering and observing, remembering the creation of the world (Ex 20:11) and the exodus from Egypt (Deut 5:15) expresses the meaning and the role of the Sabbath: the universal and the particular meaning entrusted to Israel; this role is entrusted to Israel as God's collaborator in the creation of the world and in its redemption. It is difficult not to hear the way in which this resonates with the Christian faith in Jesus Christ.[42]

The conclusion's second recourse is to Jeremiah (23:29): *Is not my word like a fire, word of the Lord, and like a hammer that breaks the rock?* The text does not develop the interpretation of the verse, but here we can suggest: the Word of God is the Oral Torah (implemented by the masters of midrash), which strikes the rock of the writ-

---

39. The Shema Israel (Deut 6:4) illustrates this: Hear, O Israel, the Lord [*YHWH*, mercy], our God [*Eloheinu*, Elohim, justice], the Lord [*YHWH*, mercy] is One.
40. The verse of the Shema Israel lets us see that the duality points towards the original Unity. It is not possible to go so far as to say, like Luther, that this verse teaches the Trinity.
41. It is difficult to give a better description of the value of Two. Nevertheless let us say that the Two and the duality that it signifies, deserve more and better than what the medieval theologians said, as quoted by H de Lubac, *Exégèse médiévale II* (Paris: Aubier, 1964), 13–16.
42. *Cf* H de Lubac, 'La réalité du sabbat, c'est le Christ', in *Exégèse médiévale II*, 22.

ten Torah like a hammer and causes an infinite number of sparks to spring forth. In text 14 on Deuteronomy 32:4, which we saw above, the rock was the symbol of divine Unity, dense and impenetrable, non-divided, perfect, whose deeds are perfect. In our text 19, the rock is Scripture, rigid and closed, which living Tradition must open up, and it does that to infinity. The interpretation of Jeremiah offered here is not at first sight based on the literal meaning. For according to the literal meaning, the (intangible) Word of the Lord has the strength to break the (unbreakable) rock. This statement remains so to say banal. The interpretation by the midrash, which is moreover explicitly suggested by the Talmud (*B.T. Shabbat* 88b) uses the literal sense to draw the better meaning out of it: the strength of the Word can be heard in the strength of the oral Torah, which acts like a hammer on the impenetrable (non-divided, perfect) rock of the written Torah, causing the multitude of sparks that are the possible and real interpretations to spring forth to infinity. Rashi, in his commentary on the *Talmud*, lets us understand that the hammer causes sparks to come forth out of the rock. Moreover, disciples can be seen praising their master by calling him 'powerful hammer'.[43] For it is the Master who shows the strength of the oral Torah and the infinite wealth of its possible interpretations.

Let us also note the importance of referring to the Psalm and to Jeremiah. Through this reference it becomes possible to 'bring out' the duality and plurality from the Unity. Duality and plurality have their origin in the Unity; thus they cannot be degraded in division.[44] Our text showed how the multiplicity of interpretations in the domain of practice has its origin in the divine Unity and receives its legitimacy from that Unity. Let us note that in this text, the duality of prescriptions in opposition to one another does not go so far as to contradict one another.

The following text (text 20) deals with the possibility of contradiction. It shows that it is rather a matter of differences that are connected to the time and the context.

43. Rabban Yohanan ben Zakkai's students *(B.T. Berakhot* 28b*)*.

44. From a Christian point of view, the pharisaic-rabbinic teaching on the divine origin of duality is a precious point of reference for understanding better that the Incarnation of Jesus Christ proceeds from Unity.

'The Words of these and The Words of those are Words of The Living God'

The *Jerusalem Talmud* transmits a tradition according to which the heavenly Voice teaches with authority that every responsible opinion can be accepted as an expression of the Word of God. This tradition teaches that the manifestation of the heavenly Voice occurred at the beginning of the Yavne period. Later, also at Yavne, the Sages, following Rabbi Yehoshua and against Rabbi Eliezer, would decide that the heavenly Voice must give way to the opinion of a good majority of masters. We shall see how God himself approves of this decision by saying: 'My children have vanquished me.'

J.T. Berakhot 1, 7 3b (Text 20)

> Ever since the Heavenly Voice came forth [made itself heard], the halakhah is always according to the words of Beit Hillel, and whoever transgresses against the words of Beit Hillel is liable to death.
>
> It has been taught: a Heavenly Voice came forth and said: 'These and those (words) are words of the living God, but the halakhah is according to the words of Beit Hillel.'
>
> When the Heavenly Voice came forth, Rabbi Bibi said in the name of Rabbi Yohanan: 'The Heavenly Voice came forth in Yavne.'

It is impossible to study in detail such a rich and complex reality as the fact that the written Torah presents contradictions and that the oral Torah transmits many controversies that end up with contradictory opinions and teachings.[45] However, because this touches on the subject of Unity, we must at least broach it.

The divergences in opinion between Hillel and Shammai and controversies between their pupils, 'the House (*beit*) of Hillel' and 'the House of Shammai', occupy a place of honor in rabbinic literature. When badly imitated, badly interpreted or badly developed, they risk

45. On the importance of controversy *(mahloket)* cf R Fontana, 'Tarbut ha-Mahloqet, Una cultura della discussione', *in Cahiers Ratisbonne,* No 2 (June 1997): 118–136.

undermining the Unity of the Torah.[46] Our text testifies to the intervention of a *Heavenly Voice* (*Bat Kol*) at Yavne after the destruction of the Second Temple, which confirms the legitimacy of the controversies. They are not only legitimate because they submit to the living God; they are seen as the expression of God's Unity. It is not possible to go further than this in recognizing the power of the oral Torah. Each person or each group in Israel has his and her voice and light from Sinai and must not abandon his or her piece of Truth.[47] Certainly, one must find a *modus vivendi*, as the text indicates, and it is found. The most reasonable solution is to vote and to decide according to the majority. The minority is not discredited. Its position is noted and it is kept in case, in the future, it must be adopted in place of that of the present majority.[48]

This helps to understand why Israel and the Church insist on maintaining the at times contradictory diversity of testimonies. Thus the conviction expressed above is translated: Unity comes about through convergence and not through conformism. The diversity of the gospels was maintained, contrary to the good intentions of Tatian and Tolstoy. As for the mystery of the Trinity, since it is a mystery, why should Western and Oriental Christians not hold together the two versions of the Creed, with and without the *Filioque*?[49]

---

46. The scourge of bad division, which was rife before the destruction of the Second Temple, was denounced by Rabbi Yosse (pupil of Rabbi Akiba–middle of the second century CE), and this tradition is reported in the Talmud (B.T. Sanhedrin 88b). In his famous letter (967), Rav Sherira Gaon cites the essence of Rabbi Yosse's tradition: 'When the disciples of Shammai and of Hillel who had not served sufficiently (their masters: who had not gone to them enough and who had not learned what was necessary) became more numerous, the controversies multiplied in Israel and the Torah became like two Torot', in *Iggeret Rav Sherira Gaon*, edited by BM Levine (Jerusalem: Makor, 1972), 22–23.
47. See Akabia ben Mahalalel's admirable fidelity to his truth (to the tradition he had received from a majority, which itself had received it from a majority, Mishnah Ediyyot 5, 6–7.
48. *Cf* Mishnah Ediyyot 1, 4–6; Tosefta Ediyyot 1, 1.
49. On the importance of paradoxes and contradictions, *cf* H de Lubac, *Paradoxes* (Paris: Livre français, 1946), 13; 35; 111; 143; 162; 180; and above all, *Le mystère du surnaturel* (Paris: Cerf, 2000), Chapter IX, 'Le paradoxe surmonté dans la foi', 208–229.

PARADOXICAL Unity

Having seen the relationship between Unity and multiplicity, diversity, difference and contradiction, let us get to know some traditions that manifest what one might call the paradox. We have seen how the One God and God's One Torah express themselves in the legitimate diversity of human testimonies. With the paradox, we enter into what God reveals of God's own self and no longer into what God wants the human person to be and to do in order to testify to God.

Let us say what we mean by paradox, first of all in general and in ordinary language, and then in a particular way in theological and spiritual language.

In ordinary language, a paradox is the reality that runs counter to reason or to common meaning.[50] Thought or words also present a paradox, announce it or reveal it in a way that runs counter to reason or to the common meaning.

In theological and spiritual language, paradox is the divine, paradoxical reality to which Israel testifies through its inspired Tradition, prayer and practice.[51]

---

50. I am offering this definition for lack of a better one, without quoting authors or authorized dictionaries. My main support is the work of H de Lubac, in particular *Paradoxes and Nouveaux Paradoxes* (Paris: Seuil), and *Paradoxe et Mystère de l'Eglise* (Paris: Aubier, 1967), 71–72: 'For a paradox is everywhere in what is real before being in thought. And paradoxes: the word thus means first of all the things themselves, not the way of saying them.' By insisting on the significance of this support for me, I do however have one regret. Father de Lubac praises the paradox, but he does not say what it is and he only gives a few examples of it. See however: H de Lubac, *Le Mystère du Surnaturel* (Paris: Cerf, 2000) (first edition, Paris, Montaigne editions, 1965). In this book, H de Lubac speaks of paradox in three very rich chapters. In spite of this wealth, I cannot benefit from this study of paradoxes that are assumed by the Christian faith; for I must remain in contact with Israel's Tradition so as to hear how it resonates.
51. I am not at all claiming that the paradox of the Unity of the Absolute or of the Infinite as expressed in the Hindu tradition of the non-duality (*Advaita*), or also the paradox of the divine Unity as perceived in the experience of Sufi Muslims is in relation with the paradox of the divine Unity taught by Israel's Tradition. I lack the competence and therefore am not suggesting any approach to these magnificent experiences. However, I have two positive reasons for favoring the experience of Israel. The first is that the paradox of Unity is presented by Israel to every person in Israel and not only to the learned. The second is inspired by what H de Lubac expressed beautifully in the epigraph to *Paradoxes and Nouveuux Paradoxes* and in the foreword to *Nouveaux Parodoxes*. The paradoxes that are

The word *paradox* has entered into the Hebrew language of today, but Marc M Cohn in his excellent dictionary suggests translating it as *hiddush* (renewal, innovation, novation). In fact, *hiddush*, the new interpretation, the new practice, goes against the grain of habit or against the common meaning and remains suspect so long as it has not been possible to verify its usefulness and compatibility with the old teaching that precedes it. It is the same for the paradox, which people believe must be rejected because it is contrary to reason, but which is accepted if it renders an account of an experience that in the end is recognized as authentic.

The paradoxes that we shall study have been accepted and are taught by Israel's Tradition, even though they are not described as paradoxes.[52] They are of capital importance for a Christian, as the fundamental paradoxes of Christian faith are based on them and have their foundation in them: the paradox of the Incarnation and the paradox of the Trinity.[53] Let us develop in several stages this encounter with the paradox.

---

specifically vital for Christians are above all the paradox of the Incarnation and the paradox of the Trinity, but also the paradox of the Church. These paradoxes are accepted, held and maintained in Christian thought and life, which are illuminated by the mystery of the Incarnation, of the Trinity, and of the Church.

52. This is a difficulty that should be discussed at greater length. But the study of the texts will make it possible to encounter the paradox, even if it is not named as such. Israel's tradition does not like to use philosophical terms that get into the way of the reality that is being presented. The texts that we are studying are from ancient Tradition that precedes the Middle Ages, and this tradition never uses philosophical vocabulary. It uses only the ordinary language and images, sentences, proverbs, parables of popular wisdom. Starting with the Middle Ages, spiritual and mystical currents appear that use a more sophisticated terminology. Within the limits of this study, we shall favour the terms closest to the Jewish context that is contemporary with the editing of the New Testament.

53. A paradox most often presents two realities or two formulations which human reason cannot reconcile. It can present more than two realities, for example the three persons of the Trinity or the infinite multitude of particles of the One Torah, or again, over and beyond the two main and fundamental divine attributes (*middah, middot*), mercy and justice, the many attributes or divine names. We must distinguish between paradox and dyad, of which we shall speak further on. A dyad is a paradoxical reality that unites perfectly by distinguishing without separating two divine entities, which Christian dogma, for lack of a better word, calls Person (*persona, hypostasis*).

We shall see first how three aspects of reality and of divine activity manifest themselves in a paradoxical way: *Justice and Mercy, the Old and the New, the Unknown (transcendent) and the Known (immanent).*

We shall then go further in our study by following the pedagogical order offered by the *established and obligatory prayer* for *Reading the Shema* and for *Shabbat.* Thus we shall speak successively of God's paradoxical activity as the author of creation—*The Paradox of Creation*—of revelation—*The Paradox of Revelation*—and of redemption—*The Paradox of Redemption.*

Let us begin with the three paradoxical aspects of reality and of divine activity.

Justice and Mercy

The qualities of God, God's ways of being and of doing that are manifested to human beings, are called *attributes* (in Hebrew *middah, middot*). These attributes are made known by means of names or formulas that God indicates to Israel through Scripture or Tradition. The most fundamental attributes are mercy and justice, which are made known respectively by means of the two main names of God: God's own ineffable Name, indicated through the tetragram YHWH in which God reveals his mercy, and the common name ELOHIM, which can signify *judge* (*cf* Ex 22:8 when correctly understood and translated), but which signifies God's justice, when applied to God.

Mercy and justice seem to be incompatible, but because God is One, God unites them by enveloping his justice in his mercy. That is what the preacher in the *Pesikta de-Rav Kahana* teaches in his homily calling to repentance.

The *Pesikta de-Rav Kahana* is a *midrash haggadah*; it is homiletic from the period of the Amoraim, and came out of the same schools as *Genesis Rabbah, Leviticus Rabbah*, and *Lamentations Rabbah.*[54] The *Pesikta* brings together homilies that were given in the Land of Israel on the readings from the Torah or the Prophets established for the feasts and for the important Sabbaths during the course of the liturgical year. Text 21 is taken from a homily given on *Shabbat Shuvah* or *Teshuvah*, which is lived during the *Ten Days of Repentance*, between

54. *Cf* above note 21.

the feasts of *Rosh ha-Shanah* and *Kippur*. The prophetic reading established for this Sabbath is Hosea 14:2–10, which begins with the word: *Return* [shuvah], *Israel, to the Lord your God*!

Pesikta de-Rav Kahana on Hosea 14:2, *Piska* 35, 355 (Text 21)

> Psalm 25:8: *The Lord is good and upright; that is why he teaches the sinners the way.*
>
> Wisdom (the Holy Writings) was asked: 'The sinner, what is his punishment?' She answered (Prov 13:8): *Misfortune will pursue the sinners.*
>
> Prophecy (the Prophets) were asked: 'The sinner, what is his punishment?' She answered (Ezek 18:4): *The sinful soul shall die.*
>
> The Torah (Pentateuch) was asked: 'The sinner, what is his punishment?' She answered (Lev 5:6): *Let him bring a sacrifice for the sin and he will benefit from the atonement.*
>
> The Holy One, blessed be He!, was asked: 'The sinner, what is his punishment?' He answered: 'Let him repent and he will benefit from the atonement.' And that is what is written: *The Lord is good and upright, that is why he teaches the sinners the way.*
>
> Rabbi Pinhas said: 'How can the one who is upright be called "good", and how can the one who is good be called "upright"?' *That is why he teaches the sinners the way*, which is to say: he teaches the sinners the way so that they will repent.

The preacher knows the rhetoric which personifies Wisdom, Prophecy and the Torah. He has them say verses that leave no hope whatsoever to the sinner. The Torah (the Pentateuch) itself leaves no hope, for since at the time of the preaching the Temple was destroyed, the sinner can no longer offer a sacrifice. Therefore, he must call on God himself. The text thus shows the strength of the oral Torah, which through the mouth of the preacher, lets God himself speak and has God say that God goes beyond the letter of Scripture in order to show mercy.

As we saw in texts 2 and 10, mercy is the creator God's essential attribute, the attribute that envelops and unites all the others.[55] Mercy is characteristic for the heavenly Father, for Christians the first Person of the Trinity. It has its origin in the Father, it reveals itself in the Son. In the Spirit, mercy enlightens and leads the sinner on the way of repentance (*teshuvah*, return to God, return as far as God, according to Hos 14:2).

The liturgy for the *Ten Days of Repentance*, from *Rosh ha-Shanah* to *Kippur*, proclaims *the thirteen attributes of mercy*, which Tradition reads in the Book of Exodus (34:6–7), while taking care to stop the reading when Scripture (Ex 34:7) begins to speak of punishment: *but leaves nothing unpunished*. The text we are going to study shows that mercy is One as God is One. This Unity makes itself known in thirteen aspects, which must always be explored.

Rashi gives us an introduction to this exploration. He quotes literally the *Mekhilta de-Rabbi Ishmael*, to which he refers. Thus we have with Rashi and the *Mekhilta* a double authority that guarantees the legitimacy of the interpretation of Psalm 22:2: *My God, my God, why have you abandoned me?*

Let us note that the anonymous, age-old Tradition believes that in Exodus 34:6–7, Scripture makes known *Thirteen Attributes of Mercy*. The masters diverge on how to divide the words of Scripture in order to reach the number thirteen, but they are unanimous in teaching that the text speaks of attributes of mercy, even though the end of the scriptural passage talks of punishment and chastisement, as I have indicated in brackets in the text quoted below. The *established and obligatory prayer* has the reading of the beginning of the passage in several places during the community prayer for the feasts of *Rosh ha-Shanah* and *Kippur*.

Rashi on Exodus 34:6–7 (*Mekhilta de-Rabbi Ishmael* on Exodus 15:2, 128) (Text 22)

> Exodus 34:6–7: *The Lord [YHWH] passed before him and called out: "Lord [YHWH], Lord [YHWH] God [El] of tenderness and pity, slow to anger, rich in grace and faithfulness; who keeps his*

55. This can be shown through the following clarification of the first verse of the Reading of the Shema (Deut 6:4): Hear, O Israel, the Lord (*YHWH*: Mercy), our God (*Eloheinu*; *ELOHIM*: Justice), the Lord (*YHWH*: Mercy) is One. *Cf* Text 10, which speaks of the mercy of the creator God (the heavenly Father in Mt 5).

> *grace for thousands, tolerates error, transgression and sin* [but does not leave unpunished, and chastises the errors of the fathers on the children and the grandchildren to the third and fourth generation]."
>
> *Ex* 34:6: *Lord* [*YHWH*], *Lord* [*YHWH*]. This is the attribute of mercy, once before the human person sins, another time after he has sinned and repented. *God* [*El*, not *Elohim*], this is again the attribute of mercy, and that is truly what Scripture says (Ps 22:2): *My God, My God* [*Eli, Eli*]! *Why have you abandoned me?* For there is no cause to say to the attribute of justice: *Why have you abandoned me?* That is what I found in the *Mekhilta* [*de-Rabbi Ishmael on Ex* 15:2, p. 128].

Age-old Tradition sees in the proper, ineffable name (YHWH, pronounced *Adonai* in prayer), the expression of mercy, whereas the common name *Elohim* signifies justice. As for the name El (God of tenderness and pity), even though it appears here next to the mercy (tenderness and pity), according to its etymology it evokes rather power, domination, and justice. It is interesting to see how recourse to Psalm 22 is going to make it incline its meaning towards the side of mercy. This is not obvious and one can understand that Rashi insists on indicating from where he is getting his interpretation. We shall see again how to hear that this interpretation resonates with the cry of Jesus before his death according to the Gospels according to Matthew (27:46) and Mark (15:34).

For the Unity-Trinity that interests us, recourse to Ps 22:2 underlines that the trial of the human being's abandonment by God does not bring with it separation from God. In faith, the faithful person remains united with the hidden God who is abandoning him or her. We shall see further on that we must affirm that Jesus Christ is the presence of God in the world and among human beings. He is the *Shekhinah* (habitation) *par excellence*, which confirms and enlightens all the experiences that Israel had of the *Shekhinah* in the course of its history. Jesus abandoned by the Father is not separated from the Father. He remains One with the Father.

The Old and the New (Mt 13:51–52)

Sifra on Lev 26:9, *Weiss Edition 111a (cf. Rashi)* (Text 23)

Lev 26:9: *And I shall turn* [*u-paniti*] *to you.*

> A parable was created [to show] what the matter is like. [It is like] a king who had engaged many workers. There was one worker who had done work for him for many days. The workers entered [to the king] to take their salary, and this worker entered with them. The king said to this worker: "My son, I shall make myself free [*eppaneh*] for you. [Word play on "and I shall turn" (*upaniti*) and I shall make myself free (*eppaneh*)]. These who are numerous did little work for me, and I give them a salary that is not very high. But as for you, in future I shall make a large account." Thus it is for Israel. In this world, they ask their salary of the Place [God] and the nations of the world ask their salary of the Place. And the Place says to Israel: 'My sons, I shall make myself free for you. These nations of the world did little work for me and I give them a salary that is not very high. As for you, however, in future I shall make a large account.' That is why it is said: *And I shall turn to you* (Lev 26:9): with good things. *And I shall make you grow*: through fruitful propagation. *And I shall make you multiply*: through an upright stature. *And I shall accomplish* [*wa-hakimoti*: I shall make to keep standing, I shall establish] *my covenant with you*: not like the first covenant, which you violated, as it is said (Jer 31:32): [*Not like the covenant that I concluded with their fathers . . . my covenant*] *which they themselves broke, etc*, but a new covenant which from now on will no longer be violated, as it is said, (Jer 31:31): *Behold, days are coming, word of the Lord, when I shall conclude a new covenant with the house of Israel and with the house of Judah.*

In this world, during the time of the 'first covenant'—first in relation to the last covenant that is the new covenant of which Jeremiah is speaking—Israel violates the covenant by not fulfilling the commandments, but on the other hand, Israel acquires merit through the practice of the commandments. In the coming world, which is not necessarily the future world after death, but could be the world at the time of the Messiah, the 'first covenant' will be maintained, fulfilled in a 'last covenant.' This covenant will be new because it will no longer be violated by Israel.

Mekhilta de-Rabbi Ishmael on Exodus 13:2–3, 58–59 (*cf B.T. Hagigah* 3a-b) (Text 24)

> Jeremiah 23:7–8 (Jer 16:14–15): *And behold, days are coming when one will no longer say: the Lord is living who brought the children of Israel up from the land of Egypt, but: the Lord is living who brought up and brought home the race of the house of Israel from the lands of the North.* What is this matter like? It is like a man who greatly desired to have children. A daughter was born to him; he swore only by her [literally: by her life]. Afterwards a son was also born to him. He left the daughter [ceased swearing by the daughter] and only swore by his son.

The message is clear: Jeremiah wanted to say that the last messianic redemption, from the land of the North, will cause the first redemption from Egypt to be forgotten. Let us note that the parable does not allow us to think that the father ceases to be a father to the point of forgetting his first child, even if it is only a daughter. But of course we are dealing with a parable and not an allegory, and the parable should not serve as a key to the message in all its detail. What remains is that the suggested interpretation through the use of the parable does not take Jeremiah literally and does not teach that Israel will forget the first redemption from Egypt. In the parable, Israel and the father are carried away by the joy of the great and last newness, which transforms their life. That feeling is very natural and contains nothing worrisome. But this way of presenting the joy does include a certain danger.

Another parable, attributed to Rabbi Shimeon ben Yohai and placed by the *Mekhilta de-Rabbi Ishmael* immediately after the one we just saw, already speaks in a different tone:

> *Mekhilta de-Rabbi Ishmael* on Exodus 13:2–3, 58–59 (*Cf B.T. Hagigah* 3a-b) (Text 25)

> Rabbi Shimeon ben Yohai said: What is the matter like? [It is like] a man who was walking on a road. He encountered a wolf and he was saved from it; he told the miracles that had happened to him with the wolf. He encountered a lion and was saved from it; he left the matter with the wolf to tell the miracles that had happened to him with the lion. [According to certain versions, cf. Lauterbach edition, p. 133, the parable continues and ends as follows:] He encountered a snake and was saved from it. He forgot the matter with the first two and continued to tell of the matter with the snake. Thus it is with

> Israel. [The deliverance from the] last misfortunes makes them forget [the deliverance from the] first [misfortunes].

The message is clear and sharply decoded; in spite of the distance that must remain between the parable and the message, we are obliged to see that the joy of deliverance from trial colors Israel's forgetfulness with a negative nuance. There is a certain thoughtlessness on the part of Israel when it speaks only of the last deliverance.

At this point, we can suppose that Rabbi Eleazar ben Azariah suggested a homiletic interpretation of Jeremiah 23:7–8 that does not imply taking a position as regards *halakhah*. He wants us to understand just how far the joy will go that is given by the new and last redemption. With his parable, Rabbi Shimeon ben Yohai lets us understand that an exaggeration of that joy can be considered to be thoughtlessness. There is no question yet of *halakhah*. However, it is possible that Rabbi Shimeon ben Yohai gives his parable with the intention of strengthening the positions taken by the Sages against Rabbi Eleazar ben Azariah and against Ben Zoma in a discussion that incontestably bears on the *halakhah*. This discussion is the second possible origin of our debate on Jeremiah 23. As we shall see, it is situated in the context of the liturgical remembering of the exodus from Egypt. However, it is useful first of all to get to know a last series of homiletic units that, according to the *Mekhilta de-Rabbi Ishmael*, can also be attributed to Rabbi Eleazar ben Azariah:
Mekhilta de-Rabbi Ishmael on Exodus 13:2–3, 59 (Text 26)

> In the same way, he [Rabbi Eleazar ben Azariah] interpreted (Gen 17:5): *And you will no longer be called Abram, but your name will be Abraham*: the first name will pass [*'abar*], but the second is maintained [*nitkayyem*]. In the same way, he interpreted (Gen 17:15): *You will no longer call your wife Sarai; but her name is Sarah*. The first passes, but the second is maintained. In the same way, he interpreted (Gen 32:29): *You will no longer be called Jacob, your name will be Israel*. The first name was maintained for him [*nitkayyem lo*] and the second name was added to him [*nittoseph*]. For Isaac, his name did not change because he had been named by the Holy One, blessed be He (cf Gen 17:19).

Mishnah Berakhot 1, 5 (Text 27)

> One must remember the exodus from Egypt at night. Rabbi Eleazar ben Azariah said: Now I am as if I were seventy years old and I have not deserved that it be said [that I know how to base on Scripture the obligation to remember] the exodus from Egypt at night, [this] until Ben Zoma drew it out through interpretation [of Scripture], as it is said (Deut 16:3): *So that you remember the day of the exodus from the land of Egypt all the days of your life.* [We would only be obliged to remember the exodus from Egypt] during the day, [but it is said:] '*all* the days of your life'; (this includes the obligation) during the night. But the Sages say: 'the days of your life', this world, 'all the days of your life', this includes the days of the Messiah.

Tosephta Berakhot 1, 10, *Lieberman editition*, 4–5 (*Cf B.T. Berakhot* 12b–13a) (Text 28)

> One must remember the exodus from Egypt . . . so as to include the days of the Messiah [*Mishnah Berakhot* 1, 5]. Ben Zoma told them [the Sages]: But must one remember the exodus from Egypt in the days of the Messiah? Is it not said elsewhere (Jer 23:7–8): *Behold days are coming, word of the Lord, when one will no longer say: the Lord is living who brought the children of Israel up from the land of Egypt, but the Lord is living who brought up and brought home the race of the house of Israel from the land of the North?* They [the Sages] told him: Not that the exodus from Egypt is uprooted [*te'aker*] from its place, but that the exodus from Egypt is supplementary [*mussaph*] to the kingdoms [to the liberation from all servitudes in the foreign kingdoms], the kingdoms [then being] the main matter [*ikkar*], the exodus from Egypt the relative matter [*tephelah*]. Analogously (Gen 35:10): You will no longer be called Jacob but Israel, etc, not that the name of Jacob is uprooted [*yeaker*], but that [from now on] Jacob will be supplementary [*mussaph*] to Israel, Israel [being] the main [matter] [*ikkar*] and Jacob the relative [matter] [*taphel*].

The One and Only, Old and New Covenant

Since the Second Vatican Council, the Catholic Church recalls and teaches that 'the Old Covenant was never revoked'. For a long time, this was ignored and/or forgotten by many Christians, among them important Church Fathers, exegetes and theologians. Still in our day, certain exegetes who take a few verses in the Letter to the Hebrews literally affirm that the New Covenant takes the place of the Covenant at Sinai.

It is true that the relationship of the New Covenant to the Old is paradoxical and difficult to explain. However, it is possible to say how the paradox must be assumed. For Israel's Tradition, the 'new', which must be taught for the sake of the necessary renewal (*hiddush*) of the Torah, is radically new because it was not known, not heard of before it was taught. This does not mean just any newness that is suggested irresponsibly and erroneously, but the 'new' which the disciple uncovers in the presence of his master or at least with the conviction that his master would teach it if he were still alive. This newness existed in reality already from time immemorial, from the origin of the Torah.[56] In that sense, the 'new' is not new. It is 'old'. This is a paradox of revelation, which must be assumed as such by every good scribe *who draws from his treasure new and old* (Mt 13:52).[57]

The liturgy for the feast of *Rosh ha-Shanah* teaches that ever since Noah, God concluded the one and only covenant with humanity.

The blessing *Zikhronot* is one of the three blessings in the Additional Prayer (*Mussaf*) for the feast of *Rosh ha-Shanah*. The first of these blessings, *the Malkhiyyot* (Royalties) *blessing*, celebrates God as King of the universe. We shall study it at the end of the first part (text 49). The third blessing, *the Shofarot* (Shofars) *blessing*, celebrates God who instituted the blowing of the shofar, the main rite of *Rosh ha-Shanah*, which signifies judgment and announces redemption. The Additional Prayer for *Rosh ha-Shanah* is the only one that includes

---

56. *Cf* JT Peah 2, 6 on Koh 1:10.
57. Rabbi Eliezer the Great mourned after the destruction of the Second Temple: 'When the Temple was destroyed, the Sages began to be like the Scribes . . . No one asks, On whom can we lean for support? On our Father who is in Heaven.' (Mishnah Sotah 9, 15) The *request*, the *search*, the *question* are necessary so that the Torah will develop and be renewed. The paradox of the Torah, which is New and Old, must be assumed by the Sages, by the Masters. It must remain open to the question, to the search, to the request. To abandon this by teaching that the New takes the place of the Old or abolishes it, is to behave like a [bad] scribe who ignores Israel's Tradition and Scripture's literary genres. This is how the name Israel [New] does not uproot the name Jacob [Old]. (*Cf* B.T. Berakhot 12b–13a on Gen 32:28–30; 35:10; 46:1–3; Rashi on B.T. Berakhot 12ba–13a).

three blessings at its center. Each of these three blessings implements the *necklace* (*harizah*), of which we spoke in connection with text 18.

The Zikhronot [*Remembrances*] *Blessing in the Additional Prayer* [mussaf] *on* Rosh ha-Shanah (Text 29)

> You remember the everlasting deed, and you recall all the former creatures.[58] All hidden things are unveiled before you as well as the multitude of mysteries since the beginning . . . This day was the beginning of your works, it is the remembrance of the first day, *for it is a law, a prescription of the God of Jacob* (Ps 81:5). For the remembrance of every deed presents itself before you, and you examine the deeds of each one . . .
>
> Thus in your love you remembered Noah . . . as it is said in your Torah (Gen 8:1): *Then God remembered Noah.*
>
> And it is said (Ex 2:24): *God heard their groaning and he remembered his Covenant with Abraham, with Isaac and with Jacob.* And it is said (Lev 26:42): *And I shall remember my Covenant with Jacob, and also my Covenant with Isaac, and also my Covenant with Abraham I shall remember; and I shall remember the Land.*
>
> And in your holy Words [holy Writings] it is written, saying (Ps 111:4): *He established a remembrance, the Lord is clement and merciful.* And it is said (Ps 111:5): *He gives food to those who fear him, he always remembers his Covenant.* And it is said (Ps 106:45): *And he remembered his Covenant for them, he let himself be swayed according to his great love.* And by the hand of your servants the prophets it is written, saying (Jer 2:2): *Go and cry this in the ears of Jerusalem: Thus the Lord has spoken: 'I remember for you the tenderness of your youth, the love of your betrothal, when you followed me in the desert, in an uncultivated land.'* And it is said (Ezek 16:60): *And I shall remember my Covenant with you in the days of your youth,*

58. For the translation, 'the everlasting deed' (*maaseh olam*) and 'all the former creatures' (*kol yetsurei kedem*), cf Judah Goldin in *Days of Awe* (New York: Schocken Books, (1948) 1965), 87. This book is a faithful adaptation of S Agnon, *Yamim Noraim* (Tel Aviv: Schocken Publishing House, 1973). In contrast to other extant translations, this translation is coherent with what is said at the beginning of the blessing: 'the beginning of your works', 'the first day of creation'.

> *and I shall fulfill for you an everlasting Covenant.* And it is said (Jer 31:20): *Is Ephraim thus for me a beloved son, a child who is so cherished that every time I speak of him, I again want to remember him: Truly, my entrails are moved for him, I will have mercy on him, word of the Lord.*
>
> Our God and God of our Fathers! Remember us with a good remembrance before you and visit us with a visit of salvation and of mercy from the height of the eternal Heavens; and Lord Our God, remember for us the Covenant, the love and the oath that you swore to Abraham our Father on Mount Moriah. May be seen before you the binding by which Abraham our Father bound Isaac his son on the altar! He held back his mercy in order to do your will with an undivided heart. You as well, may your mercy hold back your anger against us! Through your great goodness, may your anger turn from your people, from your city and from your inheritance!
>
> Lord, our God, fulfill for us the promise that you made us in your Torah, through Moses your servant, the promise that came from your Glory, as it is said (Lev 26:45): *And for them I shall remember the Covenant of the First Ones whom I brought out of the land of Egypt in the eyes of the peoples in order to be their God, I, the Lord.*
>
> For you remember everything that is forgotten for ever; and there is no forgetting before your glorious throne; and you will remember today the binding of Isaac in favor of his descendants.
>
> Blessed are You, Lord, who remembers the Covenant.

This blessing celebrates God who remembers all the covenants with humanity since the covenant with Noah (Gen 8:1; 9:8–17) even to the everlasting covenant announced to Ezekiel (16:60). In its conclusion, it teaches that the stages which the Lord remembers are the stages in a covenant that is One and Only. The stage of the covenant with the 'First Ones whom He brought out of Egypt' is the covenant concluded at Sinai (Ex 24:7–8), which will never be revoked and which will be fulfilled in an everlasting covenant. The Sinai covenant was decided by common accord between God and Israel, who committed themselves to do everything that the Lord said (Ex 19:5–8).

The blessing that precedes the *Reading of the Shema* in the morning confirms the present-day validity of this biblical message and the permanence of Israel's election as willed by God, who loved Israel 'with great love' and 'with eternal love' (text 2). We saw that this blessing committed Israel on the path of unification: unification of the heart, unification of the fear and the love of God, unification of humanity through its relationship with God, whose Unity Israel proclaims and whose program of unification Israel adopts out of love. It can be surprising to see that the Zikhronot Blessing does not mention the New Covenant announced by Jeremiah (31:31). The reason for this absence is purely 'technical'. The verse in Jeremiah does not say that the Lord will remember this Covenant in order to conclude it. This covenant thus does not have its place in a blessing that is built on remembrances. From the point of view of the contents, the New Covenant is a stage in the future, which the Only Covenant has not yet reached; this comes out clearly in the prophetic text as well as in rabbinic interpretations of it.

This blessing is pertinent in what it says concerning Unity. For the diachronic diversity of the Covenant's stages is the guarantee that the Covenant is One and True, that no stage is useless. No stage can allow one to forget that God does not destroy what God wanted out of love. The New and the Old support one another and the one is illuminated by the other. Christian exegesis must be that of the good scribes, in the image of the *scribe who has become a disciple of the Kingdom of Heaven . . . who draws from his treasure new and old* (Mt 13:52). No recourse to a few verses in the New Testament allows one to replace the Old with the New.

The blessing uses the *necklace* procedure (*harizah*), which is well known in pharisaic and rabbinic Tradition and by Jesus, who uses it twice according to the Gospel of Luke (24:27, 44). The *necklace* is made up of verses drawn from the three parts of Scripture: Torah (Pentateuch, Moses), Prophets, holy Writings (Psalms). The procedure presupposes the conviction that the Torah is perfect and that the oral Torah (*midrash*) can show the Unity and the divinity of 'the whole Torah'. The symbol of the *necklace* evokes the beauty of the Beloved (woman) in the Song of Songs (1:10), who is Israel and the oral Torah, whom the Beloved (God) adorns with the necklace made of the pearls of Scripture. There is perfect Unity in the love of the Beloved (male). It is obvious that the Beloved (woman) is more important than the *necklace*, but in looking upon her, the Beloved (male) unites the beauty of the Beloved (woman) and that of her necklace. This lets us understand that the oral Torah (Tradition) is so to say preferable to the written Torah (Scripture).

The Remembrances blessing teaches with the authority of the oral Torah that there is one single covenant between God and humanity, represented by Israel. The Old Covenant at Sinai is thus not revoked by the Everlasting Covenant which Ezekiel announces (16:60). From the Christian point of view, this Everlasting Covenant is already inaugurated in this world's time through Christ's resurrection.

We noted that the blessing does not include Jeremiah 31:31 in the verses quoted to make its necklace. However, Jeremiah is quoted twice in the verses mentioning the remembrance (Jer 2:2 and 31:19, which is close to 31:31). All in all, there can be no doubt that the New Covenant of Jeremiah is included in the One and Only Covenant, which the conclusion has in mind. From the Christian point of view, we understand that the *New and Everlasting Covenant* mentioned by Jesus in the words instituting the Eucharist is the fulfilment of the Covenant.[59]

With the resurrection of Jesus, resurrection that is definitive and that has entered into this world, the Covenant has already become New and Everlasting. The newness is radical, invincible, but it does not abolish the continuity on which it rests and without which it could not be taught. Saint Paul says this clearly: '*If there is no resurrection of the dead, Christ is not risen either*' (1 Cor 15:13). Thus we must hold in faith the paradox of the 'new' which assumes the 'old', an old which is never revoked.

The Unknown (transcendent) and the Known (immanent)

Once again, the established and obligatory prayer is the place where a fundamental characteristic of Judaism is taught, the paradox of the Unknown and the Known, one of the aspects of the paradox of God's Unity.

59. This Word of Jesus in the liturgy mentions the Everlasting Covenant (Ezek 16:60), but it does not appear in the New Testament.

The paradox of the unknown and the known is expressed in the first blessing preceding the *Reading of the Shema* in the morning and in the third blessing of the community prayer on Shabbat and feasts.

Above, we studied the *Yotser* Blessing, the first blessing before the *Reading of the Shema* in the morning (text 10) in order to illustrate God's mercy as creator.

We shall take up this text again so as to better assume the paradoxes that it teaches, which are the paradox of creation and the paradox of revelation. According to the prayer's pedagogical order (Creation, Revelation, Redemption), we shall begin with the paradox of Creation, without forgetting that the insertion of the *kedushah* in the *Yotser* blessing already shows the paradox of Revelation, which is the fact that God wants to be known as the unknown God.[60]

With this beginning on the paradox of Creation, we shall see how the paradox of Revelation enables one to deepen the paradox of Creation: for how can one assume that the good and merciful Creator God could remain unknown and absent from the reality of the world that he created?

The Paradox of Creation

So as to hear the paradox taught by the Yotser blessing, which is the double paradox of creation and of revelation, we shall quote a shortened form of the text starting with the *kedushah*,.

The Yotser Blessing, the First Blessing before the Reading of the Shema *in the morning* (Text 30) (returning to a summary of Text 10)

> Be blessed, our Rock, our King and our Redeemer, Creator of saints . . . Who forms servants . . . All beloved, all chosen . . . all do the will of their creator [*konam*, their producer] in fear and trembling . . . All open their mouth . . . All together, they begin to sing the *Kedushah* and to say with fear (Isa 6:3): *Holy, Holy, Holy, the Lord of Hosts, all the earth is filled with his Glory*! And the Wheels and the holy Living Ones raise themselves with great noise before the Seraphim and say (Ezek 3:12):

60. This is not to say that the insertion of the kedushah was decided in order to show the paradox. Other reasons could be put forward, none of which is certain. What is important here is that the text as it is expresses the paradox of creation and invites one to reflect on it.

> *Blessed is the Glory of the Lord from his Place!*[61] They address their songs to the blessed God . . .

The *Yotser* blessing speaks of the Creator God and of God's creation. The heavenly liturgy that was revealed to Israel through Isaiah and Ezekiel entered into the blessing because of the experience of a group that was interested in contemplation and meditation on the mystery of creation. The prayer of the synagogue adopted this version of the *kedushah* because it is simpler. This version makes it possible to present the paradox of revelation within the blessing, the main aim of which is to teach creation.

The prayer received from Isaiah the vision of the Glory of the Holy God in his Temple. This Glory appears in the world. As Israel's later Tradition will say, the Glory is the reality of God's presence in the world. It is the *Shekhinah*, the particular *real Presence* of God in the Temple and in the world. Isaiah's seraphim acclaim this presence, which is seated on an elevated throne, and Isaiah, who has this vision, is sent to communicate it to Israel. From this point on, the heavenly liturgy has come down to earth, but by its origin it remains in contact with the Holy God, whose Place remains unknown. The Living Ones of Ezekiel communicate their experience to the prophet: the Glory of the *Shekhinah* manifests itself in the world, in the known Place in the Temple, but it proceeds from its Place which remains unknown.

The paradox of the known *Place* that reveals the unknown *Place* is so fundamental that it will be used to justify one of the names given to God by Tradition. God is called the *Place* (*hamakom*), because God is the Place *par excellence*, the Place of the world, which does away with the cosmic illusion according to which the world is the real Place, the Place that counts (*cf Genesis Rabbah* on Gen 28:11, Par. 68 & 69, 777–778).

The paradox of revelation is expressed here in the simplest possible way: God wants to make himself known as Holy, as Separate, as Other, as Unknown in the Temple, *the Known Place* that points to *God's Unknown Place.*

---

61. This must be translated as 'from his Place' (*mi-mekomo*) and not 'in the place of his abiding' (French Jerusalem Bible). The latter misses the point and eliminates the paradox. *Cf* the explanation of § 5 of Text 10.

We shall return to this teaching when we look at the paradox of revelation. However, here we must first enter into the primordial paradox, which is that of creation.

The *kedushah* in our blessing does not lead us to understand that God and God's *Shekhinah* are One single and same reality. Israel is not yet at the point of saying this. But Israel will say it in the *Great Kedushah* that we shall study later (text 38).

The insertion of the *kedushah* in the blessing that speaks of creation makes it possible to assume in depth the paradox of creation and openness to the question that constantly comes up: how can God, who creates the world through kindness and who remains present in it in order to sustain its existence, remain in silence and absence in God's transcendent holiness, abandoning the world to misfortune, to evil, to the suffering of those who are innocent?

Many texts would enable us to enter more deeply into this debate on the absence and silence of the Creator God.[62] All in all, the paradox is assumed and God's kindness is affirmed despite all opposition. It seems to me that it would be useful to present the main lines of what comes out of these texts and the questions they raise.

Psalm 119:68 presents a starting point: *You are good* [*tov*], *You, and you do good* [*metiv*]. Tradition leaves no doubt whatsoever concerning the meaning of this verse and the obligation to proclaim it in prayer and in deed.

In prayer: The *Mishnah* (*Berakhot* 9, 5) teaches that 'the human person must bless [God] for misfortune just as he blesses God for happiness.'[63] By referring to these written and oral texts, Tradition makes it an obligation to bless, and the Talmud discusses the way in which this precept is to be observed.

B.T. Berakhot 60b (Text 31)

> What does it mean, 'the human person must bless for misfortune just as he blesses for happiness'? Shall we say that: Just as one blesses for happiness: 'You are good and you do good', one blesses for misfortune: 'You are good and you do good'? However, we have taught (Mishnah Berakhot 9, 2):

---

62. *Cf* below Appendix I.

63. This is what Job said and did in his time (Job 1:20–22; 2:9–10). Whether Job was a Jew or not, whether he existed or not, the Book of Job is inspired, and Job is a model to be imitated.

> 'One blesses upon receiving good news: "You are good and you do good"; upon receiving bad news, one blesses: "Blessed is the Judge of Truth"!' Rava said: 'The [Mishnah] was only necessary so as to [make clear] the obligation to receive the [two possibilities, bad and good] with joy.' In fact, the rite of blessings prescribes the blessings that are in conformity with these teachings:
>
> - For happiness: 'Blessed are You, Lord, our God, King of the universe, who is Good and who Does Good.'
>
> - For misfortune: 'Blessed are You, Lord, our God, King of the universe, Judge of Truth.'[64]

In deed: Nahum Ish Gamzo (*a man of Gimzo,* 2 Chr 28:18, *at the end of the first century, beginning of the second century CE*) is famous for having welcomed all misfortunes with the expression: *gam zo le-tovah* ('this too is for good'; *B.T. Taanit* 21a). His student Rabbi Akiba received from him the conviction that every detail, every repetition, every 'anomaly' in Scripture is significant.[65] If Scripture says (Deut 6:5): *and you shall love the Lord your God with all your heart, with all your soul, with all your power*, each injunction must be given its place: *with all your heart*, with the good (altruistic) instinct and with the bad (selfish) instinct; *with all your soul*, even if God takes your soul (in death by martyrdom). We have seen how, according to the Babylonian Talmud [*B.T. Berakhot* 61b (*text 12*)], Rabbi Akiba fulfilled this exegesis through his deeds by dying with "One" (Deut 6:4) as the last word on his lips. According to the Jerusalem Talmud, he lived this death in joy in the midst of suffering, in the joy of non-division (*J.T. Berakhot* 9, 14b (*text 13*)]. This supreme deed by Rabbi Akiba was fulfilled in conformity with the teaching of the mishnah, to which the Talmud gives the key thanks to Raba, as we have just seen (*B.T. Berakhot* 60b): the *Mishnah* was only necessary so as to make clear the obligation to receive the two possibilities, bad and good, with joy.

---

64. The fourth blessing that is said after meals (*Birkat ha-Mazon*) must also be mentioned. This long blessing develops on Ps 119:68 by applying it to the past, the present and the future. This praise of the Lord who is Good and who Does Good is especially surprising because this blessing was established in reference to the dead at Betar at the end of the Bar Kokhba revolt in 135 CE (*cf* B.T. Berakhot 48b).
65. According to Mt 5:17–19, this is also how Jesus sees things.

The *justification of judgment* (*tsidduk ha-din*) lived by Rabbi Hananiah ben Teradion, his wife and his daughter, is also fulfilled in the joy experienced upon receiving *good news* (*basorah tovah*: gospel), the announcement of their entrance into the world to come [*Sifre Deuteronomy* on Deuteronomy 32:4 (text 14); Lk 23:42–43].

We again find the non-division, the negative way that leads to the positive proclamation of Unity. The masters who die out of love, Nahum Ish Gamzo, Rabbi Akiba, and before them Jesus, witness to the One God. When in the Gospel according to Matthew (19:16–22), Jesus teaches that *One* [alone] *is* the *Good* one, his words are to be heard in the rich context we have explained based on Ps 119:68: *You, the Good, the One who Does Good, teach me your will.* In his commentary on Matthew 19:17, Paul Billerbeck returns to this context. He mentions in particular *Mishnah Avot* 6, 3: 'And there is no Good if it is not the Torah, for it is said (Prov 2:2): *Listen, sons, to the lesson of a father . . . For it is a good teaching [lekhah tov] that I have given you; do not abandon my Torah.*' The use of the double negative, 'there is no . . . if it is not . . .', is the way to affirm even more strongly what one wants to affirm. The formula used by Jesus: *One* [alone] is *the* Good, cannot contradict the fact that the Torah is (alone) the eminently Good. God and the Torah are the Good *par excellence.* The One God (*eis*, One and thus Only, alone) is the Good.[66] In order to do Good, one must observe the commandments of God's Torah (Mt 19:17).

Summing up, we can say: *God* and the *Torah* are *One* (single) reality, and *Israel* is the witness to this.[67] God and the Torah are one (single) reality, who/which in its Kindness creates the world and sustains its existence. We saw this affirmation of ongoing creation, which the *yotser* blessing renews each morning (text 10). The verse Isaiah 45:7 that is used to support this teaching and which stands in the present tense, is modified in order to avoid anyone saying in prayer that God created evil, but its difficult wording remains. One such difficulty is linked with the one that never ceases to torment Israel and believing

---

66. The Greek in Mt 19:27 is ***eis** estin o agatos, eis and not monos*, and in Latin, *unus and not unicus*. In German ***einer** ist der Gute* [one is the Good One], *einer* and not *einziger*. It is too bad that in French one has to say *Un seul est le Bon* [One alone is the Good one]. Once again, one must first teach the Unity, which for a Christian is the basis of the Trinity.

67. God, the Torah, Israel: we see a triad appearing. Cf. the recapitulation of the triads at the end of this chapter.

humankind. How can the Creator God, the All-powerful, the Good, tolerate the existence of misfortune, of suffering and of the omnipresence of evil?

One answer can be sought first of all based on a verse in the same chapter of Isaiah (45:15), an isolated verse that speaks of God in the third person in the midst of declarations about God in the first person.

Isaiah 45:15: Truly You are a God who conceals himself, God of Israel Saviour

This isolated verse in Isaiah 45:15 can be taken as a starting point for an answer: the silence of God is that of the God who conceals himself in order to give salvation, who hides his creative Word so as to triumph over evil. For one can hear the verse in the third person as the reaction of the prophet, and after the prophet of the believer, who react to God's discourse in the first person in the whole of chapter 45. As we saw, the more difficult affirmation is that in verse 7: I *form* [*yotser*] light and I create darkness, I make good [happiness] and *I create evil* [misfortune]. As we saw, the prayer corrects this formula. Nevertheless, it remains that through the prophet, Scripture passes on a word of God which is 'scandalous'. The response suggested by verse 15 would be that God certainly always remains the *One who forms* (*Yotser*) who, like the potter, forms and maintains creation through the ongoing work of his hand, but that God is always the *transcendent Creator* (*bore*) who is independent of his creation, who is always beyond it and within it. As Creator, God eludes evil and dominates it from above and from below. God can save his creature from evil because God is concealed.

Many ancient and modern masters, both Jews and Christians, and in particular Pascal in his *Pensées*, have spoken of God's silence, especially based on Isaiah (45:15).[68]

Another answer can be suggested based on the first verse and the first chapter of the Bible, according to which God creates the world and creates it by means of a series of *Sayings* (*God said*, Gen 1).

68. *Cf* J Briend, *Le Dieu caché, Dieu de l'Ecriture* (Paris: Cerf, 1992).

The 'Saying that is not said': Genesis 1:1: In the beginning God created the heavens and the earth

The teaching that can be drawn from the first verse of the Bible (Gen 1:1) is not well known: *In the beginning God created the heavens and the earth*, compared to the rest of the first chapter. *Mishnah Abot* (5, 1) teaches: *Through ten sayings the world was created.*

Independently of the significance of the number *ten* in this sentence, we would like the *Mishnah* to say precisely which 'sayings' it is talking about, but it does not do so. It is not certain that it is talking about Scripture. However, the treatise *Abot de Rabbi Nathan*, Version B, chapter 36, which transmits the anonymous Tradition, does try to relate it to Scripture. The result of this attempt is that *God said* appears nine times in chapter 1 of *Genesis*, and that a tenth time must be included, in which God created without it being written that *God said*. This time, when God's saying is not said, is the beginning of the whole of creation as declared in Genesis 1:1: *God created the heavens and the earth*. The Talmud (*B.T. Rosh ha-Shanah* 32a) makes it clear that *In the beginning God created* must be counted among the *sayings*, since it is written (Ps 33:6): *Through the Word of the Lord the heavens were made*. There is a difficulty here and one might be surprised that the significance of the *saying that is not said* is not sought as intensely as one would wish.[69]

I suggest here a passage from the teaching of *Rav Nahman of Bratslav* (177–1810), who sought the meaning of Gen 1:1 and of the *saying that is not said* in his work *Likutei Moharan*:[70]

Likutei Moharan 2, 12 – *Mishnah Abot* 5, 1 (Text 32)

69. Rashi has the verse in Gen 1:1 say: 'Seek me!', that one might seek the significance of 'In the beginning'. His search finds in the treasure of Tradition the interpretation whose light we have received. I think the verse Gen 1:1, as it is situated in the whole of chapter 1 with its nine sayings, might mean: Seek me!, seek why Ps 33:6 says that through the word of the Lord the heavens were made, whereas (Gen 1:1) does not say: God said: 'May the heavens and the earth be'.

70. I would like to be able to indicate the sources and the close and more distant supports to Rav Nahman's teaching. *Cf* A Green, *Tormented Master. A Life of Rabbi Nahman of Bratslav* (New York: Schocken Books, 1979). *Cf* the French translation and introduction by M-A Ouaknin, *La sagesse dansante de Rabbi Nahman, biographie d'un maître hassidique* (Paris: Albin Michel, 2000).

> Know this: The root of all creation is the Glory. For all that the Holy One, blessed be He, created, He only created for his Glory, as it is written (Isa 43:7): *Everything is named after my Name, I have created it for my glory* [*cf B.T. Yoma* 38a]. From the moment everything was created for his Glory, blessed be He!, it follows that his Glory, blessed be He!, is the root of all of creation. And although He is entirely One, there are various parts in creation, and in each part of creation, there is an aspect of glory that is particular to it and that is its root, as we have said. And this resonates with [*Mishnah Abot* 5, 11] 'The world was created through ten words'. Could it not have been created through one word? But in view of the reward and of the punishment, the world was created through ten words. In each word there is an aspect of glory that is particular to it and that is its root, for the Glory is the root of everything, as we said. And this is what the Psalm (29:9) has in mind: *In his Temple everything cries 'Glory'!* For each word is clothed with his Glory, blessed be He! And it is by means of this Glory that the world was created, for (Isa 6:3): *All the earth is filled with his Glory.* 'All the earth', even in the transgressions and the bad things, may God preserve us! There his Glory is certainly not, according to (Isa 42:8): *And my glory I shall not give to another.* For there is a limit beyond which the Glory does not spread, even though *All the earth is filled with his Glory.*
>
> But know this: In spite of everything, the places [that remain outside of his Glory] receive their vitality [*hiyyut*] from Him, blessed be He! And even the soiled places, the houses of idolatry, also receive necessarily their vitality from Him, blessed be He! However, know this: They receive something from the saying that is not said [*maamar satum*], which is 'In the beginning', a *saying that is not said* which encompasses all the sayings. And all things receive their vitality from this. And the way in which the Glory of the *saying that is not said* is not said and is concealed, is an absolutely radical way, and from there they receive vitality.

The key words in this passage are glory (*khabod*), the root of creation (*shoresh ha-beriah*), and vitality (the vital strength, *hiyyut*):

- Glory is the *Shekhinah*, the presence of the Creator God in the world.
- The root of Creation is the Creator God who creates through the *Shekhinah.*
- The vitality (*hiyyut*) is the vital strength that comes from God through the Torah, or again, *from God himself* 'who is your life', according to Rabbi Akiba's interpretation and its extension through Rab Baer of Lubavitch, which we heard in the context of Text 12 (*B.T. Berakhot* 61b).

In order to shed light on this teaching by Rav Nahman, let us point out that in the blessing after eating certain foods, God is called the life of *the worlds* (*hei ha-olamot*). Here is the text of that blessing:

Blessing after eating certain foods (Text 33)

> Blessed are You, Lord, our God, King of the universe, Creator of many souls [living beings] and of their lack, for all that He created in order to give life to the soul of every living being. Blessed is the *Life of the Worlds* [*hai ha-olamim*].[71]

The text addresses God in the second person, but then speaks of God in the third person and calls God '*the Life of the Worlds*'.

In an important litany written by the Hasidim of the Rhineland entitled *Song of the Angels* (thirteenth century), God is also praised as '*the Life of the Worlds*'; it comes from the *Great Hekhalot*, an anthology of Jewish mysticism on the *Merkhabah*, a mysticism that is con-

71. On the life of the worlds, *cf* G Scholem, *Les Grands Courants de la Mystique juive* (Paris: Payot), 71–72, 377, and the *Sefer ha-Bahir*, 183–184. *Cf* the Book of Revelation 4:9–10 in reference to Daniel 4:31 and 12:7. The Hebrew of Daniel: *hai ha-olam* is taken up in the Book of Revelation as *to zonti eis tous aionas ton aionon, viventem in saecula saeculorum*, which in English is: who lives forever and ever. In the Jewish blessing, contemporary with the Book of Revelation, *the Life of the Worlds* understands *olam, olamot* as 'world, worlds', which signifies space and no longer time. The *Sefer ha-Bahir* in referring to this blessing, interprets *olamot* as 'worlds', a spatial reality. All this brings out significant resonances if we see that Jesus Christ can be understood as *the Life of the Worlds*, as *the Life* (Jn 14:6). The blessing and the *Sefer ha-Bahir* would give a basis for christological hearing. The blessing with its *You* and *He* teaches the paradox of the God who makes himself known by making himself present (*Shekhinah*), but who leads to his transcendence. *The Life of the Worlds*, the presence to his creation of the Forming God (*Yotser*), comes forth from the unknown God and leads to Him.

temporary with the New Testament. This litany is included in the liturgy of Kippur.[72] For this liturgy, G. Scholem translates *hai ha-olamot* as *eternally living*. One can ask oneself if this translation, which corresponds with that of the *Book of Revelation*, is appropriate for a text of ancient mysticism from the first centuries CE. For at that time, the word *olam* already meant the world in the spatial sense (cf. the *Kedushah*, the third blessing of the *Amidah* for ordinary days: *Let us sanctify your Name in the world* (*ba'olam*) *as it is sanctified in the heavens above*). What is more, in his German edition of *Sefer ha-Bahir*, G. Scholem translates *hei ha-olamim* as *Leben der Welten*, which is to say, *Life of the Worlds*.

In any case, the root *alam* suggests that the divine reality is concealed, cannot be seized, is infinite, beyond the time and space of this world.

To conclude this study of the paradox of creation, I suggest a few texts that speak of creation *ex nihilo*, of the creation of the world from nothing.

Creation ex nihilo. God made from his Nothing (ayn, eyno) his Being (yesh, yeshno). Creation, the First Miracle. The hidden miracles

Creation *ex nihilo* is the most radically paradoxical reality. How can one say, teach and believe that from nothing can come something?

Philosophers ask this from their point of view, for example:

- Leibnitz: The first question that a person has the right to ask is: *Why is there something rather than nothing?*[73]

---

72. Morning Prayer, *Mahzor le Yamim Nora'im*, volume II, Yom Kippur (New York: Leo Baeck Institute, 1970), 143.

73. *Principes de la nature et de la grâce* (Paris: Flammarion, 1996), 228. Leibnitz's question is preceded by the following reflection: 'Until now, we have only spoken as simple physicists; now we must rise up to metaphysics by using the great principle that is in general not used much and which says that nothing happens without sufficient reason . . . Having stated this principle, the first question that one has the right to raise would be: why is there something rather than nothing?' Having the question depend on the principle of sufficient reason is a philosophical position. The believing person does not start with such a principle.' *Cf* also Lossky, *Théologie mystique de l'église d'Orient* (Paris: Montaigne ed, 1944).

- Heidegger: *All in all, why is there being rather than nothing?*[74]

A Jewish or Christian believer prefers to ask the following question: How is it possible that God wanted to create the world? What was God's aim in creating it? This preference is inspired by the search to which Israel's Tradition invites persons based on the first verse of the Bible (Gen 1:1): *In the beginning* [*be-reshit*] *God created the heavens and the earth.*

Rashi invites the believing person to seek the meaning of this Scripture, as did the ancient masters: In the foreword to his commentary on Scripture, Rashi, *the commentator par excellence*, bases himself on the Tradition according to which Scripture must begin with the *Genesis* narrative, with the Creation narrative, and not with the first commandment revealed to Israel, the beginning of the calendar (Ex 12:1–23ff).

After that foreword, Rashi begins his commentary on the text, starting with Geneis 1:1. Instead of beginning with the *perush* that seeks to establish the literal meaning (*pashut-peshat*, the unveiled meaning, the simple meaning), Rashi first suggests the midrashic meaning (*midrash, derash*), the present-day meaning, the deepest meaning, the meaning that God wants one to seek and to hear based on the question a person never ceases to ask: 'Why did God create the world?' or, in the form the question took ever since Leibnitz: 'Why is there something rather than nothing?'

Rashi on Geneis 1:1 (Col 1, 15–20) (Text 34)

> Genesis 1:1: In the beginning God created *[be-reshit bara elohim*] (the heavens and the earth). This Scripture says nothing other than 'Seek me! [*dorsheni*]'. [Let us seek him] as our Masters sought him: [the world was created] in view of the Torah, which is called 'the beginning of his way [*reshit darkho*, Prov 8:22]' and in view of Israel, who have been called 'the beginning of his harvest [*reshit tevu'ato*, Jer 2:3].' And if you have come to explain it [*le-parsho*] according to its simple meaning [*pashut*, unveiled, literal], explain it thus: In the beginning of the creation of the heavens and of the earth . . .

74. *Cf* M Heidegger, 'Warum ist überhaupt Seiendes und nicht vielmehr Nichts?' *Einführung in die Metaphysik* (Tübingen: Max Niemeyer Verlag, 1998), 1. This question is at the root of all of Heidegger's philosophical searching. His search is that of a non-believer for whom being is surrounded by nothing.

> This Scripture does not come to teach the order of creation so as to say that these [the heavens] preceded . . . Here you must explain thus: 'In the beginning when God created, as if there were at the beginning of the act of creation [*be-reshit bero*].'

Rashi has God speak and say from the depth of Scripture: 'Seek me!' Rashi takes the responsibility for saying what he thinks is the best interpretation (*midrash*) of the ancient masters. Such an interpretation presupposes that the preposition *be* in *be-reshit* (*in the beginning*) can be understood as meaning: for, in view of. Thus the question is: in view of which beginning was the world created?

People sought what could be *the beginning*. Several *beginnings* were found. Among them, Rashi chooses those that are the most fundamental: The beginning which is Wisdom, identified with the Torah (at least since Ben Sirach 24), is the beginning of the way that God goes within God's own self as a prelude to God's revelation to the exterior. Wisdom or Torah is *begotten, not made.*

The beginning that is *Israel* is the *beginning of the harvest* that God expects from humankind. Israel is the beginning, but it is only the beginning. The Nations will come to complete the crop. The election of Israel is the result of God's love, *the affection of your youth* (Jer 2:2–3) that confers upon Israel forever the *Israelite dignity*, in which the nations of the entire world are called to participate.[75] The particularity of the beginning of the harvest, of Israel's election, is in view of the universality of revelation and of redemption, of which we shall speak later.

God, the Torah, Israel thus constitute a fundamental triad since the creation of the world.[76] Israel, to whom is given responsibility for revelation, makes this triad known to the nations. The particular election of Israel is paradoxically the narrow path of an election that is open to all.

In order to remain within the study of the paradox of creation, let us see at this point how Israel's Tradition presents this paradox, starting with the most ancient text containing the vocabulary of creation *ex nihilo*. This text appears in *Sefer Yetsirah*, the *Book of Creation*. We shall study it now in this stage dedicated to Creation. We shall return

75. Prayer after the second reading of the Easter Vigil (Ex 14:24–31; 15:1–2); Catechism of the Catholic Church 528.

76. *Cf* the recapitulation of the triads at the end of this chapter.

to it in the stage dedicated to Redemption conceived as the return of everything to the nothing of the beginning.

Let us already say that this teaching on creation *ex nihilo* will be doubly pertinent to our study of Unity-Trinity. By assuming *the paradox of creation*, the believer will see how God wanted to beget the Torah within God's own self, going forth so to speak from God's self, from God's ineffable nothing. Israel is the first witness of this first *going forth*. From this follows the existence of a *ternary* reality: *God, the Torah, Israel . . .*

By assuming *the paradox of redemption*, the believer will see how God entrusts to humankind, supported and led by the righteous, God's will that everything return to God, the return to the divine nothing before the creation of the world. This divine nothing recapitulates all things without destroying the diversity founded through creation. The result of the return to God confirms the identity of each person in Israel and in the world, identity that is in the image and likeness of God. The Unity lived with the One God is lived by Christians as Unity with God through Jesus Christ and in the Spirit.

According to Gershom Scholem, the *Sefer Yetsirah*, the *Book of Creation*, attributed to Abraham, is probably at the earliest a text of the second or third century CE.[77]

Sefer Yetsirah, chapter 2, 6 (Text 35)

> From the *tohu*, he formed what is solid [*mammash*], and he made from his nothing [*eino*] his being [*yeshno*].[78]

77. G Scholem, *The Origins of the Kabbalah* (Princeton: Jewish Publication Society, 1987), 24–25. The book's title should have been Book of Formation (*yetsirah* and not *beriah*) and not Book of Creation. This lets one think that the ancient tradition which transmitted the book understood creation as the deed of God who forms (*yotser*), who like the potter maintains contact with his work. The creation of the world is ongoing creation (*cf* text 10).

78. *Eino:* can be translated as his nothing; *yeshno*, his being, could be translated as his to be or his something. Here, we do not want to speculate, but to remain as close as possible to the concreteness of the thinking and the expression of Jewish Tradition. The text speaks of God in God's elusive aspect: God is nothing, nothingness, and in God's perceptible aspect, God is *mammash*, being. According to Rabbi Nathan of Nemirov, a student of Rav Nachman of Bratslav, the nothing-*ayin* and the being-*yesh* appear in the verse Ex 17:7: Is the *Yesh*, the Lord *[YHWH]* among us or not *[Ayin]? The Zohar (II, 64b)* sees in this question the expression of a doubt regarding God's presence in Israel and the form of this presence. This doubt, this wavering in Israel's faith, gives Amalek

The *tohu* of Genesis 1:2 is understood as unformed and insubstantial first matter (nothing), which God makes solid (being).

He made from his nothing his being. This develops and clarifies the beginning of the phrase; the nothing is *God's* nothing, from which God makes *God's* being.

Azriel of Gerona (beginning of the thirteenth century) underlines that the nothing is not *the* nothing, independent of God, but *God's* nothing. The transformation of the nothing into being is an event which occurs in God's own self; as Azriel understands it, it is the deed through which divine wisdom manifests itself. 'And the two, the nothing and the being, are only aspects of the one and differentiated *above-being*.'[79]

To complete this explanation, it is useful to cite a passage from the Sefer Yetsirah that precedes the one we are studying, which is to say Sefer Yetsirah 1, 7:

Sefer Yetsirah 1, 7 (Text 36)

---

the possibility to know how to live its relationship with God in faith. Should it waver between the present God *(Yesh)* and the absent God *(ayin)?* Certainly not. It must attach itself to the God *Yesh* in order to go to the God *Ayin (Likutei Halakhot, Hilkhot Geviat Chov Mihayetomin, 3).* The biblical *Yesh* also appears in the Book of Proverbs (Prov 8:21): so as to bring the *Yesh* to those who love me. Wisdom, which speaks in this verse, is the Word of God, identified with the Torah by Israel's Tradition based on Ben Sirach (Ecclesiasticus) (Sir 24:23). This *Yesh,* the being of God's own self, is given to those who love God, in particular to Rabban Yohanan ben Zakkai, whose knowledge of the entire Torah and of all its disciplines is praised by Tradition *(B.T. Sukkah 41a).* The Talmud says that Rabban Yohanan ben Zakkai fulfills *the verse from Proverbs.*

This fulfilment does not exhaust all the possibilities given in this verse. It is used as a "sign-siman" in order to praise those who love God for God's own self and not for the advantages that God can give. This is what Rabbi Yaakov Yoseph of Polonoe (died 1784) taught, Toledot Yaakov Yoseph, Par. Ethanan, based on Psalm 102:1: Prayer for a poor person. This psalm, as interpreted by the Besht (Baal Shem Tov), teaches that the prayer of a poor person can be understood as the prayer that is addressed to the Poor par excellence, which is to say to God, as seen by the *Yesh* of Prov 8:21. Influenced by my faith, I receive from the Sefer Yetsirah that God 'makes his being of his nothing'. God's Nothing is God's transcendent, unknowable aspect. God's Being is what proceeds from God's Nothing through begetting and not through creation (begotten, not made). This Being is the Torah through which everything was created. The word Being, which is better than To Be, expresses the concreteness of the Torah entrusted to Israel, concreteness which, for a Christian, points towards the Incarnation

79. *Cf* G Scholem, 430ff.

> Ten *sefirot* [numbers] *beli mah* [without which], their end is planted in the beginning and their beginning in their end, like a flame is attached to embers, for the Lord is only and He does not have a second, and before the One, what do you count?

Sefirah, plural *Sefirot*, from the root *safar*, to count. Sefirah, a number that is not an ordinary numerable (*mispar*) number, but a principal number of the universe or a degree of creation.[80]

Beli mah can be interpreted as 'without which', without reality, thus 'ideal'.[81]

The text is talking about the ten *sefirot* that are the non-created principals of creation, and which remind one of the 'uncreated energies' of Gregory Palamas.[82] The image of the flame and the embers is very suggestive for teaching the perfect Unity of all that is within divine life, in particular the Unity of the divine Nothing and the divine Being.

The passages from *Sefer Yetsirah* that we have just looked at would merit being studied at greater depth together with several texts, for which the references are the following:

- Sefer Yetsirah 2, 6 and 1, 7;
- *Commentary* by Nahmanides (1195–1270) on Sefer Yetsirah 2, 6 and 1, 7;
- cf. Gershom Scholem, *The Origins of the Kabbalah*, Jewish Publication Society, Princeton, 1987, pp.430ff;
- *Commentaries* by Nahmanides (1195–1270) on *Gen* 17:1; 46:15; *Ex* 6:2; *Lev* 26:11;
- Eckhart (1260–1328), *Sermon* 6;
- R. Abraham Kalisker (died 1810), *Sefer Pri ha-Aretz*, Jerusalem, Miktavim, 1964, pp. 54–55;
- Shneur Zalman of Liadi (1745–1812), *Portique de l'Unité et de la Foi*, chapters 1 and 2 with the Commentary by Adin Steinsaltz.

From these texts it is to be understood that Creation is the first, the most fundamental of all the miracles of which Scripture and the Tra-

80. Scholem, 35.
81. Scholem, 37. Scholem prefers to interpret the obscure *beli mah* as 'closed', 'closed in on itself'. He does not give reasons for his preference.
82. *Cf V Lossky, Théologie Mystique de l'Eglise d'Orient* (Paris: Aubier Montaigne, 1944), 'Energies incréées', 65–86.

dition of Israel (and of the Church) speak. Some of these miracles are *manifest*, others are *hidden*. We shall look at these miracles later in the context of the Paradox of Redemption.

The Paradox of Revelation

Every community prayer includes nineteen blessings on ordinary days and seven blessings on Shabbat and feast days. Every day, the first three and the last three blessings are considered to be blessings of praise. The third blessing is that which proclaims God's sanctity based on Isaiah 6:3, completed by Ezekiel 3:12. These two verses constitute the core of the *Kedushah* in the strict sense, of the proclamation made in the first blessing of the *Reading of the Shema* in the morning, as we have seen (text 10), and in the *Kedushah* of the *Amidah* in the morning and the afternoon of ordinary days:

Kedushah *of the* Amidah *in the morning and the afternoon of ordinary days* (Text 37)

> Let us sanctify your Name in the world as it is sanctified in the Heavens above, as it is written by your prophet (Isa 6:3): *And one cried to the other and said: Holy, Holy, Holy is the Lord Sabaot* [of hosts], *all the earth is filled with his Glory.*
>
> And opposite them they said (Ezek 3:12): *Blessed be the Glory of the Lord in his Place!*
>
> And in the Holy Words [the Holy Writings] it is written (Ps 146:10): *The Lord reigns forever, your God, O Zion, from age to age, Hallelu-Yah!* From age to age we shall speak of your greatness and from eternity to eternity we shall sanctify your sanctity. Your praise, O our God, will never leave our mouth, for you are God, great and holy King.
>
> Blessed are You, Lord, the holy God.

Through the two *kedushot*, that of *Yotser* (text 10) and that of the *Amidah* on ordinary days, Israel manifests its commitment to proclaiming that God is One and Only. Certainly, the *kedushah* of *Yotser* (text 10) does not mention Israel, but Israel received it from Isaiah, and says it in the *Reading of the Shema* in the morning. In the *Kedushah* of the *Amidah* on ordinary days, Israel is not named, but it is clearly

Israel that proclaims Isaiah 6:3 and Ezekiel 3:12 because of what the angels have revealed to it. The angels are not named explicitly, but it is clear that Israel receives from them the words of the *Kedushah* in the strict sense, the *Trisagion* of Isaiah 6 and the acclamation from Ezekiel 3.

In the additional prayer for Shabbat and feasts, the whole of the third blessing solemnly proclaims God's sanctity. This proclamation of sanctity is called *Kedushah rabbah*, the *Great Kedushah*:

Third Blessing [Kedushah rabbah] *of the additional Prayer for Shabbat and Feasts* (Text 38)

> We exalt you and we sanctify you according to the mysterious word of your holy seraphim who sanctify your Name in the sanctuary, as it is written by your prophet [Isa 6:3]: *One addressed the other saying: Holy, Holy, Holy is the Lord Sabaoth, all the earth is filled with his Glory.*
>
> His glory fills the world.
>
> His servants ask one another: Where is the place of his Glory? Opposite them [others] say: Blessed! (Ezek 3:12) '*Blessed is the Glory of the Lord from His Place!*'
>
> May he turn [to us] from His place with mercy, and may he be gracious to the people of those who unify his Name in the evening and in the morning, every day without ceasing, twice, saying the *Shema*: *Hear, Israel, the Lord, our God, the Lord is One.*
>
> Our God is One. He is our Father, our King; He saves us and he causes us to hear twice in the eyes of every living thing (Num 15:41): *so as to be your God, I am the Lord your God*, and it is written in Your holy words (Ps 146:10): *The Lord will reign forever, your God, Zion, from age to age, Hallelu-yah!*
>
> From age to age we shall proclaim your greatness and from eternity to eternity we shall sanctify your sanctity; and your praise, O our God, will not cease from our mouth forever, for you are God, a great and holy King.
>
> Blessed are you, Lord, the Holy God.

From the start, the blessing teaches that Israel's liturgy repeats the heavenly liturgy.

The *Kedushah* in the strict sense, the proclamation of holiness by Isaiah and Ezekiel, is the essence of the blessing. This proclamation is made explicit through one connecting text and is completed in such a way that the blessing merits being called the *Great Kedushah* (*kedushah rabbah*).

First of all, the connecting text between Isaiah and Ezekiel completes the message of the *Kedushah* by saying precisely that the Glory fills the world and not only the earth; the Latin liturgy does this when it says: 'Heaven and earth are full of your Glory.'[83]

Secondly, the connecting text explicitly asks about the place of origin of the Glory. As we have seen, this place is not known.

The *Kedushah* ends with the request for mercy and gives to understand that the mercy comes from the unknown Place, which is coherent with all that is said about the Creator God, the heavenly Father, who is unknown except through his mercy.

Finally, and above all, Israel not only takes charge of the heavenly liturgy. This liturgy finds its accomplishment in the earthly liturgy that leads to the unification of the Name entrusted to Israel. This is when God can declare that he is the God of Israel.

The paradox of the revelation of the God who is known as the unknown is assumed by the paradox of Unity. In order to appreciate better the message of the *Great Kedushah*, we have situated it in relation to the *Kedushah* that is included in the *Yotser* blessing (text 10) and to that of the *Amidah* for ordinary days.

The *Great Kedushah* begins with the revelation of the angels who are mentioned explicitly and in detail; this revelation culminates with the proclamation of Unity: *Hear, Israel, the Lord our God, the Lord is One.*

Israel's role is thus presented as the main one in relation to that of the angels, and it underlines the importance of the particular revelation made to Israel in view of the universal revelation.

Two verses make it possible to shed more light on this aspect of the paradox of revelation: *the paradox of the particular, which reveals and gives foundation to the universal.*

83. The Lutheran liturgy does not have the Latin liturgy's complement, which is inspired by Israel's Tradition.

We shall begin by returning to Rashi's interpretation of Jeremiah (2:3), which we already studied above (text 34). Then we shall see how *Sifre Deuteronomy* speaks of the particular search with which God seeks the Land of Israel (Deut 11:12).

Israel, the beginning of God's harvest (Jer 2:3)

Rashi on Genesis 1:1, *cf* Colossians 1:15–20 (looking again at text 34; Text 39)

> Genesis 1:1: *In the beginning God created* [*be-reshit bara*] (the heavens and the earth). This Scripture says nothing other than 'Seek me! [*dorsheni*].' [Let us seek him] like our Masters sought him: [the world was created] in view of the Torah which is called 'the beginning of his way [*reshit darkho*, Prov 8:22]' and in view of Israel, who were called 'the beginning of his harvest [*reshit tevuato*, Jer 2:3].' And if you have come in order to explain it [*le-parsho*] according to its simple meaning [*pashut*, unveiled, literal], explain it thus: In the beginning of the creation of the heavens and the earth . . . This Scripture does not come to teach the order of creation so as to say that these [the heavens] preceded . . . Here you must explain thus: 'In the beginning when God created, as if there were at the beginning of the act of creation [*be-reshit bero*].'

As we have seen, Rashi drew from Tradition the simplest and the best of what can be taught in order to respond to the most fundamental question, which is: 'Why is there something rather than nothing?' Rashi's answer is that of Jewish faith, which Christian faith must assume, but which can only irritate certain agnostics. For why do Jews and Christians jeopardize their God with Israel, a particular people that claims to be the beginning and the principal of the universe?[84]

The traditional answer transmitted by Rashi identifies biblical Wisdom in the *Book of Proverbs* with the Torah, through which and for which God created the world, 'the start, the principal, the beginning of His way.' This identification was made two centuries before Jesus Christ, as is attested by Ben Sirach (Sir 24). As for the 'begin-

84. Roland Goetschel underlines the role of Israel as 'the beginning of His harvest' in 'Le visage du premier homme,' Rashi, collected works (Paris: 1974), 217–128.

ning of His way', this gives one to understand that God goes out of himself, so to speak, in order to make himself known through his Torah, through a Torah that is nothing other than God's own self, that is begotten, not made (Prov 8:22), according to the meaning that must be given here to the Hebrew verb *kanah*.

God creates the world in view of Israel, chosen from all eternity to make God known through the Torah, so as to work at the unification of all things through love. We saw this when we looked at the blessing *Ahavah Rabbah* and *Ahavat Olam* (text 2). With Rashi, we find again this message concerning Israel, of which Jeremiah (2:3) teaches that it is *the beginning of his harvest*, the particular beginning on which the universal is founded.

The following text confirms that the true universal, the universal desired by God, passes by way of the particular of love, God's love for Israel, for the Land, for Jerusalem.

Seeking the Land of Israel, guarding Israel, the preference for Jerusalem and the Temple

The midrash *Sifre Deuteronomy* clearly teaches the paradox of the particular that leads to the universal, of which it is the foundation. The point of departure is the verse Deuteronomy 11:12, which must first be translated correctly in order to understand its interpretation. It says that *the Lord seeks the Land* in an apparently exclusive manner. This causes difficulty and gives rise to an interpretation that sheds light on the relationship between God and Israel and the Temple.

Sifre Deuteronomy on Deuteronomy 11:12, 80 (Text 40)

> Deuteronomy 11:12: *The land which the Lord your God seeks* [the eyes of the Lord your God are always on it from the beginning of the year until the end of the year]. But does he only seek it? And does he not seek all the lands, as it is said (Job 38:26–27): to *make it rain on a land without any human being . . . to satisfy the dry emptiness*?! And what does the Talmud say: 'The land that the Lord your God seeks'? If one can say: he only seeks it; but because of the search with which he seeks it, he seeks all the lands with it.
>
> In an analogous way (Ps 121:4): *Behold! He neither sleeps nor slumbers, Israel's Guardian*. But does he only guard Israel?

> And does he not guard every being, as it is said (Job 12:10): *He holds in his hand the soul of every living being and the breath of all human flesh*? And what does the Talmud say: 'Israel's Guardian'? If it is possible to say: he is only Israel's Guardian; but because of the way he guards them, he guards all beings with them.
>
> In an analogous way (1 Kings 9:3): *My eyes and my heart will always be there.* But is it not said elsewhere (Zech 4:10): *The eyes of the Lord go through all the earth*? And the Scripture says (Prov 15:3): *The eyes of the Lord are in every place, they observe the wicked and the good.* And what does the Talmud say: 'My eyes and my heart will always be there'? If it is possible to say: his eyes and his heart are only there.
>
> In an analogous way you say (Ps 29:8): *Voice of the Lord, it shakes the desert, the Lord shakes the desert of Kadesh.* What does the Talmud say? The latter [the desert of Kadesh] is the first goal.
>
> Deuteronomy 11:12: *Seek* [*'otah*: her. The Lord seeks her]. She [the land] was given for the seeking [*derishah*], so that starting with her, the *hallah* (*cf* Num 18:17–21), the *terumah* (*cf* Num 18:8.25–29) and the tithes (*cf* Num 18:26; Lev 27:30; Num 18:21–24) be separated. Or [must it be said that] the other lands were also given? [No!], the Talmud says: 'her [*otah*]': it is 'she' who was given for seeking and not the rest of the lands that were not given for the seeking.

It is said that the Lord seeks (*doresh*) the Land. The search is intense. It is inspired by the love (or the hatred) of the person or the reality that one wishes to find.[85] God is at the origin of the search, and God is the first to seek.[86]

Tradition knows the scandal of God's apparently exclusive love of the Land, of Israel, of the Temple. It is able to bring out the particular love in order to teach that it is the authentic foundation for the

85. One must seek in order to find. That is what Jesus says in the Gospel according to Matt 7:7.

86. The Bible does not say that God seeks Israel. The established obligatory prayer says it in the preamble to the processions on Sukkot. God is called 'our God, our Creator, our Redeemer, our Seeker (the one who seeks us)'.

universal love. From the exegetical point of view, the end of the text gives the key to the paradoxical interpretation. Mentioning the desert of Kadesh has no other reason than to teach a preference that is not exclusive. Kadesh is not the only goal; it is the first goal because love is always first of all preferential.

The text returns to Israel's obligation to seek the Land of Israel. This search is put into practice by means of observing the commandments that are connected with the Land. The obligation to dwell in the Land is not mentioned. It could have been. Here it is enough to see that the search for the Land points towards the search for God's presence in the Temple. Returning to the beginning of our text, it is possible to find there a ternary structure. It begins with the search for the *Land*, it continues with the guardian of *Israel*, and it ends with the House (the Tent of Meeting, the *Temple* of Jerusalem) 'in order to place my Name there forever'. God's particular love of the Land and the Temple is coherent with God's love of Israel. This points towards three possible *triads: God* (Land-Temple), *Name, Israel; God, Israel,* the *Land* (Jerusalem, the Temple); *God, Presence* (in the Temple, *Shekhinah*, the Name), *Israel.*[87]

I first mentioned the triad **God, Name, Israel** because through its resonance with the Trinity in Christian faith it is the most pertinent. However, we cannot minimize the importance of the triad **God**, the **Land, Israel** as a support for religious Zionism. Ignoring the significance of the Land in Israel's Tradition alters the integrity of the Word of the One God, which the Church receives from the Jewish people.[88]

The Paradox of Redemption: God Wants Redemption, But God Causes the End to be Awaited

The paradox of Redemption is that God wants this Redemption of the world, but God delays it until Israel returns to God.

Some preliminary remarks:

The Unity of the All-Powerful God and the mute God.

---

87. *Cf* the recapitulation of the triads at the end of this chapter.
88. *Cf* Pinhas H Peli, *Leçons sur la philosophie de l'Etat Juif (in Hebrew), (Beit El, 1990). Cf also P Lenhardt,* 'La Terre d'Israël; Jérusalem, le Temple; leur valeur pour les juifs et pour les chrétiens', in *A l'écoute d'Israël, en Eglise*, chapter VII, 241ff.

'God's silence is His might'[89] (*shetikato shel elohim hi gevurato*).

The *Mekhilta de-Rabbi Ishmael* offers splendid interpretations of the *Canticle at the Sea* (Ex 15). It teaches that the canticle was sung in contact with the presence of God (*Shekhinah*), which was recognised and pointed out through the Holy Spirit. Each word gives rise to various interpretations. Our passage offers a paradoxical interpretation of God's Might.

Mekhilta de-Rabbi Ishmael on Exodus 15:11, 142 (Text 41)

> Exodus 15:11: *Who is like you among the gods* [in Hebrew, *elim*, gods, but one wants to read *illemim*, the mute]?
>
> Who is like you among the mute? You hear the insult inflicted on your sons and you are silent, as it is said (Isa 42:14): *For a long time I remained silent, I contained myself!*
>
> [God answers:] In the past, *I remained silent, I contained myself*; from now on (Isa 42:14–15), *like a woman giving birth, I will cry out . . . I will ravage mountains and hills.*

The anonymous interpretation responds to several difficulties:

- The first and most serious would be to believe that God is one god 'among the gods'. In reading 'among the mute', the gods are lowered to the level of the idols that are the mute and false gods.
- The second no less serious difficulty is to have to praise God, God's sanctity, God's might, as does the *Canticle*, although Israel only knows God's silence and muteness.

The answer is clear. God acknowledges his absence and his silence. God admits that throughout its history and everywhere in the Bible, Israel reproaches God for this silence. This reproach must not be concealed. It always serves as a motive for vehemently affirming the salvation of the believers who 'await the end'.

The text teaches the paradox of the powerful and the powerless, the present and the absent God. Unity is the basis for the duality of suffering and of joy, of death and of life, and for Christians, of the Cross and the Glory. 'My being lowered is my elevation, my elevation is my being lowered.' (Hillel; *cf* Jesus, Lk 14:7–11; 18:14; Mt 23:12).

89. E Urbach, *The Sages* (Jerusalem: Magnes Press, 1975), 95.

Let us return to this saying by Hillel and see how it appears in the midrash *Leviticus Rabbah.*

'My being lowered is my elevation, my elevation is my being lowered.' (Hillel)

Leviticus Rabbah, a homiletic *midrash Haggadah*, offers an opening or proem (*petihah*) to the deep meaning that the first verse of Leviticus might have. The proem returns to this verse; it arrives there by way of several stages, the sequence of which cannot be clearly recognised. The written notation from oral tradition available to the scribe is not well preserved. One could try to reformulate it through recourse to parallels. However, it is better to be satisfied with the version available to us; for in its roughness it gives the message that interests us in a form that has the advantage of corresponding with the genre of notations in oral traditions.

Leviticus Rabbah on Leviticus 1:1 *Par. 1, § 5* (Text 42)

> Leviticus 1:1: *The Lord called Moses* [and spoke to him from the Tent of Meeting saying . . .]
>
> Rabbi Yehoshua of Siknin explained this text (Prov 25:7): *For it is better to say 'come up here!' rather than to be lowered before the prince.* Rabbi Akiba taught this in the name of Rabbi Shimeon ben Azzai [*cf Abot de-Rabbi Nathan A*, chapter 25, 41a; *cf* Lk 14:7–11; Mt 23:12]: 'Go away from your place by the space of two or three seats and remain there until you are told: Come up! And do not go up out of fear that you be told: Go down! It is better to be told: Come up, come up! And that one not be told: Go down, go down!'
>
> And that is what Hillel said: 'My being lowered is my elevation; my elevation is my being lowered.'
>
> What is the [scriptural] justification [for this sentence]? (Ps 113:4–6): *He who raises himself in order to sit* [is] *he who lowers himself in order to see* [in the heavens and on the earth]. You see that at the hour when the Holy One, blessed be He!, revealed himself to Moses from the midst of the bush, the latter hid his face from him, as it is said (Ex 3:6): *And Moses hid his face, for he feared to fix his gaze on God.* The Holy One,

> blessed be He!, told him (Ex 3:10): *And now go [lekhah]! I send you to Pharao*. Rabbi Eleazar said: 'There is an 'h' at the end of the word "go" [*lekhah*] in order to tell you that if you do not redeem them, there will be no other who will redeem them.' On the shore of the sea, Moses remained standing aside. The Holy One, blessed be He!, told him (Ex 14:16): *Lift up your staff, stretch out your hand and split it*. This in order to say: 'If you do not split it, no other will split it.' At Sinai, Moses remained standing aside. The Holy One, blessed be He!, told him (Ex 24:1): *Go up to the Lord!* This in order to say: 'If you do not go up, no other will go up.' In the Tent of Meeting, Moses remained standing aside. The Holy One, blessed be He!, told him: 'How long will you lower yourself? The hour is only awaiting you!'
>
> Know that it is really like this, for from among everyone, the Word called only Moses (Lev 1:1): *The Lord called Moses*.

The verse from Proverbs (25:7), on which a series of traditions shed light, will *open* the mind of the listeners to understand Leviticus 1:1, a verse which, when first heard, only gives simple information. The mention of the Tent of Meeting merits the question as to how the transcendent and infinite Lord can limit himself to the space of the Tent. The preacher turns to Rabbi Akiba, who himself had recourse to Hillel, in order to teach that one must lower oneself in order to be raised up. Hillel's sentence, spoken in the first person, makes one think that it is God himself who teaches this. Then one must ask oneself what scriptural justification can support the paradox of the lowering that is elevation. Psalm 113:4–6 is called upon, according to which it is God himself, the Most High, who lowers himself. After this, the preacher shows how God, the master in the lowering of self, is irritated to see Moses lowering himself when he should not do so. Humility runs the risk of being bad when it paralyses the deed. Certainly, one must imitate God's humility, but one must also know that *there is a time for acting for the Lord* (Ps 119:126). The Lord knows the humility of Moses and God appreciates it. Because of it, God judges Moses to be apt for teaching the Torah and for guiding his people.

The text teaches that one must imitate God along the lines of humility. The reference to Hillel's sentence sheds light on Jesus' teaching in the Gospels (Lk 14:7–11; Mt 23:12; Lk 18:14[95])[90]. Israel's Tradition teaches the imitation of God as regards humility in many ways. Recourse to this Tradition has the advantage of shedding light on the teaching of Jesus through that of Hillel and of supporting these teachings through Scripture.

As for the Trinity, it is enlightening to see how the humility and the lowering of self of Hillel and of Jesus are the conditions for the Incarnation of Jesus, through which one encounters the reality of the Trinity.

God limits himself; God hides his might in order to save: *Truly, you are a hidden God, God of Israel, Savior* (Isa 45:15; Lk 9:20; 23:35–43).

The all-powerful, transcendent Lord lowers his Presence (*Shekhinah*) in order to be with those who suffer (Ex 3:7–8; Isa 49:13–17; 63:9; Zech 2:12; Ps 91:14–16).

The *Mekhilta de-Rabbi Shimeon ben Yohai*, like the *Mekhilta de-Rabbi Ishmael*, which we have already encountered, is a *midrash halakhah* that also speaks of *Haggadah*. It does this in particular in the beginning, when it offers several interpretations of God's manifestation in the Burning Bush. This grandiose beginning is the reason for the name *Mekhilta of the Bush*, given it by Tradition. It is usually called *Mekhilta de-Rabbi Shimeon ben Yohai* because the first master who appears in the text is Rabbi Shimeon ben Yohai.

Mekhilta de Rabbi Shimeon ben Yohai on Exodus 3:1–2, 1–2 (Text 43)

> Exodus 3:1–2: *And Moses was keeping the flock of Jethro . . . and the angel of the Lord appeared to him.*
>
> Rabbi Shimeon ben Yohai said: 'Why did the Holy One, blessed be He!, reveal himself from the heavens above and did he speak with Moses from the midst of the bush? Now just as this bush is more harsh than all the trees of the world, for every bird that goes into it does not come out in peace before it is torn in all its members, so the enslavement of Israel was more harsh than all the enslavements of the world . . . And whence do we know that the enslavement of Israel was more

90. It would be inappropriate to compare Jesus' sentence (Lk 14:11) in the third person with that of Hillel in the first person and thus to draw inappropriate conclusions.

> harsh than all the enslavements of the world? Because it is said (Ex 3:7): *I have seen, I have seen [ra'oh ra'iti] the misery of my people.* And why does the Talmud say, *I have seen, I have seen* twice? After they had plunged their sons into the water, they buried them in the construction . . . Thus the enslavement in Egypt was more harsh than all the enslavements of the world, and this was manifest and known before the Place [God]. That is why it is said (Ex 3:7): *Yes, I know their sufferings.* Rabbi Hiyya and Rabbi Yehuda say: Come and see the mercy of 'Him who spoke and the world was'. For at all times when Israel is delivered to distress, the pain, if it is possible [to say it], is before him, as it is said: *In all their pain, the pain is his.* I have only the pain of the community; for the pain of the individual, whence [do I know that it is also thus]? The Talmud says (Ps 91:15): *Let him call me, I will answer him; I am with him in distress.*
>
> Rabbi Eleazar ben Arakh says: 'Why did the Holy One, blessed be He!, speak with Moses from the Heavens above in the bush? Would it not have suited him [to speak] from [the height] of the cedars of Lebanon, from the summits of the mountains or the summits of the hills? But the Holy One, blessed be He!, lowered his *Shekhina* [*hishpil et shekhinato*] and acted according to good manners, so that the nations of the world would not say: "because he is God and master of his world, he acted without respecting what is right."' That is why the Holy One, blessed be He!, undertook to convince Moses for six days, and on the seventh day, Moses told him (Ex 4:10): *Send, I pray you, whom you wish,* as it is said (Ex 4:10): *And Moses said to the Lord: Excuse me, Lord, I am not a man of words.* The Lord swore that he would not enter into the Land of Israel, as it is said (Num 20:12): *That is why you shall not cause to enter.*

The written notation, which is better preserved than that in the preceding text, manifests several aspects of the oral nature it reflects. First of all, there is the vehement insistence on the *leitmotiv* contained in the question, 'Why did the Holy One, blessed be He!, lower himself?' This insistence is brought about through the repetition, which permeates the memory and touches the heart. There is also relentlessness in finding in Scripture what makes it possible to hold that the

Lord is always with his people and with each person of his people who is in distress.

The text ends tragically by speaking of Moses' punishment.

As in the preceding text, God's lowering of self is connected with that of Israel. But Israel's being lowered precedes God's being lowered and gives rise to it. God lowers himself at all the levels of Israel's being lowered: the slavery, the forced labor, the moral degradation . . . In rabbinic tradition, the lowering, the humiliation of the Shekhinah correspond with the *kenosis* and the lowering of which the New Testament speaks in connection with Jesus (Phil 2:7–8). Here again, for the Christian, the Lord's lowering of self points to the Incarnation.

We see again the question of Israel's suffering and of God's suffering. This shared suffering is caused by *the delay and the awaiting of the End*. Several texts indicated in Appendix II make it possible to get to know better this paradoxical aspect of Redemption.

Other texts from the established obligatory prayer and for the feast of the State of Israel's Independence can let one feel *the people's tension in awaiting the end of history and the unification of all of creation with its Creator*. These texts are indicated in Appendix III.

It would be useful to speak of their pertinence in shedding light on the Christian faith in the Trinity. Everything would have to be studied in order to avoid the risk of damaging the integrity of the One Torah of the One God. However, we have to renounce studying these texts in order to remain within the limits we have imposed upon ourself.

The delay in the Redemption desired by God and by Israel is conditioned by the possibility of the *return of all things to their origin* and by Israel's will to work for this return, which is foreseen and willed by God. The *return* to God must include the *repentance* that is necessary after the sin of the human person, who was created free and who became a sinner.

The Return to the Original Unity. Repentance

Speaking of this return, which is called *teshuvah*, will show us that this process is greater than what is normally called repentance, also *teshuvah*, a return to God after the separation brought on through sin. Repentance is necessarily interior to the return, for the human person's sin exists since the beginning, as Scripture says: *The human instinct is bad since his youth* (Gen 8:21).[91] The human being must always be delivered from evil. Many texts ought to be studied in order to feel the coherence of the One and Perfect Torah as regards this fundamental reality. Since it is impossible to present them within the limited frame of these written notes, I shall content myself with giving their references in Appendix IV, as I have done above for other texts.

Let us start first of all with the New Testament (in an analytical process), with the link that Jesus establishes already at the beginning of his ministry between repentance and the nearness of redemption in the coming of the Kingdom of God (Mk 1:14–15; Mt 4:17). The repentance demanded by Jesus is situated within a large process taught by Peter in his preaching (Acts 3:18–21). Peter announces the universal restoration, the breadth and modalities of which he does not say clearly.

In order to shed light on this point, we can have recourse to the tradition transmitted in the *midrash* (Gen *Rabbah* 12, 6 on Gen 2:4 and Ruth 4:18) concerning Perez, who in the genealogy of the Gospel according to Matthew 1:3 and in Luke 3:33 is named as an ancestor of Jesus.

Genesis Rabbah on Genesis 2:4 Par. 12 § 6 Text 44

> Rabbi Berekhiah said in the name of Rabbi Shemuel bar Nahman: 'Even though the things were created in their fullness, because the first Adam sinned, they were degraded and they will only return to their order [*tikkun*] when the Son of Perez comes, as it is said (Ruth 4:18): *And these are the begettings* [*toledot*] *of Perez: Perez begot Hezron* [. . .] *and Jesse begot David*; begettings [*toledot*] is written in full [with a full *vav*, and the letter *vav* has the numerical value of six] in view of the six things that will return: his splendor, his life, his height, the fruit of the earth, the fruit of the tree, and the luminaries.'

91. *Cf* the tradition on this verse in *Exodus Rabbah* Par. 46 & 4. *Cf* the traditions on death as a consequence of Adam's sin or/and of the sin with the golden calf. *Cf* the interpretation of the word *harut* (inscribed) in Exodus 34:16, which is read as *herut* (freedom, liberation from death). The gift of the Torah, accepted by Israel, was supposed to bring with it liberation from death, but the sin with the golden calf made this liberation impossible (*Exodus Rabbah,* Par. 32 & 1). Cf the interpretation of Ps 82:6 *(Exodus Rabbah, Par.* 32 & 1). *Cf* E Urbach, *The Sages,* 420ff.

The referral to Scripture and to the numerical value of the letter *vav* will not convince everyone. What is important is that the Tradition transmitted by Rabbi Berekhiah teaches that with the Son of Perez (the Messiah, the Son of David), Adam, humankind, will regain their state before sin, in particular life. Creation, dependent on the human being, will regain its productivity.

This is speaking of a return to the origin that presupposes the deletion of sin, the destruction of death and the restoration of all things. In the New Testament, this return is called the *apokatastasis* of all things (*apokatastaseôs pantôn, restitutionis omnium,* Acts 3:21), which is to say, *restitution* or *restoration* of all things.[92]

It is not possible to attribute dogmatic value to this tradition transmitted by Rabbi Berekhiah. However, it exists and sheds light on what for Christians has dogmatic value: Jesus Christ as Messiah, descendant of Perez and of David, calls to repentance as a necessary step in order to come to the Kingdom of God, to redemption, to the return of all things to their state before the sin committed by human beings.

The *process* I now suggest (a synthetic process) will show in several stages:

- how Israel's Tradition teaches the necessary repentance after sin;
- how this Tradition can give importance to the work of the righteous in such a way that repentance can lead to the restoration of all things;
- how the day of Kippur, the culmination of repentance, leads to Unity through the abolition of whatever separates human beings from one another and from God;
- how the Sabbath announces and prefigures the Unity of God, of God's Word and of Israel; and how it leads to Israel's unification with God.

92. *Cf Appendix IV.* The word *apokatastasis* in the New Testament (Acts 3:11) is defined by the Littré (dictionary) as: 'An ideal revolution that, according to the ancient philosophers, brings the stars back to a certain point that is seen as the starting point.' The word does not frighten G Scholem, who uses it in connection with the *apokatastasis* of all things in the sense given by Nahmanides to the 'return of the things to their owner [to the Creator]', to the 'return to pure mystical nothing' *(Commentary by Nahmanides on the Sefer Yetsirah I, 1. Cf* G Scholem, *The Origins of the Kabbala, 449, footnote 201).*

Repentance (Hos 14:2): Return, Israel, to the Lord your God!

In speaking about the paradox of revelation, text 34 (Rashi on Genesis 1:1) was already introduced and explained. We saw how it presents the paradox of the particular, which is the foundation for the universal. We shall return to this text in order to show that the return is foreseen and willed by God from all eternity.

Rashi on Genesis 1:1, *cf* Colossians 1:15–20 (returning to text 34: Text 45)

> Genesis 1:1: *In the beginning* [*be-reshit bara*] *God created* (the heavens and the earth). This Scripture says nothing other than, 'Seek me! [*dorsheni*].' [Let us seek him] as our Masters sought him: [the world was created] in view of the Torah, which is called 'the beginning of his way [*reshit darkho*, Prov 8:22]' and in view of Israel, who have been called 'the beginning of his harvest [*reshit tevu'ato*, Jer 2:3].' And if you have come to explain it [*le-parsho*] according to its simple meaning [*pashut*, unveiled, literal], explain it thus: In the beginning of the creation of the heavens and of the earth . . . This Scripture does not come to teach the order of creation so as to say that these [the heavens] preceded . . . Here you must explain thus: 'In the beginning when God created, as if there were at the beginning of the act of creation [*be-reshit bero*].'

According to a text that will be cited and studied at the end of this study [*Mekhilta de-Rabbi Ishmael* on Exodus 12:41 (text 104), God becomes involved in the redemption of the world to the point of redeeming His own self. That is to say that God cannot leave the last word to the evil that exists in his creation because of the freedom God gave to his creatures who are gifted with reason, both the angels and the human beings. As we have seen, prayer does not keep the expression in Isaiah 45:7: *I make peace and I create evil*, but it assumes it while blessing God who 'makes peace and creates everything.'[93] The prayer thus confirms that God is responsible for his creation.

God creates the world and the human being in view of Israel, who was chosen from all eternity in order to make God known through the Torah, in order to work for the unification of all things through love. We saw this when we spoke of the blessing *Ahavah Rabbah* or

93. *Cf* the Blessing *Yotser* (text 10).

Ahavat Olam (text 2). We also heard this message in connection with the 'Israelite dignity', to which Christians and all human beings are called.

The Tradition transmitted by Rashi confirms Jeremiah 2:2–3: Israel is the beginning of God's harvest. Creation is made in view of a harvest, a response of love to God's love. The point is to return to the love of the beginning, of which Jeremiah speaks. Israel is the beginning of this return. The return of humankind and of the world presupposes Israel's return. From the point of view of redemption, we again see the paradox of the particular, upon which the universal is founded.

If it is thus, one can understand that Israel's Tradition gives tremendous importance to the return of Israel, of all human beings, and of all of creation to the Creator of all things. Through its origin in the will of God, the return, *teshuvah,* is greater than repentance and penance, necessary as these steps are after sin. Because the return, *teshuvah,* can take place only through repentance (the knowledge of sin, the confession of that sin, the request for and obtaining of forgiveness) and penance (the purifying fast of Kippur). For every human being was created with the freedom to sin, and ever since Adam and Eve every person is, in fact, a sinner. God in his omniscience foresaw the possibility of sin and the means to repair it. That is what Tradition teaches, without imposing it as a dogma: the possibility of returning to God after sin was created before the creation of the world.[94]

It is obviously impossible to study in detail the debates that surround this teaching on *teshuvah.* I shall content myself with indicating their existence and summing up the essential of what they convey. The human being is free and a sinner, but God does not abandon the person to his and her sin. The person is given freedom, as Rabbi Akiba teaches in accordance with the *Mishnah.*[95] *Teshuvah* is offered the human being. It is not imposed on him or her, at least according

94. *Genesis Rabbah* on Genesis 1:1, Par. 1, & 4: B.T. Pesahim 54a; Pirkei de-Rabbi Eliezer, chapter 3.

95. *Mishnah Abot 3, 15.* According to the majority of masters, the Mishnah is not a code but a collection of authorized teachings. *Cf* the rich commentary on this Mishnah by A Guggenheim, *Pirqé Abot* (Paris, C.L.K.H, 1988).

to the masters, who did not believe that it was commanded.[96] One knows that it is asked for by God, that God invites to it in many declarations (*Haggadah-haggadot*) and warnings (*hazharah-hazharot*), while leaving the human person the freedom to commit him- and herself to it or not. It would be interesting to debate this freedom, as do the sages of Israel when they teach that the love and the fear of God are inseparably obligatory.[97] The famous saying of Rabbi Haninah: 'Everything is in the hand of the Heavens except the fear of God', is of course a general maxim that certainly raises difficulties, as S Schechter says.[98] What is at stake in such debates is knowing how far human freedom goes in *teshuvah*, and how God supports the human person in this process.

Jewish prayer in its profound simplicity gives the answer that sheds light on our study of Unity. This answer does not dispense from seeking how better to understand what the human person is, what his and her sin is, and what the divine mercy is that grants forgiveness in abundance.

God calls the human being to *teshuvah* so that through it, the person may come to God, according to the call of the prophet Hosea, which is read on the Sabbath that lies within the *Ten Days of Teshuvah*, between Rosh ha-Shanah and Kippur: Hosea 14:2: *Return* [*shuvah*], *Israel, unto (in Hebrew ad) the Lord your God! Teshuvah* enables one to go unto God, and if the human being does not succeed in this, God will come to meet him and her.[99]

---

96. *Cf* B Gross, *Les lumières du retour* (Paris: Albin Michel, 1998), 12–16. With the support of Scripture (Num 5:6–7, positive commandment 73), Maimonides teaches the confession of sins as a commandment. For him, this confession is the consequence of *teshuvah*, which is not commanded. Nahmanides teaches that *teshuvah* is commanded by Scripture (Deut 30:2).
97. E Urbach, *The Sages*, 400–419. We have seen that the Reading of the Shema and the tradition that sheds light on it in prayer and in midrash calls for the unification of fear and of love. It is also the role of the liturgy of the Ten Days of Fear (literally, the terrible days, *yamim noraim*) to educate to the fear of God, who liberates from false fears and who leads to love of God and to joy. Jesus also teaches the fear of God, which frees from all other fear (Mt 10:28–31). He precedes Rabbi Eliezer ben Hyrkanos, who taught the same after the destruction of the Temple (B.T. Berakhot 28b).
98. S Schechter, *Aspects of Rabbinic Theology* (New York: Schocken Books, (1909), 1961), 264–292.
99. *Cf Pesikta Rabbati* on Hos 14:2, Pisk. 44.

Divine mercy inspires and supports Repentance

God comes to meet the sinner because of the mercy that characterises God as Creator, as we saw when getting to know the Unity of God's mercy and God's justice.

In the following text, Rashi gives us to understand that the divine mercy precedes justice (ontologically and not chronologically).

Rashi on Genesis 1:1 and Genesis 2:4 (Text 46)

> Genesis 1:1: *God* [*Elohim*, Justice] *created the heavens and the earth*. It is not said: 'The Lord [*YHWH*, Mercy] created'. For in the beginning, God had the idea of creating it through the attribute of justice. God saw that the world would not be maintained. God caused the attribute of justice to preceded and to be associated with the attribute of mercy. Thus it is written: *The day the Lord* [*YHWH*, Mercy] *God* [*Elohim*, Justice] *made the heavens and the earth.*[100]

We have seen that repentance is necessary within the return to God. Let us study the texts that show how this repentance is organised and taught in and through Jewish prayer.

We shall hear first the message of the community prayer for ordinary days. It organizes the *teshuvah* that is imposed daily on every human person according to what Rabbi Eliezer said: 'Return one day before your death', which implies daily *teshuvah.*[101]

We shall complete our listening with some passages from the *liturgy for the ten days of repentance*. Through God's Holy Spirit, God inspires, accompanies and supports *teshuvah* until it reaches its goal: the encounter with God in the joy of unification through love. God, the merciful Father, calls the sinners to return unto him through repentance.

---

100. This way of speaking of the attributes as if they had an existence separate from God in order to serve God as the Angels of Service must not lead to confusion. As the wording of the prayer during the Closing Liturgy of Kippur (the Neilah Liturgy) shows, this danger does exist: 'O Attribute of Mercy, spread yourself over us and flow out before your Creator and ask mercy for your people!' Rav Soloveitchik denies this by claiming adherence to several great masters (J Dov Soloveitchik, *L'homme de la halakhah* (in Hebrew), [Jerusalem, Eliner Editions, 1981], 56).

101. Mishnah Abot 2, 10; B.T. Shabbat 153a.

The prayer for ordinary days

The *Amidah*, the community prayer for ordinary days, includes nineteen blessings.[102] The first three and the last three are blessings of praise or are considered as such; the thirteen intermediary blessings are blessings of petition. The blessings four, five and six constitute the daily liturgy of repentance.

Through the Holy Spirit, God gives knowledge

The daily liturgy of repentance begins with the *fourth blessing* of the *Amidah*. Knowledge (*daat*) is what initiates the return to God. Knowledge of God and knowledge of oneself, which let one feel the abyss of separation caused by sin.[103]

Fourth Blessing of the Amidah *for ordinary days* (Text 47)

> Through grace you give the human person knowledge [*daat*] and you teach the human being discernment. Give him knowledge of you, discernment and intelligence . . .
>
> Blessed are You, Lord, who gives knowledge [*daat*] through grace.

Knowledge is the highest of the three faculties mentioned in the blessing. It appears first and above all, it is the only faculty that appears in the conclusion. What is meant is the knowledge of God, a knowledge which God expects of Israel. As far as it is possible and to the extent to which God gives it through grace, it is this knowledge of God that enables the human person to know himself or herself in relationship with God and to recognise himself or herself as sinner. How is this free gift given? Rashi indicates this in his commentary on the Book of Exodus (31:2–3).

Rashi on Exodus 31:2–3 (Text 48)

---

102. Although today there are nineteen blessings, the Amidah is always called the 'Eighteen' (*Shemoneh Esreh*). The transition to nineteen is best explained by the division of the earlier fourteenth blessing, which became the fourteenth and fifteenth blessings. *Cf* J Heinemann, *Prayer in the Talmud* (Berlin/New York: de Gruyter, 1977), 224–226.

103. *Cf* Isa 59:2 and Sifre Deuteronomy on Deut 18:12, 220.

> Exodus 31:2: *Know that I have called Bezalel . . . I have filled him with the Spirit of God, of wisdom, of discernment and of knowledge.*
>
> 'Wisdom': What the human being hears from others and learns.
>
> 'Discernment': What he understands of himself based on the things he has learned.
>
> 'Knowledge': the Holy Spirit.

With his usual terseness, Rashi teaches that it is the Holy Spirit given to Bezalel who enables him to build the Tent of Meeting that is capable of receiving the Holy God.

The masters who have recourse to Rashi's interpretation of the gift of God's Spirit to Bezalel (Ex 31:2–4) invite us to understand that the free gift of knowledge requested in the blessing implies the gift of the Holy Spirit.[104] The first stage of *teshuvah* is the knowledge of God and the knowledge of oneself before God.

One significant clarification is given through the request for knowledge as presented in the version established for the evening prayer that follows the closure of Shabbat:

Fourth blessing of the evening Amidah *after the Exit of Shabbat* [Motsaei shabbat] (Text 49)

> You give knowledge to the human person through grace, you teach the human being discernment, you give us knowledge of your Torah [*madda' toratekha*] through grace.

This completes the teaching given above. Knowledge of God is made possible through the Holy Spirit who makes effective the knowledge of God and of self taught by the Torah and the practice of the commandments prescribed by it.

After this preparation, the *fifth blessing* offers the following stage.

Fifth blessing of the Amidah *for ordinary days* (Text 50)

> Our Father, cause us to return to your Torah and bring us near, our King, to your service, and cause us to return before you through complete return [*teshuvah shelemah*]!

104. Cf E Munk, *Le monde des prières* (Paris: C.L.K.H., 1970), 154–156.

> Blessed are You, Lord, who take delight in repentance [*teshuvah*].

We return to the Torah, the way that leads to God. God, who is Father and therefore merciful, is also King. Repentance, *teshuvah*, is what brings the person close to God's Kingdom, as Jesus knows and teaches (Mt 3:2; 4:17; Mk 1:15).

Complete return clearly excludes that a person compromises and falls back into sin, but above all, it enables the person to reach God. This ultimate goal, which according to the prophet Hosea (14:2) God demands: *Return* [*shuvah*], *Israel unto the Lord your God!,* can only be reached if God gives the sinner the ability to encounter God. God, who has pleasure in repentance, acts through the Holy Spirit in order to support the sinner's free progress. If the sinner cannot go as far as God through his or her own strength, God comes to meet the sinner and makes himself present to him and her.[105]

Here we have a hint of a trinitarian reality: *God the Father* (all-powerful, transcendent), God's *Presence* (*Shekhinah*, immanent) to the sinner, and the *Holy Spirit* who makes the encounter between the human being and God possible.[106]

The last stage of the prayer: the request for forgiveness

Sixth blessing of the Amidah *for ordinary days* (Text 51)

> Forgive us, our Father, for we have sinned, be indulgent with us, our King, for we have erred. For you are he who is indulgent and who forgives.
>
> Blessed are you, Lord, who are gracious and multiply forgiveness.

This last stage shows the superabundance of the Creator God's mercy. The prayer takes the expression for this superabundance from Isaiah 55:7, as does Saint Paul (Rom 5:20). This shows that the return to God goes further than the necessary forgiveness of sins. The point is that all of creation should recognize its Creator and return to him. Israel

105. *Cf* Pesikta Rabbati, *Piska* 44, *Shuvah* on Hos 14:2, 184b-185a; *cf* Lk 15:20.
106. *Cf* the recapitulation of the triads at the end of this chapter.

was chosen to be 'the beginning of the harvest'. *Through its repentance, Israel makes the redemption of the world and the establishment of the Kingdom of God possible.*

The following text states this conviction and discusses it.

Rabbi Eliezer and Rabbi Yehoshua are the two great disciples of Rabbi Yohanan ben Zakkai who, together with him, taught before and after the destruction of the Temple. Because they were very conservative, they transmitted traditions from before their time:

B.T. Sanhedrin 97b–98a (Text 52)

> Rabbi Eliezer said: 'If Israel repents, they will be redeemed; if they do not repent, they will not be redeemed.' Rabbi Yehoshua told him: 'If they do not repent, they will not be redeemed?! But [no!], the Holy One, blessed be He, will raise up for them a king whose decrees will be as harsh as those of Haman; then Israel will repent and will return to the good.'

The two masters agree in teaching that there will be no redemption for Israel if Israel does not repent. One more complete version of the debate is given by the Talmud after the passage given here. It shows how the masters find support for their positions in Scripture. They end up by giving the last word to Rabbi Yehoshua. Thus God must intervene so that Israel will repent.[107]

The debate does not speak of the consequence that Israel's redemption will necessarily have for the redemption of the Nations and of the whole world. The masters and the Talmud, which transmits their teaching, do not need to say what is obvious.

The essential role attributed to Israel and to its repentance for the redemption of the world can surprise and even scandalise people who see things from the exterior. However, the Christian knows that Jesus makes repentance the condition for the coming of the Kingdom of Heaven (Mt 4:17; Mk 12:15).

As we have seen (texts 47 and 48), the *fourth blessing* of the *Amidah* for ordinary days launches the daily process of repentance by requesting the free gift of the knowledge obtained through the inter-

107. For a Christian, God's intervention began irreversibly through the Incarnation of Jesus Christ. As Messiah, Jesus brings about the restoration of all things (Acts 3:21). His work does not at all abolish the role that Israel keeps for the redemption of the world through its own repentance.

vention of the Holy Spirit. Through the Holy Spirit who inspires Israel (or through the *Bat Kol*, the *Heavenly Voice* that speaks to Israel), Israel knows God and recognizes God's Presence (*Shekhinah*). Without the Holy Spirit who inspires and supports repentance, Israel cannot witness to the Unity of the Son and the Father.

The Ten Days of Repentance (the terrible Days, the Days of Fear: *yamim noraim*) go from *Rosh ha-Shanah* (the beginning of the year, the New Year) on the 1st day of the month of Tishri, to *Yom ha-Kippurim* (or Yom Kippur, the Day of Atonement), on the 10th of Tishri.

They place repentance at the summit of the religious year, before the third feast of pilgrimage, the *Feast of Sukkot* (of Tabernacles). This latter feast, which Tradition simply calls 'the Feast' (*he-hag*), celebrates in anticipation the joy of humankind reconciled with God, united with Israel in the adoration of the One and Only God as announced by the prophet Zechariah (14:9).

Let us listen to the message of the prayer for *Rosh ha-Shanah* and then to that of the prayer for Kippur.

The prayer for Rosh ha-Shanah

Shortened version of the Malkhiyyot *Blessing in the Additional Prayer* [mussaf] *for* Rosh ha-Shanah (Text 53)

> [*YHWH*] is our God in the heavens above and on the earth below; nothing else [*ein 'od*].
>
> That is why we hope in You . . .
>
> All the inhabitants of the universe will recognize and know that before you every knee must bow, by You every tongue must swear [. . .]
>
> And all will receive the yoke of your Kingdom and soon you will reign over them forever, as it is written in your Torah (Ex 15:18): *The Lord will reign forever.* And in your holy Words [the Holy Writings] it is written (Ps 22:29): *For to the Lord belongs the Kingship.* And through your servants the prophets it was written (Isa 44:6): *Thus said the Lord, the King of Israel and its redeemer.* It is our task [*aleinu*] to praise the Lord of

> all, the 'one who formed the beginning' [*yotser bereshit*]. The seat of his Glory is in the heavens above and the Presence [*Shekhinah*] of his might is at the highest height; He is our God, nothing else in truth. He is our King; nothing that is not He, as is written in his Torah (Deut 4:39): *And you will know today and you will establish in your heart that the Lord is Redeemer.* And it is said (Zech 14:9): *And the Lord will be King over all the earth, and on that day, the Lord will be One* [*ehad*] *and his Name will be One* [*ehad*], and in your Torah it is written (Deut 6:4): *Hear, Israel, the Lord our God, the Lord is One.*

The *necklace* (*harizah*) illustrates God's kingship through Scripture. It culminates in the verses from Zechariah (14:9) and from Deuteronomy (6:4). Zechariah announces the final unification of which Moses traced the program in the *Shema Israel.*

The prayer for Yom Kippur: the reunion of Israel and of all of humankind

The immense Kippur prayer begins with the proclamation of joy. This joy is sown by those who rectify their heart (through repentance, Ps 97:11). The last, the closing prayer (*neilah*), culminates in seven appeals for mercy and for forgiveness, which are called *Selihot.*

Each of these appeals is addressed first of all to 'God, the King who is seated on the throne of Mercy'. The prayer then goes on from the third to the second person in order to remind God that he has established the recitation of *the thirteen attributes of mercy*. This reminder of 'the Covenant of the Thirteen' means that the recitation of the attributes is effective for the forgiveness of sins. For God communicated them to 'the Humble [Moses, Num 12:3]' when God descended in the cloud and remained with him (Moses) when he called upon the Name of YHWH (mercy). *And the Lord* [*YHWH*] *went before him and proclaimed: 'Lord, Lord'.*

Each of the seven appeals is followed by *a justification or explanation of this process*. The repetition of the requests is always intense. In the *fifth selihah*, the community goes so far as to personify the attribute of mercy in a surprising way:

> *Fifth selihah in the closing prayer for* Yom Kippur (Text 54)
>
> O Attribute of Mercy, pour yourself out over us; cast our supplication before your Creator; ask mercy for your people, for every heart is in pain and every head is sick. Uphold my trust in the Thirteen Words.

Many masters do not accept this formulation for obvious reasons, and they manage to avoid it. Without intervening in a debate internal to the Jews, it is permitted to note that the personification of the Attribute of Mercy is analogous to the personification of the Torah and of the commandments in Psalm 119.[108]

The closing prayer is extended by one last call for forgiveness, addressed in the form of a litany to 'Our Father, our King [*avinu malkenu*]'. It ends with the proclamation of the *Shema Israel* (Deut 6:4): *Hear, Israel, the Lord our God, the Lord is One*, and with that spoken by Moses, Solomon, and the people together with Elijah (Deut 4:35, 39; 1 Kings 8:60; 18:39): *The Lord is God.* The shofar is sounded to announce the redemption that is possible and that will be confirmed in the building of Jerusalem, which is desired and announced in the expression: 'Next year in Jerusalem (re) built!'

The building of Jerusalem, which is to say of the Temple, is requested in the fifteenth blessing of the *Amidah* on ordinary days. Because of *Psalm* 147:2, the prayer knows that the Lord builds Jerusalem. It confirms that this is so by ending the blessing without the citation formula: 'Blessed are you, Lord, who (re) builds Jerusalem.' Certainly, the Lord is at work in building Jerusalem, Zion, to which he will cause his Presence (his *Shekhinah*) to return. That is what Israel requests at the end of the daily *Amidah.*

Thus, repentance will come to its fulfillment in the reunion of Israel and of all of humankind with God who is present in the Temple.

108. Yom Kippur Machzor, with commentary adapted from the *Teachings of Rabbi Joseph B. Soloveitchik* (New York: The Kasirer Edition, 2006), 818–819. *Cf* also J. Dov Soloveitchik, *L'homme de la halakhah* (Jerusalem: Eliner Editions, 1981), 55–56. On Psalm *119, cf Y Amir, Psalm 119 als Zeugnis eines proto-rabbinischen Judentums* (Frankfurt: Studien zum antiken Judentum, 1985), 3ff; *E Zenger, 'Comme j'aime Ta Torah (Ps 119, 97), La signification de la Loi juive pour le christianisme', Sens,* 5 (2003): 211–228.

Kippur is *the day One* that removes the abyss of separation between human beings and God, which was caused by sin (Isa 59:2).[109] It is the Day (the Day *par excellence*, *Yoma*) that opens the Temple to the prayer of all peoples (Isa 56:7).[110] The unification of human beings among themselves, the unification of Israel and of all human beings with God—it all depends on Israel's repentance. We can understand why God insistently asks for it and why Israel commits itself to it.

Central Blessing in the Additional Prayer for Kippur, *before the confession of sins* (Text 55)

> Hear our voice, Lord, our God; have pity and compassion on us; receive our prayer with mercy and good will; cause us to return to you, Lord, and we shall return; renew our days as formerly; do not send us away from you; do not take your Holy Spirit from us; do not reject us in our old age; do not abandon us when our strength is exhausted.

At the end of repentance, we again encounter the Holy Spirit, just as we saw the Holy Spirit at its beginning. This Spirit is the one who unifies and balances the human person's freedom with the will of God.

We have just seen that repentance is the activity that again unifies after the forgiveness of sins. We saw that God in his mercy multiplies forgiveness over and beyond what justice would require. The return to God that God's love desires must be in accord with the superabundance of God's love. It is not enough to feel God's mercy and the benefits of that mercy. The joy of the repentant sinner must be in accord with the greatness of the joy of heaven. Mercy must be sought by going to its origin, by returning to the divine nothing that precedes creation.

The acclamation that ends the prayer of Kippur (Deut 4:35.39; 1 Kings 8:60; 18:39) benefits from being re-situated in the context of Deuteronomy. Let us look again at the verses and see how their interpretation opens up a reflection on the Unity-Unicity (the fact that God is the Only) which completes what we studied at the beginning of these pages.

---

109. *Cf* Genesis Rabbah on Gen 1:5, Par. 3, 8; Sefat Emet, le-Yom Kippur (1891), 5, 171–172 (text 61).

110. *Cf the central blessing (kedushah ha-yom) of the Additional Prayer for Kippur.*

> *Deuteronomy* 4:35: *You were made to see* [or: it was given to you to see] *so that you might know that the Lord* [*YHWH*] *is* [the] *God* [*Elohim*] *and that there is nothing other than he* [*ein 'od milebaddo*] (text 53).

Rashi explains 'You were made to see . . . (*atta hor'eta la-daat*)' according to the targum: *at hithazeta*, 'you were made to see'. He explains that the Holy One, blessed be He!, opened the seven firmaments and that they saw that God was the Only One (*yahid*).

This *does not teach the Unity of God, but that God is the Only One.* Listening to the verse in Deuteronomy 4:39 enables one to go further:

> Deuteronomy 4:39: *And you shall know today and you shall cause to return to your heart that the Lord* [*YHWH*] *is* [the] *God* [*ha-Elohim*] *in the heavens above and on the earth below, nothing other* [*ein 'od*, nothing more, nothing beyond].

The expression 'ein od' is absolute, which it isn't in the preceding verse. Most translations—'he and no other' (French Jerusalem Bible), 'there is no other' (TOB), 'no other is' (Cerf edition of the translation of E Urbach's book, 27)—do not take its radicalness into account. *Its formulation goes further than indicating that God is the Only.* Being the only in itself is not unfathomable, whereas the Unity is. We can regret that E Urbach did not see any point in saying what seemed to him to be obvious. We can rejoice that a late master of the Hasidic movement HaBaD, Rav Aaron ha-Levi of Starosselia, interpreted magnificently Moses' absolute expression of God's being One and Only.[111]

In order to enter more into the mystery of the divine Unity and of the mercy that characterizes this Unity at the origin of the creation of the world, it is good to follow the steps of the righteous who bring creation back to its origin.

The Work of the Righteous is Greater than the Work (of Creation) of the Heavens and of the Earth

We shall begin with a saying by Bar Kappara that causes us to reflect on the role of the righteous in the redemption of the world. This ancient saying, contemporary with the establishment of the New Tes-

111. L Jacobs, *Seeker of Unity* (New York: Basic Books, 1966), 105–110.

tament, is taken up again by the Hasidic masters whose message we shall study. These masters at the end of the eighteenth century and of the nineteenth century are much later than Bar Kappara. The gap in time does not take anything away from the pertinence of these masters who have to their credit that they understood and lived in depth the spiritual traditions that they transmit.[112] I acknowledge that in choosing these texts, I am inspired by their resonances with the Christian faith in Jesus Christ, the Righteous and the Redeemer *par excellence*. Such as they are, these texts are independent of the Christian faith, and listening to them in no way means that Christians 'take possession' of their message. We shall return to these resonances later.

Bar Kappara is one of the last Tannaim, a student of Rabbi Yehudah ha-Nassi at the beginning of the third century CE. 'He is known for his sharp and agile mind.'[113]

B.T. Ketubot 5a (Text 56)

> Bar Kappara said: 'The work of the righteous is greater than the work [of creation] of the heavens and of the earth. For concerning the creation of the heavens and of the earth it is written (Isa 48:13): *Certainly, my hand founded the earth, my right hand stretched out the heavens*, whereas concerning the work of the righteous it is written (Ex 15:17): *The place that you, Lord, made your dwelling place, the sanctuary that your hands prepared*.'

The statement by Bar Kappara is typical of this master, who disconcerted people both by his message and by the way in which he based it on Scripture. Certainly, in his recourse to Scripture, he is not using Scripture as proof but as a support. Thanks to Rashi, we can accept that 'your hands' in Exodus 17:17 are not the hands of God but the hands of the righteous (Moses, Bezalel, Solomon, the Children of Israel) who built the dwelling place in the desert and the temple in Jerusalem in accordance with the will of God. This interpretation of Scripture is not necessarily convincing. For it is significant that Rashi finds support from the same verse in Exodus 17:17 when he

112. R Meshullam Feibush of Zbarah in his book *Derekh Emet* vehemently criticizes the masters who do not study the Torah for its own sake *(li-shemah)* and who do not pray *(cf L Jacobs, Hasidic Prayer* [London/Washington: The Littman Library of Jewish Civilization, 1993], 2–21).

113. *Cf* Ketubot 1, *Steinsaltz Edition* (Paris: Jean Claude Lattès, 1994), 41–44.

teaches that 'the temple of the future', the one we await, will be built and accomplished; it will manifest itself coming from heaven, as it is said (Ex 15:17): *The sanctuary that your hands will have prepared.* The same verse can thus be interpreted and translated in two ways: 'Your hands': the hands of the righteous who work in your Name, or 'your Hands', and not human hands.[114]

Even if the scriptural support is controversial, Bar Kappara's message deserves to be heard because it is pertinent to this study.

In order to show this pertinence, I would like to study one text from the Babylonian Talmud and three texts of Hasidic masters. The fact that I find support in these Hasidic texts is more influenced by the New Testament than by ancient rabbinic literature. I do not have the right to make the ancient Jewish texts say what I hear in the New Testament about Jesus Christ, but I do believe that I can call upon Jewish teachings that are rooted in the message of Bar Kappara and that are based on traditions from ancient mysticism, the most ancient we can know: the Merkhabah or Heikhalot traditions that were known and lived by Saint Paul and Rabbi Akiba.[115]

The Talmud transmits a series of traditions on Rabbi Hanina ben Dossa, a student of Rabban Yohanan ben Zakkai. He was a respected master who was known for his close relationship with God and his power to work miracles. Upon the request of his wife, he obtained a miracle from God and then a second miracle, which annulled the first in order to satisfy a second request by his wife. Concerning this, the Talmud passes on an authorized commentary on the two successive miracles:

B.T. Taanit 25a (Text 57)

> A tanna taught: 'The last miracle was greater than the first, [the following is in Aramaic] for we have learned [through tradition] that what has been given is given, what has been received is not taken back.'

114. *Rashi on B.T. Sukkah 41a.*

115. On Rabbi Akiba and Saint Paul, *cf* P Lenhardt, P von der Osten-Sacken, *Rabbi Akiva* (Berlin: Institut Kirche und Judentum, 1987), *Gefahren der Mystik,* chapter 6, 122–153; on Saint Paul: A Schweitzer, *Die Mystik des Apostels Paulus* (Tübingen: Mohr Siebeck, (1930), 1981), 152–153.

The expression 'a tanna taught' is often used in the Babylonian Talmud. It introduces an authorised commentary on the tradition that precedes it. Through a miracle, God had taken back a gift that God had given through a miracle. Tradition teaches that in this case, the second miracle is greater than the first, because God does not take back what God has given.

This teaching will be taken up again in the following texts that speak about the first great miracle, the miracle of the creation of the world, and a second miracle, that of the de-creation of the world, which occurs through the deeds of the righteous.

> *Dov Baer of Mezeritch* [*the great Maggid*, died in 1772], Maggid debarav le-Yaakov 9, 24 (Text 58)
>
> The works of the Righteous are greater than the work [of creation] of the heavens and of the earth. Explanation: For the work of the heavens and of the earth was [to make] being from nothing [*yesh mi-ayin*], whereas the righteous make nothing from being [*mi-esh ayin*]. For based on everything that they do, even material things such as eating, they raise up holy sparks from that eating to the Height. And thus they do with everything. Thus it happens that they make nothing from being.

The Maggid bases what he says on the famous expression in the Book of Creation (*Sefer Yetsirah* 2, 6), a work on mystical cosmogony that can be traced back to the fourth century CE:[116] 'He made his being from his nothing (*asah eino yeshno*).'

The Maggid's disciples, especially Abraham Kalisker (died 1810), applied his message to spiritual life and taught that if the human person makes him- and herself nothing before God and follows the Torah for the good of his or her neighbour, they attain their own unification and that of their community.[117]

R. Meshullam Feibush Heller of Zbarah (died 1795), a disciple of R Menahem Mendel of Peremyshlany, who was himself a disciple of R

116. This expression from the Sefer Yetsirah, a book attributed to 'Abraham our Father', was nourished by many speculations especially in the Kabbalah of Gerona.

117. *Cf* J Weiss, 'R. Abraham Kalisker's concept of communion with God and men', in *Journal of Jewish Studies*, VI (1955): 87–99.

Israel ben Eliezer (Baal Shem Tov, died 1760) and of R Jehiel Michael, the Maggid of Zloczov (died 1786), is known for his profound interpretations of the teaching of R Dov Baer (the great Maggid).[118]

R Meshullam Feibush Heller of Zbarah, *Yosher Dibrei Emet 12* (Text 59)

> When we recognise that in truth we are nothing and when we take into account that there is nothing in the world except the Name, blessed be He! as it was before the creation, then there is for the Name, blessed be He!, if one can say this, real enjoyment, which he expects us to give him. This is like a father and a mother who hope to give birth to a son and to carry him in their arms. Thus there is for the Name, blessed be He! an enjoyment that comes to him from his sons when they come into his arms in order to embrace him and to attach themselves to him, as has been said above.
>
> This is what was said [B.T. Ketubot 5a]: 'The work of the righteous is greater than the work [of creation] of the heavens and of the earth', and Rabbi Dov Baer, the man of God, said: 'Because the work of the heavens and of the earth was a derivation of being coming from nothing, a descent from the superior to the inferior, whereas the righteous through their works strip themselves of their materiality and always think of the Name, blessed be He! They see, understand and become truly aware of the fact that this [materiality] is in a

---

118. R Meshullam's importance is recognised by the best competent scholars in Hasidism. *Cf* the many citations and positive interpretations of this master in: J Weiss, *Studies in Eastern European Jewish Mysticism, The Littman Library of Jewish Civilization* (Oxford: Oxford University Press, 1985); L Jacobs, *Hasidic Thought* (New York: Behrman House, 1976), 144–154, and *Hasidic Prayer* (London/Washington, The Littman Library of Jewish Civilization, 1972, 1993); RS Uffenheimer, *Hasidism as Mysticism* (Princeton/Jerusalem, Princeton University Press, The Magnes Press, The Hebrew University, 1993). *Cf* also G Scholem, *Le messianisme juif* (Paris: Calmann-Lévy, 1974), 320–321. R Meshullam, who is mentioned by G. Scholem, teaches that 'the true mystery, the esoteric wisdom, is the communion of love with God, *devekut ha-ahavah ba-shem yitbarak*.' We shall see that R Meshullam taught that the Sabbath is the return of everything to God and leads the human being to union with God *(ahdut)*. The recent publication of all the available texts by R. Meshullam, vocalised and with cross-references, is a cause for joy: *sefer yosher dibrei emet* (Benei Berak: Tiferet ha-Sefer Institute, 2006).

> sense nothing, as [it was in God] before creation. Thus they cause being to go up again to nothing and to go up from the inferior to the superior; this is more marvelous [than to make to go down from the superior to the inferior], as was said in the Gemara [*B.T. Taanit* 25a] in the name of Rabbi Haninah ben Dossa: "The last miracle is greater than the first, for what was given [by the heavens] is given and not taken back."'
>
> And concerning this, Rab, our holy master Menahem Mendel of Peremyshlany, said: 'Thus one must explain the verse (Ps 90:1): *Lord, you have been a shelter for us from generation to generation*. This means that we, our souls, were in the Name, blessed be He! before creation. Only one thing is now necessary (Ps 90:3): *that you make the human person return to his dust*. After that, may each person strip himself of his materiality in order to return to the Name, blessed be He!, in his thinking, as in the beginning.'

R Meshullam extends the teaching of R Dov Baer and completes it by adding the very important reference to the miracles of Rabbi Haninah ben Dossa. This opens up reflection on the miracles that have their origin in God but that are done through the deeds of the righteous. R Meshullam starts with the miracle of creation worked by God and comes to the miracle of de-creation worked by the righteous. The return to the divine nothing of before creation is only possible through God's doing at the root of the deeds of the righteous. Divine nothing at the origin and at the end unites God and the righteous, the righteous such as Rabbi Hanina ben Dossa and others, in particular Jesus Christ, according to Christian faith.

Bar Kappara's saying, upon which R Meshullam calls, can shed light on a fundamental aspect of the life and deeds of Jesus, situated between those of Hillel and of Rabbi Akiba. This aspect is the value of poverty, both real and in spirit, and the importance of humility, which pharisaic Tradition taught in the context of the imitation of God.

Rabbi Shneur Zalman (1745–1813), a disciple of the Great Maggid and founder of the HaBaD movement (*Hokhmah, Binah, Daat*), saw in the work of the creation of the world the first and greatest of all miracles:[119]

---

119. *Shaar ha-Yihud ve-ha-Emunah*, chapter 2.

Rabbi Shneur Zalman, Shaar Ha-Yihud ve-ha-Emunah, Chapter 2 (Text 60)

> From what has just been explained, the answer to the heretics can be deduced of itself, as can be found the source of the error of those who deny divine Providence and the miracles and marvels reported in the Torah. These latter err by establishing an analogy between the work of G.od,[120] the Creator of heaven and earth, and the work of human beings and their plans. When a goldsmith has made a vessel, once it is finished, it escapes its maker. Even when the hands of the latter have left it and he distances himself from his work, the vessel does not preserve its shape and image less than what the artist gave it. These senseless people compare the creation of heaven and earth to this. But their eyes are veiled from seeing the enormous difference between the work of a human being, which consists in making one thing while using another thing that already exists, changing only the form and appearance, for example of a silver ingot into a vessel, and creation *ex nihilo*, which is that of heaven and earth.
>
> It is even a greater miracle than for example that of separating the Red Sea in two, where G.od made the sea to move back by means of a very strong east wind that blew all night, and the waters, separating, stood up like a wall (Ex 14:21–22 and 15:8). If G.od had stopped that wind even for an instant, the waters would inevitably have collapsed and flowed as it is in their nature to do and they would surely not have held themselves like a wall, even though this nature of the water itself is also created *ex nihilo*, for a stone wall stays standing all by itself without the help of wind, whereas the nature of water is different. Thus, if the ongoing activity of G.od was necessary for the miracle of the separation of the waters of the Red Sea, how much more is it necessary in the creation of a being starting with nothing. That created being would return to nothing if the power of G.od withdrew from him even for an instant. The might of the Creator must constantly work in the created in order to give it life and existence.

---

120. Out of respect, I maintain the word G.od as it is written in the (French) translation published in the Hasidic movement's editions.

R Shneur Zalman[121] teaches that the creation of the world from nothing is a greater miracle than that which 'the senseless people', those whose 'eyes are veiled' see in artistic creation, in 'the work of a human being' and his or her plans.

He teaches that the miracle of the creation of the world is greater than what a human being can do. This seems to contradict Bar Kappara's teaching that was mentioned above: 'The work of the righteous is greater than the work (of creation) of the heavens and of the earth.'

I shall speak of this contradiction in an excursus in Appendix V. I shall present a translation of the teaching of Nahmanides (1195–1270) *on the manifest miracles* (*nissim mepursamim*) *and the hidden miracles* (*nissim mistarim*). We shall see how it is possible to make a distinction between the manifest miracles and the hidden miracles. From the Jewish point of view, this distinction is useful for people who accept its pertinence. Listening to this Jewish reality, a Christian can better hear what his or her own faith says about the miracles worked by Jesus Christ.

So as to show how this matter is of interest, let us already give the example of the gift of manna that is recounted in the Book of Exodus (16:6–36). Scripture and Tradition see in the gift of the manna a prodigious act, a miracle worked by God who, through this gift, wants to test Israel's faith and its obedience in practicing the Sabbath, a day blessed and sanctified by the Lord (Gen 2:3; Ex 20:11; *cf* Rashi on these verses). The miracle is worked by God himself and not by Moses, which comes out clearly in Scripture, and which Jesus notes in the Gospel according to John 6:32. *The miracle is manifest* so that Israel might witness to it after having seen it, with or without the support of the vision of the *gomor* (portion) of manna that is placed before the *Testimony, in the Tent of Meeting* (Ex 16:32–34). The *hidden miracle* which flows from the manifest miracle is that of all nourishment, of every bread that is produced through Israel's work, which is brought to God through the established blessing. Jesus Christ introduces himself as manna, as the bread of life. Through the hidden miracle of the Presence of Jesus Christ in the bread and wine of the Eucharist, the Christian in a real sense already lives eternal life (Jn 6:25–40).

---

121. *Cf* Rabbi A Steinsaltz's commentary on this text: *A commentary of the Tanya (en Hebrew)* (Jerusalem: The Gate of Unity and Faith, Keter, 1989), 37–44.

This makes it possible for us to shed light on what, according to Christian faith, can be said about the manifest miracle of the resurrection of Jesus Christ and of the hidden miracle of the resurrection in Jesus Christ of the Christians who believe in him.

For Jews as for Christians, there is also the hidden miracle of the sinner who has repented and been forgiven, and who has become greater than the righteous who has not sinned.[122]

Two hidden miracles support Christian life and illuminate it: the miracle of the resurrection and that of the new creation, lived in faith in Jesus Christ. During the Easter Vigil, the Church exults for joy and sings: 'O night of true happiness when heaven is united with the earth, when man encounters God.'

These teachings, which are heard in Israel's Tradition and assumed by Christian faith in Jesus Christ, give Christians the audacity to proclaim the Unity of the One and triune God.

Here I shall risk presenting a summary of the essence of Nahmanides' teaching. I do so based on the texts translated and presented in Appendix V.

There are 'the great manifest miracles [*ha-nissim ha-gedolim ha-mepursamim*], based on which the human person can recognize the hidden miracles that constitute the foundation of the whole Torah.' (Nahmanides on Ex 13:16).

The great *manifest miracles* are, for example, the ten plagues in Egypt, the separation of the waters of the Red Sea, the manna, the wells, etc. Such miracles worked by Moses are worked by God.

The *hidden miracles* are worked by God but are only visible as miracles to the eyes of faith. The best example of such miracles is the miracle of rain in the land of Israel, which falls in its time to reward obedience to the commandments (Lev 26:4).

Based on this, two questions arise for every reader: Is the creation of the world a miracle? And if it is a miracle, is it a manifest miracle or a hidden miracle?

In response to the *first question*, the believer says that creation is a miracle, for outside of faith, there is no answer to the age-old ques-

---

122. Maimonides, *Hilkhot Teshuvah, Normes de la Repentance*, 7, 4: 'The Sages said (B.T. Berakhot 34b): The accomplished righteous would not know how to be in the place where the repentant sinners are. In other words, the penitents' degree is superior to that of the righteous who have never sinned, for the former master their tendencies more than the latter.' *Cf* Lk 15:7.10.24.32.

tion expressed by Leibnitz and Heidegger in their time: Why is there something rather than nothing?

The believer has a double answer to the *second question*:

- *Creation is a hidden miracle*, for God is a hidden God (Isa 45:15) and no theodicy can satisfy those who see the existence of unhappiness and of evil, as well as that of the suffering of those who are innocent.
- *Creation is a manifest miracle* for some believers according to Saint Paul (Rom 1:20–21), and nothing and no one can explain the beauty of the sky filled with stars except the heavens and the firmament and the psalmist (Ps 19:2ff.), except Saint Francis of Assisi, except Rav Nahman of Bratslav . . .

Now we can return to the work of the righteous, of which Bar Kappara said that it is greater than the work of Creation.

Let us first acknowledge that the teaching of Bar Kappara remains a personal teaching that is neither confirmed nor taken up by an anonymous teaching, which might represent an authorized majority. I would not dare to make it a starting point for this study of the Unity of the Trinity if it did not resonate with the miracles worked by charismatic Jews such as Honi the 'Circle Drawer', Rabbi Hanina ben Dossa and Jesus of Nazareth.

Let us return to what E Urbach writes concerning the genre of miracles. As we have seen, for him the essential is to attribute the miracle to the all-powerful God. Elsewhere he clarifies: 'An outstanding feature of the miracle stories in Rabbinic literature is the fact that the personality of the miracle-worker is not emphasized' (116–117). He continues: 'This point established a difference of principle between these stories and the tales about the miracles of Jesus, whose entire purpose is to accentuate his might and power.' What he says seems to me to be doubly inexact:

- First of all, it is obvious that the miracles worked by Honi the Circle Drawer (first century BCE) give rise to a detailed exposition of his relationship with God. He is presented as the one to whom God cannot refuse anything. This is recognized by Shimeon ben Shetah, the master Pharisee, brother of Queen Salome Alexandra (76–67 BCE) and brother-in-law of the Hasmonean king Alexander Jannaeus, and causes him to say: 'If you weren't Honi, I would decree anathema against you . . . But what can be done to you since you are cherished by God who does your will, like a child cherished by his father who does his will?' (*B.T. Taanit* 23a) It is certainly God who does the miracle, but God does it in order to please Honi, his cherished child. This resonates with the miracle of the raising of Lazarus, which God does through Jesus who asks it of God, knowing that the Father always hears him (Jn 11:41–42).

- Second, the miracle worked by Jesus does not have as its only goal to underline his power. Its goal is to manifest the power of God and the necessity to believe in God and in his power that passes through Jesus. This is underlined in the miracle accounts, very especially in the healing of the woman suffering from hemorrhages, as recounted in the Gospel according to Mark 5:25–34. Jesus is aware of a strength having gone forth from him. Thus the miracle comes from God. Jesus does not know who has touched him and benefited from the miracle. Faith in Jesus is addressed to God while Jesus remains limited in his humanity, which does not know everything.

According to Christian faith, Jesus' great miracle is that he brings all of creation and sinful humankind back to their divine origin, to Unity with the Father.

Here again, Israel's Tradition is unanimous in teaching that the repentant sinner has a higher status than the righteous who has never sinned.

In its liturgy, the Church confirms this grandiose vision of the 'happy fault (*felix culpa!*)' and of the new creation that is greater than the first. In the prayer following the first reading in the liturgy of the Catholic Easter Vigil, Christian liturgy goes so far as to say: 'Give those whom you have redeemed the grace to understand that the sacrifice of Christ our Passover is an even more marvelous work than the act of creation at the beginning of the world', or: 'Lord our God, you who have done marvels in creating man and even greater marvels in redeeming him, give us the wisdom of the Spirit that we might resist the attractions of sin and reach the eternal joys.'

The miracle of creation, a hidden miracle, is certainly the most fundamental, the greatest of all the miracles. However, Tradition goes so far as to say that the work of the righteous is greater than the work of creation.

The miracle that makes the sinner who has repented and been forgiven more righteous than those who have never sinned, is a very great miracle.[123] This second miracle can be called greater than the first. For the latter miracle fulfils God's project with Israel, which is called 'the beginning of God's harvest'.

To return to the teaching we heard above, according to which the second miracle is greater than the first, it must be emphasized first that the second miracle worked by Rabbi Haninah ben Dossa is a miracle worked by God through the action of R Haninah.

If the second miracle is greater than the first, it is because God accepts that the righteous causes God to take back what God had given. When applied to creation, this gives us to understand that God certainly does not annul creation, but God accepts that the righteous returns creation to God through an act of de-creation. The act of de-creation is miraculous, for it is God who makes it possible; but the divine miracle passes through the deed of the righteous, which is made effective through 'the divine might that goes forth from him' (Mk 5:30). The Gospel according to Mark, recounting the miraculous healing of the woman suffering from hemorrhages, notes that Jesus, aware of the strength that went forth from him, did not know who had touched him. This note is precious; it underlines that the healing comes from God without Jesus having asked for it (Mk 5:25–33).[124] These healings by Jewish charismatic masters and by Jesus are miraculous, for they come from God, whether the masters are aware of this and request them (Jesus in Jn 11:41–42; Honi the Circle Drawer, Rabbi Hanina ben Dossa . . .), or whether they are aware of it without having requested them.[125]

Thus the return to the nothing of before creation is the effect of a miracle worked by the righteous and made effective by a strength

123. *Cf* what L Askenazi writes on *La Repentance* [Repentance] and its power to reverse time: *'La Teshouvah'*, in *'Ki Mitsion' II* (Jerusalem: Manitou Foundation, 1999), 59–68.

124. Jesus' not knowing also underlines the extent to which Jesus is limited in his humanity, in the lowering of his Incarnation.

125. *Cf* E Urbach, *The Sages*, 97–123. *Cf* especially the comparison of the miracles worked by the Sages and by Jesus. For the miracles of Rabbi Hanina ben Dossa, of Honi the Circle Drawer, *cf* Mishnah Berakhot 5, 5; Ta'anit 3, 8; B.T. Taanit 23a; J Fraenkel, *Le monde spirituel des contes aggadiques* (Paris: Cerf, 1996), chapters 1 & 2 . . . *Cf* also G Vermes, *Jésus le juif* (Paris: Desclée), 77–108.

that comes from God and causes one to reach the Unity of God.[126] Entrance into the nothing of God, made possible by the nothing of the human person who makes him—or herself nothing in God, destroys the barriers that separate the human person from him—or herself, from the neighbor and from God. This is clearly taught by Rav Abraham Kalisker, of whom we spoke above.

R Yehudah Arieh, Leib Alter, called *Sefat Emet* after the title of his great collection of homilies, is the great master of the Hasidic group of Ger (Gur in Yiddish, a place near Warsaw). The Hasidim of Gur who survived the Shoah and reorganized themselves in Jerusalem, successfully spread in Israel the teaching of their master, who has become famous for his profound and clear simplicity.[127]

Sefat Emet, *Pr 12, 19 – Rabbi Yehudah Arieh Leib Alter of Ger (1847–1905)*, Yom Kippur (1891, *5, 171–172*) (Text 61)

> It is said in Mishnah Yoma [Yoma 8, 9]: 'For the faults committed by man towards the Place [God], the Day of Kippur atones; for the faults by man towards his neighbour, the Day of Kippur does not atone so long as he does not obtain reconciliation from his neighbor.'
>
> For on the Day of Kippur, the children of Israel become a Unity, as is interpreted from Psalm 139:16: 'Days were formed, and one of them is One [*ehad*] for Him.' This day is the Day of Kippur (*Seder Eliyahu Rabbah*, chap I, 4). Just as this Day unites all the days, it is on this Day that all souls are united. For in truth, the souls are close to one another; it is only through sins that distancing and separation comes about, as it is written (Isa 59:2): *It is your faults that made the separation between you and your God.* There are faults that bring about separation between man and the Place [God], and there

126. This might that comes from God and that makes effective the miracle worked by a human being in the name of God, is for a Christian the might of the Holy Spirit, who makes Jesus Christ present as the 'abridged Word' who sums up everything and leads all of creation to Unity in each believer and in the community.

127. Arthur Green, the present-day great spiritual master of the Jews in the United States, endeavours to make the Sefat Emet known: A Green, *The language of Truth, The Torah Commentary of the Sefat Emet* (Philadelphia: The Jewish Publication Society, 1998). *Cf* also C Chalier, *Le Rabbi de Gur, La langue de la vérité,* followed by *Penser avec les versets* (Paris: Albin Michel, 2004).

> are those that bring about separation between man and his neighbour. Now it is possible to interpret 'separation between you'; and so also 'between your God', as previously. These two kinds of separation must be repaired. And what is written [in the *mishnah*], 'the faults *committed* by man towards his neighbour', are not exactly stealing or similar faults. Rather, they are the faults that bring about the separation of man from his neighbour, like (Lev 19:17): *You shall not hate your brother* and similar faults. And 'as long as he does not obtain reconciliation from his neighbour', this means that he finds again good will and love for his neighbour, as our Sages wrote (Lev 19:18): *And you shall love your neighbour as yourself*; this is a great general rule in the Torah (Sifra on *Lev* 19:18). And on the Day of Kippur, when the faults are atoned, the children of Israel become *One*. That is why they were given the *Last Tables* on the Day of Kippur. For before that, because of sin, it is written (Ex 32:25): *they* [the people] *were undone*, the Unity was separated. But after that, when Moses came down from the mountain, it is written (Ex 35:1): *And Moses gathered the whole community of the children of Israel together*; they returned to the Unity and the Torah depends on this Unity, as it is written (Deut 33:4): [The Torah] *inheritance of the assembly of Jacob*.
>
> And this is what is written: 'This is a great general rule in the Torah.'

The master's teaching is based explicitly on the *Mishnah* and on Scripture.

As regards Psalm 139:16, the interpretation mentioned by the *Sefat Emet* is the one that appears in the *Midrash Seder Eliyahu Rabbah*, a popular collection that picks up and develops very beautiful ancient traditions on the value of the Torah and of the study of Torah. Rashi certainly knew the double interpretation of Psalm 139:16, which was given here and according to which 'the Day One (*ehad*) for Him' is the Day of Kippur, and the other interpretation that we shall return to further on, according to which 'the Day One for Him' is the Day of Shabbat. *Sefat Emet* presupposes that everyone knows both the *Seder Eliyahu Rabbah* and Rashi, and that no one needs to be given the precise references.

The question is to know what the word One (*ehad*) means in Psalm 139:16. The answer comes from the way *Sefat Emet* applies it to the children of Israel, who through the reconciliation and atonement of Kippur become One. The Day One is the Day of Unity of the people that has been reconciled and forgiven. Thus this people can witness in truth to the One God.

The return to God of which we have just spoken has as its goal the Unity of the people that witnesses to the One God. Can this return lead to union with God?

Here, *Sefat Emet* does not say this explicitly. As we shall see, he will say in the context of Shabbat that the practice of Shabbat can go as far as union. For the Shabbat is the impassable, definitive divine reality that Israel is called to assume by means of its study, its prayer and its practice (remembering and observing). This reality is that of the One God.

To conclude this stage, we hear that the righteous by their work of de-creating the world cause human beings and the world to return to the divine nothing, which causes all the walls of hatred and division to disappear. Union with God is attained by the negative way. For Christians, Jesus is the Righteous *par excellence* who confirms the work of all the righteous. He is the *abridged Word* who recapitulates the whole of creation. He is the Alpha and the Omega, the reality of Shabbat, as Father H de Lubac dared to say.[128] Now we must receive the message from the Sabbath.

The Sabbath as Instrument of Creation's Return to God

The Sabbath is the culmination of creation, the instrument of revelation, the fulfilment of redemption. The community's established obligatory prayer unfolds in these three stages: *Creation*, in the central blessing of the evening liturgy (*maariv* or *arvit*), *Revelation* in the central blessing of the morning liturgy (*shaharit*), *Redemption* in the central blessing of the afternoon liturgy (*minhah*).

The Testament of the Ribash (***R**abbi **I**srael **B**aal **Sh**em Tov*) is a collection of sayings spoken by the founder of modern Hasidism and collected in the school of the great Maggid of Mezeritch. The written,

128. H de Lubac, *L'exégèse médiévale,* II, 2 (Paris: Aubier-Montaigne, 1964), 22.

summarised, elliptic notation incites one to find the original of the teaching that is given orally.

B.T. Shabbat 118b – *Tsavva'at ha-Ribash* 183 (Text 62)

> To observe the Shabbat according to its norm, in all its details and minutiae . . . The sign [*siman*] to remember is Ps 90:3: *You cause man* [*enosh*] *to return to dust*. 'You cause to return [*Ta SheB*]' those are the letters of ShaBaT; 'man [*enosh*]' that is to say, even the one who practiced idolatry as in the time of *Enosh* [*cf B.T. Shabbat* 118b] is forgiven, as it is said (Isa 56:2): *Happy the man* [*enosh*] *who does thus.*

The Besht (***Baal Shem Tov***) teaches that the return to dust, to nothing, is the path to forgiveness and joy.

Along the lines of the Besht and of the Maggid of Mezritch, Rabbi Meshullam Feibush of Zbarah (died 1795) develops the interpretation of the Sabbath as restitution, as return to God.

Rabbi Meshullam Feibush of Zbarah, Yosher Dibrei Emet § 12 and 46 (Text 63)

> The Sabbath is called by a name that means restitution [*hashabah*] because there is no subsistence for any created thing in the world that is foreign to the will of the Name, blessed be He! For nothing has [its own] existence, since all things were created after the absence [the emptiness left in God, if one can say thus, by the *tsimtsum*, the restriction], all things were preceded by the absence. And for everything preceded by the absence it is impossible to subsist other than by the will of the Name, blessed be He!, who himself subsists forever, who is before everything, who is eternal without a past or future gap. As to the creatures, they were in His will; they come from the fact that he wanted them to be. Without his will, they are nothing and have no existence, as they had none before He came to will [them to be], and His will regarding the creatures is the enjoyment [He awaits] from them when they attach themselves to their root through their desire. And it is through this that they subsist before they attach themselves to Him, while he is eternal and subsisting. Thus it is still necessary that the creatures fulfil his will, that they do what He wants of them in such a way that his will is realised. And that the creature might be, for the creatures have no existence except by the subsistence of His will in

> them. But what that will wants, which is that the creatures attach themselves to their root, is impossible. For through creation itself, the creatures are at a distance from their root, as was mentioned above; they have distanced themselves because that is the constituted bodily state of men. Because of this, men have detached themselves from the root that is the spiritual state and the Unity of the One. This occurred after the creation willed by the Name, blessed be He!, so that they might subsist. But they could not [respond to that will] because of their distancing from Him. That is why He illumined their being [in the world] with a clarity that comes from what he is in himself, blessed be He! through an emanation that is of weak intensity. Then men are filled with a desire and a will that are directed to Him. This is like a small child who acts according to his age and forgets his father, but afterwards, when he sees his father, because of the great desire he has to be with his father, he rejects everything and attaches himself to him; he runs to him because he is a part of the parts [of his father]. Thus it is so to speak with the Name, blessed be He! He projects the splendor of his magnificence upon the creatures; then their faces are turned towards Him in a great desire, and that is His will, that is what He hopes from them. That is the cause of their subsistence for two reasons, as was mentioned above. This is the reality of the Sabbath, which is restitution to the root. The root sheds light on the branches, and the branches desire it; they find their delight in it and they long for it. That is union [*ahdut*] with the Name, blessed be He!

This message, expressed in the form of a spiral with repetitions that bring about an advance towards a conclusion, is typical of the Hasidic masters' style. Its heaviness, its 'imperfection' in a Hebrew that reflects the original Yiddish, makes an explanation difficult and useless. It develops at length the Besht's elliptic teaching that we heard in the preceding text. It continues this teaching and ends in union with the Name, a union that is very much that suggested in the last prayer of Shabbat.

R Meshullam dares to say that the Sabbath as lived and practiced by Israel leads to Israel's *union* with God. Such an affirmation is one of the exceptions that confirms the rule, according to which the masters consider attachment (*devekut*) to God to be more communion with God than union (*ahdut*).[129]

The Sabbath prayer suggests that union is possible. This prayer, after teaching *Creation* (in the evening) and *Revelation* (in the morning), proclaims *Redemption* (in the afternoon, in the *minhah* liturgy). The central blessing in the *minhah* liturgy describes the ultimate reality to which Israel comes through its observance. In its beginning, the blessing offers a ternary formulation that is very suggestive for our study of Unity-Trinity.

Central blessing of the Amidah, *community prayer on Shabbat afternoon* [minhah] (Text 64)

> You are **One**, and your Name is **One**, and who is like your people [*am*] Israel, **One** people [*goy*] on the earth (Deut 6:4; Zech 14:9; 2 Sam 7:23). You have given to your people the day of rest and of holiness, a jewel of greatness and a crown of salvation. Abraham jubilates, Isaac sings, Jacob and his sons rest in it in a rest of love and of generosity, in a true and sincere rest, in a rest of peace and of well-being, of security and assurance, in a perfect rest such as you love. Your children understand and acknowledge that their rest comes from you, and by their rest they sanctify your Name.
>
> Our God and God of our Fathers, receive our rest, sanctify us by your commandments and let us participate in your Torah, satisfy us with your kindness, let us rejoice because of your help, and purify our heart so that we might serve you with sincerity. Give us an inheritance, Lord our God, in love and kindness, your holy Sabbath in which Israel rests, the sanctifier of your Name. You are blessed, Lord, who sanctifies the Sabbath.

The prayer uses Scripture without quoting it. As we have already underlined, Tradition confirms through this the message of Scripture: Deuteronomy 6:4; Zechariah 14:9; and 2 Samuel 7:23, which says that God is One, that God's Name is One, and that Israel is One.

---

129. G Scholem, *The Messianic Idea in Judaism* (New York: Schocken Books [1st Edition 1971, 2nd Edition 1978]), 213–214, '*Devekut* or Communion with God'. It would be necessary to say more precisely how 'communion' *(devekut, attachment, adhesion)* differs from 'union' *(ahdut).*

Tradition puts the message of Zechariah, which in the original is in the future (imperfect tense), into the present. What was in the future and interpreted as such in the texts we studied above in *Sifre Deuteronomy* on Deuteronomy 6:4 (text 5) and in the *first central blessing (Malkhiyyot) in the additional liturgy* for Rosh ha-Shanah (text 53), is put into the present by this prayer. For Tradition wants to teach that with and in the Sabbath of every week, one lives and celebrates in anticipation the Sabbath rest of eternal life.

This text brings to closure the first part of our study. Its ternary beginning lets us hear a resonance with the Trinity of Christian faith.

Unity – The 'Jewish Trinity'

This resonance also comes out in what the great scholar Jacob Zallel Lauterbach (1873–1942) wrote in his day on the *Jewish Trinity*, which will serve us as a conclusion to this first part.

JZ Lauterbach, The Pharisees and their Teachings, Rabbinic Essays, Hebrew Union (Cincinnati: College Press, 1951), 111–112 (Text 65)

> We shall, therefore, consider primarily how the Pharisees understood the three central concepts of Judaism; *viz*, God, Israel, and the Torah, which are fundamental doctrines in Judaism, or, as one might call them the Jewish Trinity. For, the understanding and interpretation of these three concepts decides the character of Judaism and determines all its aspects, its laws and rituals, its beliefs and practices. These three ideas are in Judaism intimately connected with one another, and in Jewish thought they are inseparable. To use the words of an older Jewish mystic, 'While these three are separate and distinct concepts, they are almost like one, in that they are bound together and cannot be separated from one another.' In other words, these three ideas hang together and are inextricably interwoven.

Lauterbach could have based his words on the text of the Shabbat prayer that we just looked at. For this text begins with the triad: the Holy One, blessed be He! (God)—the Name—Israel, a triad that corresponds with the triad: God—Israel—the Torah, which Lauterbach calls 'the Jewish Trinity'.

In fact, we have two equivalent triads that are known and received by Israel:

- God, Name, Israel (in the Shabbat prayer);
- God, Torah, Israel (in the Zohar and Hasidism, *cf* Lauterbach).

It really is necessary to speak of Triads, triads made up of a Dyad (God – Name/God—Torah) and a third term, Israel, that is declared to be One like the first two terms of the Triad. However, one cannot teach that Israel is One in the same way as are without doubt God and the Name, God and the Torah. Thus it is not permitted to speak of a perfectly unified triad, as a 'Jewish Trinity' should be, according to Lauterbach.

Whatever the case may be, since the creation of the world **God, the Torah, Israel** constitute a **fundamental triad**. Israel, responsible for revelation, *the beginning of the harvest*, makes this triad known to the nations. **God** and the **Torah** are **One** (single) reality and **Israel** is the witness to it.

At the end of this first part, it seems to me that it is useful to sum up the triads or 'Jewish trinities' that we have already encountered. I shall arrange them with a look to the Christian Triad or Trinity. I shall speak of this Triad-Trinity in the third part. In order to arrive there, I would invite the reader to first listen in the second part to the message of Israel's Tradition on the numbers one, two, three and on their place in the Unity. The texts in the second part will show up two dyads: God and God's *Shekhinah* (the divine presence in the world), the *Shekhinah* and the Holy Spirit, as well as several triads that approach the Christian Trinity without them being the same. The work will end with a third part on the Christian formulation of the Trinity resonating with the message of Israel's Tradition.

Recapitulation of the triads:

- The triads or Jewish 'Trinities':
  God—Name—Israel
  God—Torah—Israel
  God—Israel—Land (Temple) God—*Shekhinah*—Israel
  God—*Shekhinah*—Holy Spirit.

I have discussed these triads in the course of this chapter.

- The Christian triad or Trinity: the Father (God)—the Son (incarnate Word)—the Holy Spirit.

2
Unity—Trinity

In the first part of this study, we saw how God's ineffable Unity gives a foundation to and legitimizes the diversity of the testimonies, the interpretations, the opinions reported in the rabbinic sources that speak of this Unity. As we saw, the diversity starts with the One, is established with the Two and then goes to the infinite.

In this second part, we shall deal first of all with Scripture as source or support for a possible teaching on the Trinity. Because the question as to the relationship between the trinitarian doctrine and Scripture precedes that of the pertinence of the number Three, of its possible relationship with the number Two and the number One, and of its status at the root of the Christian experience of the Trinity. We shall then speak of the value of the numbers, of the dyads and the triads.

We shall conclude by listening to the possible resonance of these realities in the Christian experience of the Trinity.

The Trinity in Scripture

In the New Testament, which the Church offers as Scripture, expressions and testimonies can be found that let us understand explicitly (Mt 28:19) or through hints (Lk 3:21–22; 9:34–36) what will later become the dogma of the Trinity or will permit its affirmation. According to this dogma, the God of the Christians is One, Father, Son and Holy Spirit. As we did in the first part of this study, we shall begin with a text of the New Testament, with the testimony on the baptism of Jesus as transmitted by the Gospel according to Luke (3:21–22). But before doing that, we must see whether the First Testament, which is Scripture for the Jews and for the Christians, teaches the Trinity or can serve as a support to the Christian teaching of the Trinity.

We shall present this question in the simplest and briefest way possible by returning to the large themes of exegesis (*midrash*) in Israel's Tradition, to which I shall refer.[1]

We shall get support from Rashi (1040–1105), who has very great authority with Jews and who is a very sure reference for Christians.

Jewish exegesis occurs at two levels:

- *The first level* is that of *explanation*, of *perush*, which aims at offering the unveiled meaning, the exposed meaning, the *pashut* (or *peshat*), which can be understood as the simple or literal meaning of Scripture.[2]
- *The second level* is that of *interpretation*, of *midrash*, of seeking with the aim of suggesting Scripture's present-day meaning for the community and the individual in the community. This meaning is called *midrash* (or *derash*).[3]

The two levels are connected, as required by the statement: 'Scripture does not depart from its simple meaning', according to which

---

1. *P Lenhardt*, 'L'exégèse (Midrash) de la Tradition d'Israël, sa grandeur et ses limites', *A l'écoute d'Israël, en Eglise*, volume 1, 119–155.
2. The literal meaning is never the result of a fundamentalist reading. Tradition does not allow for the literal meaning *(pashut)* to be that heard in the scriptural text when first reading or hearing it *(mishma or shamoua)*. The literal meaning is determined in a critical manner, and it is never obtained unanimously or without possible modification. *Cf* what Rashbam (**R**abbi **Sh**emuel **b**en **M**eir, grandson of Rashi) says on his grandfather's renewable determination of the literal meaning *(perush ha-torah asher katav rash//bam*, Breslau, David Rosen edition, 1882, 49).
3. There is nothing surprising in the fact that both the activity and the result of the activity bear the same name. Thus the word *Shekhinah* is first of all the active noun of the verb *shakhan*, to dwell; it then means the result of that dwelling, the presence of God where God dwells. Finally, the word *midrash* (plural *midrashim*, whereas *midrashot* was the plural preferred during the ancient period) means the collections that gather together the results of exegesis, the determinations of the literal meanings and above all the exposition of the present-day meanings in detail, verse by verse. There are two large groups of *midrashim*: the *halakhic midrashim (midrashei halakhah)*, which base on Scripture the teachings of Tradition about practice; and the *haggadic or aggadic midrashim (midrashei haggada or aggadah)*, which gather together the very rich synagogal homilies.

the *midrash* (present-day meaning) cannot contradict or ignore the *pashut* (simple or literal meaning).[4]

It seems obvious that neither for Jews nor for Christians Scripture in its literal meaning can teach that God is One and Triune.[5] For the Trinity is a teaching of the Tradition of the Church and not of Scripture. It is true that Tradition can find support in the literalness of certain verses and see the Trinity suggested there. In such cases, Scripture cannot be called upon as proof (*reayah*), but as a support (*hasmakhah, asmakhta*).[6] W Kasper mentions certain patristic interpretations that teach the Trinity based on Scripture. He declares them to be inadmissible today, for example the interpretation of Genesis 1:26, *Let us make humankind in our image*, in reference to Genesis 3:22; 11:7; Isaiah 6:8.[7] Other references, on the contrary, are accept-

4. *Cf B.T. Shabbat* 63a. The connection between *pashut* and *midrash* is postulated by the fact and the conviction that the Words of the Torah are One (single reality). This is taught by the midrash *Sifre Deuteronomy* on Deut 32:2, 339 (text 16). The connection is not always obvious. However, let us mention the *Mekhilta de-Rabbi Ishmael* on Ex 20:18, 235 (text 17), which shows how the present-day meaning *(midrash)* of Ps 29:4 confirms the simple meaning *(pashut)* while deepening it.
5. Counter to this obviousness, the surprising position of Luther is to be noted; for him, Scripture in its literal sense teaches the Trinity. Luther ignores the Jewish distinction between *pashut* and *midrash*, and with his known vehemence he reproaches the Jews for not seeing the Trinity as taught by Scripture. Because of his difficulty in recognizing that it is the Tradition of the Church and not Scripture that teaches the Trinity, Luther wants Scripture in its literal meaning *(sola scriptura)* to teach the Trinity. *Cf* P von der Osten-Sacken, *Katechismus und Siddur* (Berlin: Institut Kirche und Judentum, 1994), 127–128, and *Martin Luther und die Juden* (Stuttgart: Kohlhammer, 2002), 38–40; 118–121. The formula sola scriptura, of which moreover Luther is not the author, cannot be interpreted narrowly.
6. I am using terms from Israel's Tradition in the debate on the teaching status drawn from Scripture. Cf. the positions of Nahmanides (1194–1270) and Maimonides (1135–1204) in Nahmanides, *Book of the commandments of Maimonides (in Hebrew): sefer ha-mitsvot le-ha-ram//bam im hassagot ha-ramba//n*, (Jerusalem: Shavel edition, Mossad Harav Kook, 1981), 29–34. W Kasper explains clearly how the trinitarian interpretations of Scripture by the Fathers of the Church are to be understood *(Le Dieu des chrétiens* [Paris, Cerf, 1996], 350–351). With him and with Maimonides, one must hold on to the fact that Scripture *can* certainly support what faith teaches. For Scripture does not prove, but supports and upholds what is held by faith. And in the cases when Scripture in its literalness seems to teach what one must believe or do, one cannot be dispensed from consulting Tradition in order to confirm this teaching.
7. *Cf* W Kasper, 350–351.

able, such as Genesis 18:2 and Isaiah 6:3, if they are taken as supports for contemplating the mystery, as is the case in the Rublev icon.[8]

Israel's Tradition knows of certain references, which it attributes to Gnostic heretics and/or to Christians who are in opposition to the pharisaic-rabbinic teaching on the One and Only God. A long list of such references is given in the Talmud (*B.T. Sanhedrin* 38b).[9] We do not need to move further forward in history to see how the ancient Kabbalah, beginning in the thirteenth century and especially in the *Zohar*, finds references in Scripture which, under the influence of Christian authors, lead to ternary teachings.[10] Let us take as an example the first verse in this list, Genesis 1:26: *Let us make humankind in our image*. The Sages interpret the plural (*Let us make*) in various ways:

- either as the sign of a consultation by which God would have asked the angels for their opinion before creating man and woman,
- or as the sign of an association of God with man and woman so that their union might produce men and women in the image of God. According to this latter interpretation, man and woman with God would constitute a triad at the root of the propagation of humankind.[11]

---

8. We shall speak of the Rublev icon again at the end of this study.
9. *Cf B.T. Sanhedrin 38b:* a long list of verses in which God is mentioned in the plural. *Cf* E Urbach, *The Sages,* 206–2 and L Jacobs, *A Jewish Theology* (New York: Behrman House, 1973), 25–28. L Jacobs points out that an anti-Christian polemic seems to have been carried out in Caesarea in the 3rd century against the doctrine of the Incarnation and the dualism that was attributed to it. However, could the doctrine of the Incarnation already be spotted among the Christians and known by Jews before the Council of Nicea? Would this not rather be an anti-Gnostic polemic? As for the doctrine of the Trinity, it could not be attacked because it was not taught during the first three centuries CE. It seems useful to point out the rabbinic interpretation of the three men who stood before Abraham by the oaks of Mamre (Gen 18:1–2), offered in the second century. The teaching based on this text does not bear on the three men, but on Abraham's hospitality and humility, on the necessity to imitate Moses and Abraham, and so doing, to imitate God who receives and nourishes all his creatures *(cf Mekhilta de-Rabbi Ishmael* on Ex 18:12, 195–196).
10. *Cf* Y Liebes, 'Christian Influences on the Zohar', in *Immanuel*, 17 (Winter 1983/84): 43–67.
11. *Cf Genesis Rabbah* on Gen 1:26, Par 8 and 9, 62–64, and *Pirkei de-Rabbi Eliezer*, chapter 12.

In addition, it is interesting to look at the polemic by Rabbi Abbahu (Caesarea around 300 CE) against the Christian affirmations concerning Jesus as the Son of God and Son of man.

On Exodus 20:2: *I am the Lord, your God.* Rabbi Abbahu says: A parable, [the matter resembles] a king who has a son and a brother. The Holy One, blessed be He!, says: I am not thus (Isa 44:6), *I am first*, for I have no father, *I am last*, for I have no brother. *Aside from me there is no God*, for I have no son.[12]

On Numbers 23:19: *God is not man that he would lie, nor the son of Adam that he would retract.* Rabbi Abbahu says: 'If a man tells you he is God, he is lying, but if he declares about himself "the Son of man" he will end up regretting it; "I go up to the heavens", he will not fulfill what he said.'[13]

These polemical interpretations of Genesis 1:26, Exodus 20:2, and Numbers 23:19 together are aimed at the Christian doctrine of the Incarnation. They are not aimed at the Trinity, for the Christians are not yet offering it as such. The refutation bears on God's Unity and the fact of God's being the Only, as the masters of Israel teach. From the Christian point of view, the affirmation of God's Incarnation in Jesus Christ is the indispensable passage towards the affirmation of the Trinity.

In the first part, we saw texts from Israel's ancient Tradition that speak explicitly of the relationship between the One and the Two as the passage from the ineffable Unity to the fundamental duality, a duality which is the irreducible beginning of plurality.[14]

We have just seen how, based on Scripture, it is possible—or not—to teach a relationship between the One and the Two that sheds light on the relationship of Unity, which Christians proclaim regarding the relationship between God and Jesus Christ, Son of God and Son of Man. For the Jews, such a teaching cannot be received and is impossible. For the Christians, it is possible if Scripture is evoked based on the Christian faith, not as a proof, but as a support (an allusion, a memory).

For the passage from One to Three, from Two to Three, from One and Two to Three, we have only seen one possibility, that of the

12. *Exodus Rabbah,* Par 29, 5.

13. *JT Taanit*, 2, 1.

14. *Cf* the Texts 16, 17, 19.

triad of God with man and woman for procreation in God's image. It remains to be seen whether the Three and the Thirds have in themselves, independently of their relationship with the other numbers in the enumeration, a value that can shed light on the Christian faith in the Trinity.

In ancient literature, we did not find any possibility to give status to the number three that by resonance would enlighten the *three* of the Christian Trinity. A few texts, which pass in review a large number of examples in which the number *three* and *thirds* are mentioned, resemble school exercises.[15] They do not offer any interpretation that could be pertinent to our study. It is remarkable that these texts neither mention the *trisagion* of Isaiah 6 nor the *third days*.

Nevertheless, we would underline the importance of these two realities: *trisagion* and *third days*.

For the trisagion in Isaiah 6:3, we already saw how important it is in Israel's liturgy in the many blessings that complete it with the quotation from Ezekiel 3:12. These blessings and the commentaries on them do not underline the value of the number three. However, the version developed in the Great Kedushah (*kedushah rabbah*) of the additional prayer for Rosh ha-Shanah and Kippur emphasizes the tripling.

Kedushah Rabbah *of the Additional Prayer for* Rosh ha-Shanah *and* Kippur (Text 66)

> They [the angels] intone songs . . . In their exhortations, they call to one another; while exchanging their words, they applaud and cause the Tripling [*shillush*] to ring out of the Sanctifications in the Sanctuary.

The tripling seems only to have value as an emphasis. This is also what is to be drawn from Rashi's commentary on Isaiah 6:3.[16]

15. *B.T. Shabbat 88a; Pesikta de-Rav Kahana, Pisk.* 12 & 13, 213–214; *Midrash Tanhuma* Yitro & 10.

16. Rashi on Isa 6:3 invites one to look at the Targum ad locum, which suggests that God is triply holy: in the heavens, on earth and in eternity. The common interpretation in the different commentaries is that the tripling of the word holy is emphatic. This is the interpretation given by the liturgy of *Rosh ha-Shanah* and *Kippur* in the *Kedushah Rabbah* of the additional prayer. In that liturgy, the quotation from Isa 6:4 is preceded by a statement according to which the angels sanctify God by the tripling *(shillush)* of sanctity *(kedushah)*. Here again,

For the third days, the following tradition speaks of them in a way that is particularly interesting in view of the pharisaic-rabbinic teaching on the resurrection of the dead, as also for this same teaching in Christian tradition:

Genesis Rabbah on Genesis 22:4 *Par* 56, 595 (Text 67)[17]

> Genesis 22:4: *On the third day, he raised his eyes and saw the place from afar.*
>
> Hosea 6:2: *At the end of two days, he will have given life back to us; on the third day, he will have raised us up and we shall live in his presence.*
>
> On the third day [of the deliverance of the Fathers] from the tribes, for it is written (Gen 42:18): *Now on the third day, Joseph told them.*
>
> On the third day of the gift of the Torah, as it is said (Ex 19:16): *Now on the third day, when morning came.*
>
> On the third day of the explorers, as it is said (Josh 2:16): *She* [Rahab] *told them: '. . . You will hide there for three days.'*
>
> On the third day of Jonah, for it is written (Jon 2:1): *And Jonah remained in the belly of the fish for three days* [and three nights].
>
> The third day of the pilgrims coming from the Golah [exile], for it is written (Ezra 8:15): *I gathered them and we camped there for three days.*

---

what is taught is the emphasis and not any ternary idea of the divinity. The use of the word *shillush,* which since Maimonides *(Guide to the Perplexed I, 71)* commonly indicates the Trinity of the Christians, does not satisfy, for the word *shillush* signifies the action of tripling, the tripling. According to Even Shoshan's dictionary, another word, the word *shelshah* is used by Christians to signify the Trinity of the Christians. Even Shoshan gives no indication as to the origin of this word. His use of it seems doubtful.

17. J Theodor, in a footnote in his critical edition, 595, cites several anonymous versions that say: 'The Holy One, blessed be He!, does not leave the righteous in distress for more than three days.'

> On the third day of the resurrection of the dead, as it is written (Hos 6:2): *At the end of two days he will have given life back to us; on the third day, he will have raised us up and we shall live in his presence.*
>
> On the third day of Esther, as it is said (Esth 5:1): *At the end of three days, behold what came. Esther put on her royal garments.* She put back on the royal garments of her father's house. Because of which merit [did all these beginnings of deliverance occur on the third day]? The Sages say: 'Because of the third day of the gift of the Torah, as it is said' (Ex 19:16): *Now on the third day.* Rabbi Levi says: 'Because of the third day of Abraham our Father, as it is said: (Gen 22:4): *On the third day*, etc.'

The written notation of the Tradition given in this text is imperfect. Moreover, the *third days* are situated in a different context to ours. Nevertheless, it is interesting and important to note what the text enables us to hear: the *third day* of which our text is speaking is not to be thought chronologically. This day probably marks the *chronological* end of the trial, but the question raised at the end of the text is not one of chronology. It has to do with knowing whence comes the value of the *third day*. Does its value come from the third day of Abraham's trial (Gen 22:4) or from the third day which inaugurates the theophany at Sinai (Ex 19:16)? The answers given are not chronological but rather ontological and theological.[18] It is the (*ontological*) *Three* [and not the (*chronological*) *Third*], it is the *Three* that cannot be numbered, which draws its strength from the God who speaks through Scripture, who gives his saving strength to the third days.

The answers given are obviously pertinent to Jewish faith and to Christian faith based on the resurrection of Christ *on the third day according to the Scriptures* (1 Cor 15:4; *Nicene Creed*). Rabbi Levi's answer emphasises Abraham and corresponds with the importance given by Saint Paul to the faith of Abraham. The answer of the Sages is more in accord with the importance given by Saint James to works and not to faith alone.[19]

---

18. This nature of the number three relativises the interest of Christian research in the calendar of the Passion.
19. Listening to these Jewish opinions supports those in the Church who do not find directly the only truth in a few passages from the writings of Saint Paul.

Having said that the saving strength of the third days can flow from the value of the number *three*, we must also say that the number *three* in the *trisagion* and the number *three* of the third days can be in relation with the *three* of the Christian Trinity.

For this, I suggest two paths of reflection:

- The *first* is suggested to me by Rabbi Simai who said: 'There is no passage in Scripture that does not speak of the resurrection of the dead. But we do not have the strength to show it by means of exegesis.' (*Sifre Deuteronomy* on Deut 32:2, 341). If for a Jewish teacher, the resurrection is everywhere in Scripture, a Christian can say that the Trinity is everywhere in Scripture. We shall also say that the Trinity is always at the root of Scripture, but that we do not have the strength to show it by means of exegesis. Then nothing prohibits finding in the number three of the *trisagion* and of the third days an allusion (*remez*), a remembrance (*zekher*), a trace (*reshumah*) of the Trinity. The Trinity is so fundamental, so strong, that it is present in every reality of this world. God wants us to seek in Scripture through love the allusion, the remembrance, the trace of what God is: One and Triune. The allusion is stronger than the proof when love is the subject.
- The *second path of reflection* would be to ask about the origin of the saying: 'Never two without three.' However, this would imply that three flows from one and two. That would not be significant, for in the continuation of the numbers, why should one stop at *three*? Let us rather see what H de Lubac's summary says about the *value of the 'trinity of the number'*:

H de Lubac, Exégèse médiévale II, *la valeur de la 'trinité du nombre'*, 25 (Text 68)

> The trinity of the number symbolizes the Trinity that cannot be numbered. And this not in a banal and entirely external way because the number three reminds one that there are three persons in God, as certain modern people hear it, judging that the elders' considerations on the Trinity 'would gain by freeing themselves of the symbolism of numbers, where they easily get tangled up'; rather, this is because of an intrinsic symbolism that can be called ontological, because

> this number is truly itself through its structure, a unity in trinity, trinity in unity. In every sense, we will say together with Saint Ambrose about three: '*salutaris hic numerus*'.[20]

The Triads, The Triplicity

Walter Kasper spoke very well *of the triplicity, the triad and the triads*. We can only adhere to what he wrote:

Walter Kasper, *Le Dieu des chrétiens* (Paris: Cerf, 1996), 342–344 (Text 69)

> No less than the question of Unity, that of triplicity is a primeval problem of the human person and of humanity. Ternary schemata (triads) present themselves everywhere where reality is in opposition to the human mind's innate need for unity [342].
>
> However, one cannot deduce the Christian doctrine of the Trinity from such symbols and speculations (343).

We have no text that teaches or suggests the relationship between the number *one* and the number *three*. The texts that speak of *three* and of what is *third* do not speak of this relationship.[21] They give long enumerations, but they do not reveal the key to the excellence of the number *three*. However, let us highlight three indications of the value of the number *three*:

- The first is given by the *pedagogical structure of the Shema Israel prayer and the Shabbat*. This ternary structure can resonate with certain interpretations of the Trinity by great Christian teachers.[22] In this context, we do not need to study such interpretations.
- The second comes from *the use of the necklace* (*harizah*), by which one has recourse to the three parts of Scripture: Torah (Pentateuch—Moses), the Prophets, the Writings (the Psalms) in order

20. To understand better what H de Lubac says about the 'trinity of the number', *cf* L'Exégèse médiévale II, 25–26.
21. *Cf B.T. Shabbat 88a; Pesikta de-Rav Kahana*, Piska 12, 13, 213–214; *Midrash Tanhuma*, Yitro 10.
22. *Saint Augustine, Luther, Barth . . .*

to teach an important point of Israel's faith and hope in liturgical prayer and midrash.[23]

- The third indication, which is small but significant, is given by Rashi in his commentary on Isa 6:3. Rashi sees an emphasis in the *trisagion* and invites the student Targum of the verse, 'God is thrice Holy in himself in heaven, in the world where he makes himself known, in the coming world'.

This third indication based on Isaiah 6:3 can help to open up reflection on the relationship of the *three* to the *one*. It is surprising that Isaiah 6:3 is not included in the rabbinic lists mentioned above, which sing the praises of the *three*. Rather than imagining that the Sages intended this in order to avoid a controversy with the Christians, which would be an anachronism, it is better to note the difficulty that exists in justifying the value of the *three*. As we saw, the two is easy to justify. Other than as emphasis, the *three* is difficult to justify.

Based on rabbinic texts, it is not the value of the number *three* that could lead to the Trinity or that might be at its distant origin. This difficulty does not surprise the Christian, who knows how much time was necessary to come to the *three* and to recognize the Holy Spirit as equally glorified with the Son and the Father. What is clearly explained is the relationship between *one* and *two* as a passage from ineffable Unity to fundamental duality at the irreducible beginning of plurality. Nothing is said about the passage from *one* to *three* or from *two* to *three*. Because of its transcendent origin, the one has without doubt the strength to beget the three, as well as every other number, and to make its development possible. But there should be a text that shows how *three* as such is begotten by *one* or proceeds from it.[24]

---

23. *Cf B.T. Megillah* 31a, where God's humility is taught doubly and triply; *B.T. Sanhedrin* 90b, *where the resurrection is taught by means of a necklace; the Malkhiyot, Zikhronot and Shofarot Blessings* in the additional prayer for *Rosh ha-Shanah;* the necklaces in Lk 24:26–27, 44–45.

24. Let us again mention H de Lubac's rich exposition on the 'Symboles numériques' *Exégèse médiévale* II, 7–40. He does not say anything about Israel's Tradition, but what he teaches on the value of the number One resounds with it and enlightens Christian faith on the Unity and the Trinity of God. See in particular the praise of the number one and the number three cited above. One could try to find in H de Lubac's writings something with which to justify the passage from one to three. But in any case, this would neither be in reference to Israel's Tradition nor would it resonate with it, and that is what interests us in this study.

Let us return to the meaning and value of the number *one*. Let us then look again at the relationship between *one* and *two* as the passage from ineffable Unity to fundamental duality at the irreducible beginning of plurality. Let us finally try to see why, in Israel's ancient Tradition, nothing leads from *one* to *three* or from *two* to *three* or from *one* and *two* to *three*.

The Numbers

One

This number, *ehad* in Hebrew, is first of all the *first* in the listing of numbers, one, two, three, etc. It is then what designates the *only*, *yahid* in Hebrew, as flows from Malachi 2:10: *Have we not one Father* [*ab ehad*, one single father] *who created us*? Finally and above all, it is the number that designates the *principle of Unity*, of perfection, of non-division. As such, the *One* is over and beyond the number. It is what founds plurality and diversity, what gives its place to each number, starting with the number two, and its value in the plurality.

The relationship of One to Two

As we have seen, *two* is the beginning of plurality.[25] *Two*, nourished from within by *one*, exercises the fundamental function of teaching the paradox of the *One*.

The passage to Three?

This passage does not occur based on *two*. It occurs directly starting from *one*, if one wants to agree with H de Lubac that 'Three is the first number, because it is the first that "is tied"; it is the first organized number that includes a beginning, a middle and an end, united in one single whole, in perfect equality'.[26]

25. *Cf* Text 19.
26. H de Lubac, 25, quoted above.

Resonance with Christian Faith in the Trinity.

The Unity of God, of the *Shekhinah*, and of the Holy Spirit

Here, I shall offer texts that show two dyads:

- The first: the Unity of God and of the *Shekhinah*.
- The second: the Unity of the *Shekhinah* and of the Holy Spirit.

As in the first part, we shall begin with the New Testament (analytical process). In the account of the baptism of Jesus, the Gospel according to Luke presents three aspects of the divine reality: God (the Father), the Son, the Holy Spirit (Lk 3:21–22). Luke's testimony states that the Spirit descended upon Jesus in corporeal form as a dove and that a heavenly voice designated Jesus as the Son according to Psalm 2:7. The same realities are presented by Luke summarily in the account of the transfiguration (Lk 9:28–34). This second testimony however transmits two interesting supplementary elements: Jesus is the Chosen and the disciples must listen to him.

We shall first seek (in an analytical process) what sheds light on the link between the Holy Spirit and the Spirit's manifestation as a dove through the heavenly Voice (*Bat Kol*). We will then return (in a synthetic process) to the Jewish sources, so that we might receive from them the best possible light for Christian faith.

The study of the Jewish sources will lead the Christian to see in Jesus the Presence of God, the *Shekhinah par excellence*, which neither abolishes nor diminishes in any way the particular Presence of the One and Only God in the Temple of Jerusalem and in other places, as well as in certain groups or persons. Based on this particular Presence and together with it, the universal presence of Jesus Christ and the action of the Holy Spirit in the world unfold. We shall then see in an open conclusion how the ternary message in the New Testament testimonies to the baptism and transfiguration of Jesus are in reality an icon, a written icon of the Trinity based on what the 'Servants of the Word' saw and heard.[27]

27. I deliberately use the expression 'written icon'. For if in the tradition of the Oriental Church, one does not speak of painting an icon but of writing an icon, it is possible to say that the text of the New Testament writes the icon of the oral testimony of those who saw and heard.

The New Testament testimonies to the baptism of Jesus (Lk 3:21–22) and to his transfiguration (Lk 9:34–36; 2 Pet 1:16–18) are structured in a ternary way, which invites one to seek (analytically) in the Jewish sources what the Father, the Son and the heavenly Voice might be, as well as the relationship they have with one another.

We shall first see what can be said about the *Father* who, at the baptism and the transfiguration of Jesus, speaks through the voice coming from heaven. In doing so, we shall try to clarify the role of the *heavenly Voice* and the authority it has because of what it is. As regards the *Son*, it will not be possible to speak of him correctly before having listened more broadly to the Jewish sources (synthetic process) and having heard through resonance that the Son is the divine Presence in the world, the *Shekhinah par excellence.*

The Father

In our passages, the one who speaks of the Son is the Father, and this voice from heaven very clearly proceeds from the heavenly Father. The fact that God is the Father and that he is known as such by Scripture and by Tradition, even though God remains unknown, is the paradox assumed by the Jewish people and by the Church. As Father, God is known as the inexhaustible source of mercy and of the forgiveness of sins. As Creator, God remains unknown, in the unknown place of God's transcendence, which is paradoxically linked to the known place of the Temple, where God manifests his sanctity and his glory.[28]

In rabbinic literature, God is often mentioned in the third person as 'Father who is in heaven'.[29] God is called upon in the second person as *Our Father who art in heaven* only in the New Testament (Mt 6:9), in the Christian 'Our Father' prayer, and in the established prayer for the Day of Independence of the State of Israel.[30]

28. *Cf* above the paradoxes of Creation and Revelation.
29. *Cf* for example Mishnah Sotah 9, 15.
30. The prayer for the peace of the State established by Israel's Chief Rabbinate. *Cf* P Lenhardt, 'La fin du sionisme?', in *Sens,* 3 (2004): 124–136.

The Bat Kol (heavenly voice)

God speaks from heaven through a *heavenly voice*, as is said based on the New Testament Greek. Israel's Tradition calls this voice *Bat Kol*, which can be translated as *Daughter of the Voice* or *Echo of the Voice.*

The *Bat Kol* appears frequently in the pharisaic-rabbinic sources and in the New Testament. According to Israel's Tradition, it took over from prophecy when the latter ceased with the death of the last prophets Haggai, Zechariah and Malachy.[31] It speaks in rabbinic Hebrew with a simple and clear language so as to be heard and understood by all who hear it.[32] In the Jewish milieu, it has the authority of the Word of God, at least until a turning point in Yavne, of which a trace has remained.[33] In the New Testament, the testimonies collected by the evangelists present the *Bat Kol* as the voice of God.

Two passages shed light on the *Bat Kol*'s intervention in the baptism and transfiguration of Jesus.

The Talmud (*B.T. Baba Metsia* 59a) reports a controversy between Rabbi Eliezer and his colleagues, in which a *Bat Kol* made itself heard in order to support Rabbi Eliezer's position. Contrary to the *Bat Kol*, Rabbi Yehoshua with the support of the other masters teaches that 'the Torah is not in heaven [or: is no longer in heaven, Deut 30:12]' and that from now on, the authority of the *Bat Kol* is no longer accepted, but rather the decision is made by the majority. Thus, in relation to the tradition we saw above, according to which at the beginning of the Yavne period the authority of the *Bat Kol* was accepted, there was a turning point in Yavne.[34] What is pertinent here is that the *Bat Kol* asked that one abide by Rabbi Eliezer's opinion. That is what, in the Gospel account of the transfiguration, the *Bat Kol* asks for Jesus (Mt 17:5; Mk 9:6; Lk 9:35). Rabbi Eliezer is certainly not 'the Son', but he is Rabbi Eliezer the Great, who was considered by his disciples to be a

31. *Tosefta Sotah* 13, 3–4, 231–232; *B.T. Sanhedrin* 11a. On the ceasing of prophecy, *cf* E Urbach, *The Sages*, 564ff.
32. On the Bat Kol in the Jewish sources, *cf* S Lieberman, *Hellenism in Jewish Palestine* (New York: JTS, 1950), Appendix I, Bath Qol, 194–199. In the New Testament, the *Bat Kol* has the same characteristics as in the rabbinic sources. It speaks in order to be heard and understood by auditory witnesses (*cf* Jn 12:28–30; 2 Pet 1:16–18).
33. *Cf B.T. Baba Metsia* 59a.
34. *Cf J.T. Berakhot* 1, 7 3b (text 20).

living Torah.[35] Through the *Bat Kol*, the Holy Spirit is thus the divine force that discerns and designates the "great" teacher as living Torah for his disciples. In the New Testament, the *Bat Kol* makes known and designates 'the Son' who must be heard because he is the living Torah.[36]

In this process, a second passage sheds light on the fact that at the baptism of Jesus, the Holy Spirit is manifested in the form of a dove. The Talmud (*B.T. Berakhot* 3a) tells a legendary story according to which Rabbi Yose heard the Holy One, blessed be He!, lamenting and saying through a *Bat Kol* with the voice of a dove, 'Woe to my children, to their sins, because of which I had to destroy my house, burn my Temple and exile them among the nations of the world!' Here, let us remember the voice of the dove, a feminine voice given to the Holy Spirit, as we shall see again further on.

According to the two passages and their context, God speaks to his children or of his children. After the incident recounted in the first passage, in which the Sages refuse to go along with the position of the *Bat Kol*, Rabbi Nathan meets the prophet Elijah and asks him what the Holy One, blessed be He!, did when he heard the Sages' decision. According to Elijah, God laughed and said: 'My children have conquered me, my children have conquered me.' (*B.T. Baba Metsia* 59a) This legendary complement to the historical debate in Yavne confirms the legitimacy of the decisions taken by the majority of the Sages. 'The children', the majority of the Sages, from now on have the 'Words of eternal life'. This does not deny Rabbi Eliezer's right to maintain his position that was supported by the *Bat Kol*. He is only asked to conform in his practice to the majority decision. Because he refused to submit, he was excommunicated. This sheds light on the delicate question of Jesus' relationship with certain pharisaic teachers of his time.

In the second passage, God laments over his children and over the destruction of the Temple.

---

35. *Cf B.T.* Sanhedrin *68a and 101a*. Rabbi Eliezer is more than a father who gives life in the world. Through his Torah, he gives life in the world to come. Like Jesus, he has the words of eternal life (Jn 6:68).
36. In Mk 7:14, Jesus asks: *All of you listen to me and understand*! He is the teacher who gives with authority the best pharisaic teaching on the honour due to parents.

It is to be noted that Jesus, as son of Israel and as 'Son', laments over the destruction of the Temple (Lk 19:41–44).[37]

This (analytical) process enlightens us as regards the baptism and the transfiguration of Jesus. The *Bat Kol* designates Jesus as the Son, as the Chosen. It does not allow us to understand that Jesus is the divine Presence (*Shekhinah*) in this world. Based on the Jewish sources heard in a broader sense (synthetic process), we shall also hear in resonance that Jesus is the *Shekhinah par excellence.*

We shall now begin the (synthetic) process that goes from the rabbinic sources to the New Testament and to Christian faith. Listening to the texts will let us perceive the reality of a *first dyad*, the Unity of the *Shekhinah* and of God, whom the *Shekhinah* manifests. The process will then let us encounter a *second dyad*, the Unity of the *Shekhinah* and of the Holy Spirit.

The First Dyad: God and God's *Shekhinah*

Israel's Tradition makes known the times and the places of the *Shekhinah*'s manifestation and teaches the Unity of God and of God's *Shekhinah.*

We shall also see that in certain traditions, the manifestation of the *Shekhinah* implies the activity of the Holy Spirit. In reality, *Shekhinah* and Holy Spirit are inseparable, and the activity of the Holy Spirit must be supposed even when it is not explicitly mentioned in the texts. We place the *Shekhinah* in first place because its manifestation in the world precedes (ontologically, not chronologically) that of the Holy Spirit (or of the *Bat Kol*). The order of this presentation corresponds with that of the revelation in the New Testament. The Holy Spirit testifies to the identity of the Son. The Spirit acts, so to speak, after the Son and in view of the Son, in view of God's presence in the world. In suggesting this order, I am not constrained by Christian faith. It corresponds with the intention of the Creator God whose Spirit, manifested since the beginning of creation, indicates God's intention of being present in the world by means of the rest on the seventh day (Gen 1:2; 2:1–3; Heb 4:1–11).

---

37. On this lamentation of Jesus, which is proper to Luke, cf P von der Osten-Sacken, *Ein trauriges Kapitel*, Lk 19:41–48, *Anstösse aus der Schrift* (Neukirchen-Vluyn: Neukirchener Verlag, 1981), 169–175.

As an introduction, I am offering a brief presentation of the *Shekhinah* and the Holy Spirit, of what these two divine realities are, and of the way in which their activity in the world is described.

Shekhinah

The word *Shekhinah* is first of all an active noun. It designates the activity of the verb *shakhan*, which means to dwell. The activity of dwelling brings about a result, the habitation, which is also called *Shekhinah*. Thus the *Shekhinah* is the immanent Presence in the world of the transcendent God.

It is neither mentioned in the Jewish Scriptures nor in the New Testament. However, it appears frequently in Israel's oral pharisaic and rabbinic Tradition. In the ancient layers of the oral Tradition that are contemporary with the compiling of the New Testament, the *Shekhinah*, a feminine word in Hebrew, does not have a feminine connotation. It acts in a dynamic and personal way, distinct from the transcendent God but one with God and in no way other. It is hypostasised only late, probably in the twelfth century CE.[38]

The Holy Spirit

God's Spirit is present everywhere in the Hebrew Bible. In the last chapters of the Book of Isaiah and everywhere in oral pharisaic and rabbinic Tradition, this Spirit is called Holy Spirit (*ruah ha-kodesh*). Based on the Hebrew *ruah*, the Spirit keeps its first meaning of wind and breath. The word *ruah* is feminine, which to my knowledge is not emphasised in the ancient rabbinic interpretations that speak of the Spirit's being and doing.

As we shall see, the texts that describe the intervention of the *Shekhinah* and of the Holy Spirit use differentiated expressions, which sometimes make it possible to determine whether the text is speaking of the *Shekhinah* or of the Holy Spirit. However, since these realities are inseparable and at times interchangeable—which leads to contaminations in vocabulary—discernment is not always easy.

At the end of this process, we will have heard two messages: that of the Unity of **God** and the ***Shekhinah*** (first dyad), and that of the

38. *Cf* E Urbach, *The Sages*, 37–65, in particular 64–65.

Unity of the ***Shekhinah*** and the **Holy Spirit** or the heavenly Voice (second dyad). This double duality, these two dyads, let us hear by means of resonance the triad: **God, *Shekhinah*, Holy Spirit**.[39]

Let us first see how the *Shekhinah* is at work everywhere in the world, and how it attaches itself to certain places, to certain times, in which it manifests itself to Israel with or without the designation Holy Spirit.

No place on earth is void of the Shekhinah[40]

Pesikta de-Rav Kahana Pisk. 1, 4 (Text 70)

> A non-Jew (goy) asked Rabban Gamaliel. He asked him: 'Why did the Holy One, blessed be He!, reveal himself in a bush?' He answered him: 'If he had revealed himself on a carob tree or on a fig tree, what would you say? But it is because no place on earth is empty of the Shekhinah.'

Rabban Gamaliel, the grandson of Saint Paul's teacher, gives a good answer, even if it does not say the essential of the biblical and rabbinic message. The essential of this message is that God lowers, humbles his *Shekhinah* so as to be with Israel in distress.[41]

The response, though incomplete, remains fundamentally good. For it agrees with the message regarding the Creator God given in the first blessing before the *Reading of the Shema*, a prayer that we studied in order to speak of the paradox of creation.[42] If we return to that prayer, we can note that Tradition, which knows and mentions all the verbs used by Scripture to speak of creation, here favors the verb *yatsar* and calls God 'the one who forms' (*yotser*). This evokes the

---

39. *Cf* the recapitulation of the triads at the end of the previous chapter.

40. This conviction of the masters of Hasidism includes the moral and spiritual domains. Based on *Tikkunei Zohar* 57: 'no place is void of Him' *(leit atar panui minneh),* these masters teach that God is present everywhere, even where sin takes all the space in the sinner's soul. *Cf* P Lenhardt, 'La Terre d'Israël; Jérusalem, le Temple', in *Cahiers Ratisbonne 1,* 113, note 24, reprinted *in A l'écoute d'Israël, en Eglise,* volume I, chapter 7, note 25, 248.

41. This humiliation, this lowering of the *Shekhinah* is the great message given by the *Mekhilta de-Rabbi Shimeon ben Yohai*, the *Mekhilta of the Bush*, which was studied above, text 43.

42. *Cf* Text 10.

activity of the potter who forms his object and in the present maintains with it the contact that creates it. We saw that this term of 'the one who forms', borrowed from Isaiah (45:7.9), which is used but not cited and thus confirmed, is followed by the affirmation that God 'in his goodness [or out of his goodness] renews every day, constantly, the act of the beginning [the act of creation].'

This implies that God does not abandon his creation after the 'initial flicker', but on the contrary, maintains it in existence.[43] his conviction is age-old in Judaism as in Christianity.[44] God's constant Presence to his creation, this *Shekhinah* which is not lacking in any place in the world, is without doubt God's most fundamental activity, it is the activity which keeps the world in existence.[45]

Thus, the Presence of God is everywhere in the world. This conviction of faith makes it possible for the believer to experience this presence and to live by it, but it does not authorise him or her to prove it or to impose it on others. God, the creator who is present to the world as 'the one who forms' it, remains over and beyond all knowledge unless this knowledge comes from the Holy Spirit, who can give it through grace.[46] God is always over and beyond.[47] We shall see that to the extent to which the *Shekhinah* manifests itself in the world, it is

---

43. As regards the flicker, *cf* Pascal on Descartes, *Pensées*, Brunschvicg edition, 77.
44. On the ongoing creation, *cf* H de Lubac, *La révélation divine* (Paris: Cerf, 1983), 63–69.
45. In the ancient mystical tradition that is contemporary with the New Testament, God is acclaimed as *He who lives forever* (Rev 4:9–10; *cf* Dan 12:7). However, at that time, the word *olam* already designated the world, as is indicated by the beginning of every blessing in conformity with the model established by the Sages: 'Blessed are You, Lord, King of the world [*melekh ha-olam*].' Thus it could be that the acclamation of the Living in the *Book of Revelation* is addressed to 'Him who is the *Life of the Worlds* [*hey ha-olamim*].' (*cf* Jn 14:6) If, as we shall see, Jesus is the Presence of God in the world, the *Shekhinah par excellence*, he is first of all the *Shekhinah*, the *Life of the Worlds*, through which everything was made. A Christian knows this *Shekhinah* through the Holy Spirit whom he or she received in baptism.
46. *Cf* the fourth blessing of the *Amidah* for ordinary days and of the *Amidah* for Saturday evening: 'You graciously give knowledge [*daat*].' According to Rashi, this knowledge is a free gift of God; it is given by the Holy Spirit (Rashi on Ex 31:3).
47. Saint Augustine, *Confessions* III, 6, 11: *Tu autem eras interior intimo meo et superior summo meo*. 'You are more interior to my soul than what is most hidden within me and more elevated than what is highest in me.'

the known place which points to the unknown place. It is the known God who makes known the unknown God.[48]

If it is useful, one can speak of an interior transcendence of God or also of a transcendence of/in immanence.[49] God always remains unknown, but in faith, by the gift of the Holy Spirit, one can know God and this knowledge is already eternal life.[50] The prophets of Israel had a certain knowledge of the transcendent God.[51]

To conclude these remarks on the presence of God to his creation, it is possible to say that the Unity of God, sighted in its unknown place and revealed in its known place is perceived as the perfect Unity of God's transcendence and of God's immanence, of God's absence and of God's presence.

One can also say that the world is the known place where the *Shekhinah* is to be found, since it is everywhere. However, the *Shekhinah* only reveals itself to the human person in a particular way, in historical events and in particular places in the world.[52]

In these events and in these places, of which we will now have to speak, the *Shekhinah*, often designated and identified by the Holy Spirit, reveals that God is One, absent and present.

---

48. Cf the *Kedushot* in Jewish liturgy studied above, and Jesus according to Jn 1:18.
49. *Cf the Song of Unity (Shir ha-Yihud),* which in the 13th thirteenth century Rhineland expressed Israel's age-old faith in the One God. *Cf The Song of the Third Day,* which celebrates God as the one who 'surrounds everything' *(sovev et ha-khol)* as the superior and exterior transcendence, and who 'fills all' *(male or memale et ha-khol)* as the inferior and interior transcendence. God is over and beyond everything. *Cf* also Rabbi Hayyim of Volozhin, *Nefesh Hayim,* III, 4 and 6, translation into French by B Gross, *L'âme de la vie,* Verdier, 1986, and Rav Shneur Zalman, *Tanya*, chapters 23, 41, 46, 48.
50. *Cf* the blessing after the liturgical reading of the Torah and the words of Jesus according to Jn 6:68; Jn 17:3.
51. A partial but real knowledge of God is given to the prophets. Isaiah sees the holy God and his glory in the Temple (Isa 6). The Living in Ezekiel (Ezek 3), animated by the Spirit, see the glory and teach that its place is unknown (*B.T. Hagigah* 13b).
52. The *Shekhinah* is in the world. One cannot say that it is 'of this world'; one also hesitates to say that 'it is not of this world'. Israel's Tradition teaches that God is the Place of the world and not the world God's place *(Genesis Rabbah* on Gen 28:11*)*. Since the *Shekhinah* is the divine presence in the world, it seems that one *can say that the* Shekhinah is the world's place. A Christian can say that Jesus Christ, as the *Shekhinah par excellence,* is the known place in the world, not of the world (true God of true God), who makes known the unknown place (God, the unknown Father, Jn 1:18).

The Shekhinah *in the Burning Bush*

According to the chronology assumed by Tradition, in the history of Israel the Exodus from Egypt is announced and prepared by the manifestation of God's Presence in the burning bush.

As we saw, the *Mekhilta de-Rabbi Shimeon ben Yohai*, known as the *Mekhilta of the Bush*, begins with the interpretations of Exodus 3[53] (text 43). It explains why and how God humbled (*hishpil*) his *Shekhinah* in the thorny lowliness of the bush. From that, we hear that God in his mercy is with those who suffer, with Israel who was in the misery of slavery, with every person who is in distress, according to Psalm 91:15: *When he calls me, I answer, I am with him in distress, I deliver him and I glorify him.*

These interpretations are a preparation for hearing the traditions on Easter.

The Exodus from Egypt. The night of Egypt. The Lord's passage

The Lord saw and knows the misery and suffering of his people. God sends Moses in view of the Exodus from Egypt (Ex 3:7–10), but this exodus was the work of God alone, as the *Pesah Haggadah* teaches.

We shall listen to this *Haggadah*. It speaks of the Lord's passage during the night of Egypt (Ex 12) and mentions that in this passage, there was a 'revelation of the *Shekhinah*' (*gillui shekhinah*).

We shall encounter this revelation again in the *crossing of the Red Sea* and in *the gift of the Torah at Sinai*. In each of these stages, it is the *Shekhinah* of the same One and Only God which manifests itself in different aspects. For a Christian, this diversity opens up the

---

53. *Cf* Text 43 above. The other *Mekhilta*, the *Mekhilta de-Rabbi Ishmael* of which we studied certain passages above, begins with the interpretations of the book of Exodus (12:1–2): 'This month will be for you the head of the months, it will be for you the first of the months of the year.' The masters *(Tannaim)* who taught in Yavne after the destruction of the Temple, discussed and compiled first of all orally the traditions that have to do with practice. Thus the beginning has to do with the first commandment revealed to Israel, the commandment to establish a calendar. The *Mekhilta de-Rabbi Ishmael* is thus a *midrash halakhah*. It includes many *haggadot* which cannot be separated from the *halakhah*. The *Mekhilta de-Rabbi Shimeon ben Yohai* is also a *midrash halakhah*, but it did not reject the magnificent haggadic beginning with the traditions on the burning bush (Ex 3:1–2ff).

possibility of a manifestation of the *Shekhinah* in Jesus Christ, which takes nothing away from the manifestations preceding it. Once again, diversity and not uniformity manifests Unity. Before looking at the *Pesah Haggadah*, let us recall that the Torah is one and includes two kinds of teachings: those having to do with practice (*halakhah*) and those bearing on faith (*haggadah*).

The *haggadah* is Torah, divine Word, which expresses itself in human language, a Word which makes known *the One who said and the world was* (*cf* Ps 33:9), the (transcendent) creator of the world, *the Holy One, Blessed be He!*[54] This is paradoxical. For how can one know God, who is unknowable? Such knowledge, which is certainly partial, is nevertheless given through the study of *haggadah*, and in view of what interests us here, through the study of the *Pesah Haggadah*.[55]

Jews are obliged to observe the commandment to 'recount the Exodus from Egypt', to recount the *Haggadah* within the liturgy of Pesah (*seder ha-pesah*) during the 'night of watching for the Lord' (Ex 12:42).[56]

The essential in the *Haggadah* is a midrash on Deuteronomy 26:5–8. This midrash is preceded by many preliminary comments and is completed by several additions. From this midrash, we shall study the interpretation of Deuteronomy 26:8: *And the Lord brought us out of Egypt*, which is its conclusion. Among the complementary comments surrounding it, we shall study the teaching attributed to Rabban Gamaliel on the conditions which make the liturgy valid.

Pesah Haggadah – the midrash on Deuteronomy 26:8 (Text 71)

54. *Sifre Deuteronomy* on Deut 11:22. Within the *haggadah*, the *Pesah Haggadah* manifests and realises in the best possible way the role of every Haggadah: to make God known. For a Christian, this resounds with what is said in Jn 1:18: No one has ever seen God; the Only-Begotten Son, who is in the bosom of the Father, has made him known (*exègèsato, narravit, higgid).* Because for a Christian, Jesus Christ is the living (oral) Word who knows and makes known God the Father. It is possible to say that he is the *Haggadah* of the Father.

55. The question arises as to what the liturgy or the practice of *Pesah Eve* was at the time of Jesus, but in this question, it is impossible to go beyond learned ignorance. *Cf* K Hruby, 'La Pâque juive du temps du Christ à la lumière des documents de la littérature rabbinique', in *L'Orient Syrien*, VI, Fasc. 1, 1st tr (1961):

56. The commandment to recount (or to narrate, le-haggid) is taught in the *Pesach Haggadah*. It is taught as the positive commandment No 157 in the *Book of Commandments* by Maimonides, who bases it on Ex 13:8: And on that day you will recount (*ve-higgadeta*) to your son.

> Deuteronomy 26:8: '*And the Lord brought us out of Egypt with a strong hand and an outstretched arm, in a great apparition* (*mora*: terror, read and interpreted as *mar'eh*: apparition).'[57]
>
> *And the Lord brought us out of Egypt*: Not through an angel nor through a seraph nor through an envoy, but the Holy One, blessed be He!, through his glory and through his own self, as it is said (Ex 12:12): '*And I shall go up and down through the land of Egypt during that night and I shall strike every first-born in the land of Egypt, from man to beast, and I shall do justice to all the gods of Egypt, I, the Lord.*'
>
> *And I shall go up and down through the land of Egypt*, I and not an angel, *and I shall strike every first-born*, I and not a seraph, *and I shall do justice to all the gods of Egypt*, I and not an envoy, *I, the Lord*, it is I (*ani hu*) and not another (*ve-lo aher*).

Exodus 12:12, which is in the first person, is called upon and interpreted in order to strengthen the teaching given by Scripture in the third person in Deuteronomy 26:8: *And the Lord brought us out of Egypt*.

It is the Lord himself who acted and not an **envoy**: and not **Moses**, who is the envoy *par excellence*, sent for the gift of the Torah (*cf Sifra* on Lev 26:46); and not **Jesus** (whom the Father sent, *cf* Jn 3:17, *passim.*). It is possible that this is a polemic note and that **another** has Jesus in mind, who is considered to be **Other** (*aher*: heretical).

The verse's interpretation does not mention the *Shekhinah*. Nevertheless, we must understand well: God, the Holy One, blessed be He!: Holy is to say transcendent, blessed is to say source of every blessing; this God makes himself present to the world in order to pass over the houses of the children of Israel so as to spare them, to redeem them, to save them. God acts by God's immanence during the night of Egypt. Thus the *Shekhinah*, the Presence, is active even if it is not mentioned. It is not necessary to see it suggested by the glory that is in *by his glory*. For if Tradition often says that the glory of which

57. The age-old Tradition of Israel and of the Church wanted to interpret the biblical *mora* (fear, terror) as *mar'eh* (vision, apparition). *Cf* F Dreyfus, 'L'araméen voulait tuer mon Père: L'actualisation de Dt 26, 5 dans la tradition juive et la tradition chrétienne', in Maurice Carrez, Joseph Doré, Pierre Grelot (editors), *De la Torah au Messie . . . offerts à Henri Cazelles . . .* (Paris: Desclée, 1981), 147–161.

the written and the oral Torah speak is the *Shekhinah*, it is not legitimate to insert this interpretation onto our passage. The same goes for the expression *by his own self*; one cannot force the words in order to make them say that the Unity between God and God's activity through God's *Shekhinah* is being taught.

This said, the question remains: how can God, the Holy One, the Other, the Transcendent, pass over the houses and bring people out of Egypt (Ex 12:27–28)? The answer is that God is in God's own self paradoxical. God is One, transcendent and immanent, as we have not ceased to see.

Outside of the *haggadah*, the paradox is explained and assumed by a midrash on the verse (Ex 12:13): *and I shall pass over you*, in the first person. Let us look at this midrash, the written version of which is very terse and needs to be developed.[58]

Mekhilta de-Rabbi Shimeon ben Yohai on Exodus 12:13, 16 (Text 72)

> Exodus 12:13: *And I shall pass*. If it were not written, it would be impossible to say [but since it is written, it must be interpreted and one must understand that the Lord acted] as a father who brings to his son [what he needs], words of Rabbi Eliezer.
>
> But the Sages say [*and I shall pass, u-pasahti, u pasa'ti*]: like a king who makes his legs take big steps [*pesi'otaw*].[59]

Rabbi Eliezer taught before and after the destruction of the Temple. He was very conservative and was known as the one who taught nothing that he had not received from his teacher. What he says is contemporary with the New Testament. After demythologizing the biblical text, he re-mythologises it by suggesting the image of the father who is more than a father. He uses anthropomorphism in order to dominate it.[60]

---

58. The written note of the midrash is addressed to readers who know oral tradition and are capable of savouring what the midrash wants them to hear. I have written in brackets [. . .] what needs to be completed so as to understand the text.

59. The Sages find support in the analogy of the roots: *pasah, pasa,* the third letters of the two roots, the *het* and the *'ain* respectively, are two guttural consonants that are close to one another.

60. Tradition is not taken in by anthropomorphism. It uses it instead of discrediting it. It knows that it is better to speak the language of everybody than to abandon the source through language that requires painful decoding, which is reserved to 'specialists'.

Another interpretation is offered by the Sages through Rabbi Eliezer's colleagues. Here again, anthropomorphism makes it possible to teach a paradox that is stronger than that of Rabbi Eliezer. For who has ever seen a king of this world, a dictator of the Right or of the Left, running to serve his subjects?

Thus, the Holy One, blessed be He, is more Father than a father of this world, and more King than a king of this world. This is about the heavenly Father or the heavenly King who could deliver his children by means of angels and envoys, but who acts himself through love by 'lowering (humbling) his *Shekhinah*' or by lowering himself in his Shekhinah. Here is affirmed the Unity between the Father and the King of kings, whom no one knows, and the *Shekhinah* that is known. Thus one sees how the *haggadah*, which bases the value of Pesah on a scriptural verse in the third person (Ex 12:27), is enlightened by the midrash on Exodus 12:13 in the first person. The oral Torah, prayer and midrash, are one and coherent.

Among the complementary comments added to the midrash, it is also necessary to hear Rabban Gamaliel's teaching:[61]

Pesah Haggadah (Text 73)

> Rabban Gamaliel said: Whoever did not say [explain] the following three things on Pesah: *Pesah*, *Matsah* [unleavend bread] and *Maror* [bitter herb] did not fulfil his obligation [to recount the exodus from Egypt].

Pesah (pascal lamb) (Text 74)

> The *Pesah* that our fathers ate when the Temple existed, what was the reason for it? It is because the Holy One, blessed be He! passed (*pasah*) above the houses of our fathers in Egypt, as it is said (Ex 12:27): *And you will say: it is the Pesah sacrifice for the Lord who passed over the houses of the children of Israel in Egypt and who struck the Egyptians and who spared our houses.*

61. Certain commentators think that this is Saint Paul's teacher, the grandson of Hillel, the first to bear the title Rabban (our master), who taught before the destruction of the Temple, who defends the apostles before the Sanhedrin (Acts 5:34–39). Other commentators think more reasonably that this is the grandson of Saint Paul's teacher. This Rabban Gamaliel, called Rabban Gamaliel of Yavne, plays an important role in the reorganization of the Torah and of liturgical prayer, which had become necessary after the destruction of the Temple.

We have seen how the interpretation of the passages in the first person (Ex 12:12), *and I shall go up and down*, and (Ex 12:13), *and I shall pass*, are better for enabling one to understand the value of Pesah than the passage cited here (*Ex* 12:27), *the Lord who passed*, in the third person.

Matsah (*unleavened bread*) (Text 75)

> This *Matsah* that we eat, what is the reason for it? It is because the dough of our fathers did not have time to ferment when the King of kings, the Holy One, blessed be He!, revealed himself to them and redeemed them, as it is said (Ex 12:39): *With the dough they had brought from Egypt, they made unleavened cakes, for it had not fermented; because chased from Egypt, they could not wait and had not made themselves any other provisions.*

Before the passage just cited (Ex 12:39), Scripture says concerning Pesah (Ex 12:11): You will eat it in [great] haste, it is a Pesah for the Lord. The text does not say explicitly that the haste must be Israel's, but it is clear that it is talking about Israel's haste. Nevertheless, one must not remain with the obvious meaning, and the midrash has to seek the reason for this haste.[62]

The first stage in the search is the debate on Israel's haste, which evidently is caused by the haste of the Egyptians who want Israel's destruction. A short dialectic with not necessarily convincing references to Scripture ends with the conclusion that this is above all about Israel's haste and that this haste is explained by the haste of the Egyptians who want to destroy Israel.[63] But the *Mekhilta de-Rabbi Ishmael* dares to go further.

Mekhilta de-Rabbi Ishmael on Exodus 12:11, 22 (Text 76)

> *In great haste*. Abba Hanin in the name of Rabbi Eliezer says: It is the haste of the *Shekhinah*. Even though there is no proof for the matter, there is a memory [*zekher*] of the matter (Song 2:8): *It is the voice of my Beloved. Here he comes, jumping over*

62. The midrash does not prove. It clarifies, even though it is not based on the verse in Ex 12:22. It is necessary to go further in the coherence of Scripture as a whole. All of Scripture teaches God's love for his people.

63. Israel's haste did not come into play enough in Europe and above all in Germany. Too many Jews perished because they did not flee on time. The Haggadah's message is prophetic for all times.

> *the mountains, leaping over the hills*, and again (Song 2:9): *Here he is standing behind our wall.*[64]

Thus, it is definitely God who through his *Shekhinah* makes himself present to Israel's distress and hastens to save Israel. The feminine of the word *Shekhinah* is not emphasized. It is God who acts as the Beloved (masculine).[65]

But let us return to Rabban Gamaliel's teaching:
Maror (*bitter herb*) (Text 77)

> This *Maror* that we eat, what is the reason for it? The Egyptians made life bitter for our fathers in Egypt, as it is said (Ex 1:14): *They made life bitter for them through hard work with clay and bricks, through rural drudgery, through all the labors they imposed upon them with harshness.*

Here again, the midrash illustrates in the best possible way the value of actualizing the bitterness of the enslavement in Egypt, It is necessary again to listen to and to meditate[66] on the *Mekhilta of the Bush*, of which we have already spoken (text 43).

---

64. The midrash says clearly that it does not prove. It finds support from the Song of Songs without a quotation formula and from the coherence of Scripture as a whole, which teaches God's love for his people, and in the Song of Songs very particularly the love of the Beloved (masculine) for his Beloved (feminine). Memory (*zekher*) with the allusion (*remez*) and the trace, the traces (*reshumah, reshumot*), is one of the words by which the midrash launches a search that goes beyond the literal meaning of Scripture. God left a memory in Scripture, an allusion, traces which only those who seek traces (*dorshei reshumot*) can find, because they seek out of love. The experience of love described in the Song of Songs is much stronger than a proof. The *spiritual exegesis* of the Sages *(hakhamim)* dares to go further than the *scientific* exegesis of the scribes *(soferim),* who remain with the literal meaning.
This presupposes that the position of the Sages is known; it is unanimous since Rabbi Akiba and says that the Song of Songs speaks literally of the love between God (the Beloved, masculine) and Israel (the Beloved, feminine).
65. Christ, who for a Christian is the Shekhinah par excellence, is seen in the traditional commentaries on the Song of Songs as the Beloved (masculine) of the Church.
66. Text 43.

In this midrash, let us note above all the repetition of the paradoxical *leitmotiv* and the diversity of interpretations given to the misery of enslavement in Egypt.

With the interpretation given by Rabbi Yehoshua and its extension through that of Rabbi Hiyya and Rabbi Yehudah, let us note the amplification of the message: God's involvement in the suffering of Israel throughout its history, in the suffering of the community and in the suffering of each person, with the culmination given in the reference to Psalm 91:15 in the singular: *Let him call me, I will answer him; I am with him in distress.* Finally, let us highlight the *key* to the whole message given by Rabbi Eleazar ben Arakh: *The Holy One, blessed be He! lowered his* Shekhinah.

The pharisaic-rabbinic Tradition transmitted by these masters who taught before and after the destruction of the Temple (Rabbi Eliezer and Rabbi Yehoshua) or at any rate during the period when the New Testament was compiled, does not use the image of **kenosis**, but that of **being lowered**, of **humiliation**. In any case, the *Shekhinah*, which by its origin is divine, lowers itself as does Christ Jesus, according to the Letter to the Philippians (2:6–8).

The passage through the Red Sea (Ex 14 and 15)

The *Pesah Haggadah* teaches the manifestation of the *Shekhinah* in the passage during the night (Ex 12:13, 27). It is the Lord himself, not an envoy and no other, who by his *Shekhinah* brings about the passage.[67] According to the liturgy, the seventh day of the feast of Pesah corresponds with the crossing of the Red Sea (Ex 14). This day is marked by the Canticle of the Sea (Ex 15:1–18, *Shirat ha-Yam*).

The verse Exodus 14:31 and Exodus 15:1 are organically connected. Moses appears there in force. The people saw the hand of the Lord, and this vision gives substance to Moses.

The Canticle of the Sea confirms this vision when all the people exclaim (Ex 15:2): *This is my God* [*zeh eli*]. According to the age-old Tradition of Israel and of the Church, the *hand* of the Lord could be the *Shekhinah* or the Holy Spirit, and as we shall see, these are inseparable but not identical. Let us listen to the midrash on Exodus 15:1–2 as transmitted by the *Mekhilta de-Rabbi Ishmael* and the *Babylonian Talmud Sotah*.

67. Text 43.

Mekhilta de-Rabbi Ishmael on Exodus 15:1–2, pp. 118–119 (Text 78a)

> Exodus 15:1: *Then Moses and the children of Israel sang this song to the Lord and they said while saying.*
>
> '. . . and they said while saying.' Rabbi Nehemiah says: The Holy Spirit rested upon Israel and they said the song like men reading the Shema. Rabbi Akiba says: The Holy Spirit rested upon Israel and they said the song like men reading the Hallel. Eliezer ben Taddai says: Moses began with the first words and Israel repeated after him, and Israel continued with him. Moses began and said: 'I sing for the Lord' and Israel repeated after him and continued with him: 'I sing for the Lord, for he has covered himself with glory.'

What Rabbi Eliezer ben Taddai says does not tell us how the *Shema* or the *Hallel* were read at the time of this midrash.[68] We shall not deal further with that question, but we note the emphasis in: *and they said while saying.* This redundancy in Scripture suggests a certain repetition in the way the song is to be sung. We see that the people 'continues the song with Moses' without needing to learn it. This knowledge comes to the people from the Holy Spirit who rests upon it. The Spirit rests upon Israel, upon all the people.

This teaching is clearly given by the *midrash*, both in the *Mekhilta de-Rabbi Ishmael* and in *Talmud Sotah*. All together they say: 'This is my God.'

Mekhilta de-Rabbi Ishmael on Exodus 15:1–2, pp. 126–127 (Text 78b)

> Exodus 15:2: *This is my God* [*zeh eli*].
>
> Rabbi Eliezer says: Whence can you say that a servant at the edge of the sea saw what neither Isaiah nor Ezekiel saw? Because it is said (Hos 12:10): *And by the ministry of the prophets I shall speak through images*, and it is written (Ezek 1:1): *And the heavens opened and I saw divine visions.* A parable: This is like a king of flesh and blood who enters into a city. He is surrounded by guards, valiant knights are on his right, and on his left soldiers are before and behind him. All

68. Just before the passage that we shall cite further on, the Talmud, B.T. Sotah speaks more of the way in which the Song of the Sea is to be sung. To enter into this debate would needlessly take us away from our subject.

> ask themselves: 'Who is the king?' For he is of flesh and blood like them. But when the Holy One, blessed be He!, revealed himself at the sea, not one of them needed to ask 'who is the king?' As soon as they saw him, they recognized him; they opened their mouth and they said: 'This is my God and I celebrate him . . .'

B.T. Sotah 30b–31a (Text 79)

> Our master taught: Rabbi Yosse the Galilean interpreted: When Israel came up out of the sea, they decided to sing a song. How did they say the song? The very small child who was on his mother's knees and the infant who was sucking his mother's breast, when they saw the *Shekhinah*, the baby stretched its neck, the infant let go of the nipple with his mouth and they said: 'This is my God and I celebrate him', for it is said (Ps 8:3): *By the mouth of the very small and the infants you have founded strength.* Rabbi Meir said: Whence do we know that even the embryos in their mother's womb say the song? Because it is said (Ps 68:27): *In choir, bless God, the Lord, from the origin of Israel!* But they did not see! Rabbi Tanhum says: The abdomen became for them like a transparent glass window and they saw.

The midrash teaches that the people's vision is made possible by the Holy Spirit who is poured out upon them. For the Spirit spread itself upon all the people, including the most humble, the infants and even the embryos in their mothers' womb. Everyone together, without practicing, sang the canticle. As the Psalm (8:3) cited by Jesus in Matthew 21:16 says, the smallest are part of the people, and their testimony is privileged both in Israel's Tradition and in that of the Church.

The *midrash of the Sages* (*midrash hakhamim*) is true; it goes beyond the exactness of the explanatory commentary of the scribes (*soferim*). All saw the Lord, they saw the *Shekhinah* acting at the sea like 'a warrior' (*ish milhamah, Ex* 15:3) or like a 'courageous combatant' [*Mekhilta de-Rabbi Ishmael* on Exodus 20:2 (Text 80 below)]. The parable transmitted by the *Mekhilta* gives us a message that resonates fully with the experience of Thomas reported in the Gospel according to John (20:24–29). Thomas sees God present in the risen Jesus.

The conclusion of the Covenant at Sinai

God makes his Presence to be seen at Sinai when God gives the Torah (Ex 19–24) at the conclusion of the covenant (Ex 24:10–11).

The exodus from Egypt on the 15th of the month of Nisan, the first month of the year, opens the period of seven weeks, which ends on the fiftieth day (*pentecostes*) with the Feast of Weeks (*Hag ha-Shavuot*). Here, we shall not discuss this feast.[69] Nevertheless, let us note that ever since it was established as the feast of the gift of the Torah, Tradition has called it *Conclusion* (*Atseret*).[70]

It is the conclusion of Pesah in a double sense: at the agricultural level, it concludes with the offering of the sheaf of wheat (*omer*); at the historical level, it concludes the pascal redemption through the gift of the Torah at Sinai. Here, we are interested in noting that the *Shekhinah* revealed itself on Sinai, as the following midrash teaches.

Mekhilta de-Rabbi Ishmael on Exodus 20:2, pp. 219–220 (Text 80)

> Exodus 20:2: *I am the Lord, your God . . .* Why is this said? Because at the sea, He revealed himself as a valiant warrior (*gibbor oseh milhamot*), as it is said (Ex 15:3): *The Lord is a warrior.* At Mount Sinai, He revealed himself as an elder full of mercy, as it is said (Ex 24:10): *And they saw the God of Israel.* (Under his feet there was something like a sapphire pavement that was as pure as heaven itself), so as not to give the nations of the world the possibility of saying that in reality there are two powers, it is said: *I am the Lord your God.* I am in Egypt, I am at the sea, I am at Sinai, I am in the past, I am in this world here, I am in the world to come.[71]

The *Shekhinah* is not mentioned, but it is clear that this is what manifests itself in all the stages of Israel's first redemption. In the diver-

69. *Cf* K Hruby, 'Shavuot ou la Pentecôte', in *L'Orient Syrien,* vol Fasc 3/4 (1963). *Cf* Also J Potin, *La Fête juive de la Pentecôte,* 2 volumes (Paris: Cerf, 1971).
70. It is remarkable that the Feast of Weeks was only recognized officially as the feast of the Gift of the Torah in the fourth century CE. The Church, which celebrates the feast of Pentecost on the day of the Jewish Feast of Weeks following the Feast of Pesah, has taught since its beginnings that through the gift of the Spirit, Pentecost is the conclusion of Easter.
71. The biblical support for the manifestation of God at Sinai as an elder full of mercy is given in the verse Ex 24:10, which is completed above in brackets. *Cf* Rashi on this verse.

sity of manifestations, it is the same God, the One transcendent and immanent God who is meant.[72]

The Shekhinah *in the world below and in the heavens above*

The Shekhinah *in the Tent of Meeting*

A homily found in the Land of Israel from the time between 200 and 400 CE opens the meaning of the verse Numbers 7:1, which is read on the Sabbath during the Feast of Dedication (*Hanukkah*):[73] *And behold on the day that Moses finished setting up* [*khallot*] *the dwelling place* [*mishkhan*].

The proem is based on the Song of Songs (5:1): *I came into my garden, my sister, my betrothed* [*khallah*]. The proem repeats several times that 'in the beginning the *Shekhinah* was mainly in the inferior regions', which according to Rabbi Abba bar Kahanah points to the verse in Genesis (Gen 3:8): *And they heard the voice of the Lord God who was hopping* [*mit'hallekh*] in the garden. *God who was hopping* means that God had not decided to remain below and could rise up.[74]

The proem develops and concludes as follows:

Pesikta de-Rav Kahana, Piska 1, 1–3 (Text 81)

> In the beginning, the *Shekhinah* was mainly in the inferior regions. When the First Adam sinned, it detached itself and raised itself [*nistallekah*] to the first firmament. The generation of Enoch came and sinned, and it raised itself to the second firmament. [. . .] The Egyptians [sinned] during the time of Moses, it raised itself from the sixth firmament to the seventh.

72. A Christian can hear resonating that, according to Jn 20:28, Thomas sees God who manifests himself in Jesus.
73. Opening the meaning occurs by means of a proem (*petihah*), a homily that in general precedes the liturgical reading from Scripture and that ends with the first verse of that reading.
74. Rashi on Gen 3:8 remains with the verse's literal meaning, which according to him is that God and not God's voice hopped. However, Rashi does not disqualify the 'many *aggadic midrashim* (*midrashei Haggadah rabbim*) of his teachers'. Let us note that this verse in Gen 3:8 as interpreted by Tradition speaks of the Lord God who cannot cease being above (transcendent), of God's Presence (*Shekhinah*) situated below with human beings, and of the Voice. Is this Voice not heard through the working of the Holy Spirit?

> Seven righteous arose against them and made (the *Shekhinah*) come back down to earth. Abraham our Father rose up. He gained merit and made it come down from the seventh [firmament] to the sixth. [. . .] Amram rose up. He gained merit and made it come down from the second [firmament] to the first. Moses rose up. He gained merit and made it descend from the first [firmament] to the earth. Thus it is said (Num 7:1): *And behold the day on which Moses finished raising up the abode.*

From this proem we receive the fundamental conviction that God wants to reside among human beings and that because of this, God resided on earth and in a particular way in the abode. The biblical precepts concerning the construction of the abode (Ex 25:8, 21–22), its consecration and purification (Num 7:1; Lev 16:1–2, 16–18), and the investiture of the priests (Lev 8:34–35; 9:1, 5, 23–24) support the conviction that the *Shekhinah* came to reside in the abode (the Tent of Meeting) and that it remained there. Let us see how Tradition highlighted the *Seventh Day*, or the *First Day*, as the Day of the *Shekhinah's Habitation*, as the Day of the *Shekhinah*'s inaugural descent into the abode (the Tent of Meeting).

The inaugural descent

The *Seder Olam Rabba* (chapter 7) and the *Talmud* (*B.T. Shabbat* 87b) teach that the *Eighth Day* (Lev 9:1) or the *First Day* (Ex 40:17) received *ten crowns*. These days are not days of the week. But the fact that the one and/or the other of them are crowned with ten crowns incites one to think that the eighth day, which follows the seven days of the week but which is not one of them, is the reality of Shabbat, the fulfillment of the seventh day which opens onto the world to come.

The crown that interests us is the seventh one. Let us see how the Talmud presents this crown based on the first day mentioned in the Bible.

B.T. Shabbat 87b (Text 82)

> Ex 40:17: *The first day of the first month of the second year, they raised up the abode*. A Tanna taught: That day [the First day] received ten crowns: [First crown] it was the First [day] of creation . . . [seventh crown] the First for the *Shekhinah*'s habitation [*li-shekhon shekhinah*] in Israel.

The Shekhinah*'s activity in the Abode (the Tent of Meeting) and going out from there*

Rashi on Numbers 3:16 (Text 83)

> Numbers 3:16: *Upon the word of the Lord, Moses took their census* [the sons of Levi] *as the Lord had ordered him to do* [to take a census of the males starting at the age of one month and above].
>
> Moses said before the Holy One, blessed be He: 'How shall I enter into their tents so as to know the number of their infants?' The Holy One, blessed be He!, told him: 'Do your work and I will do mine.' Moses went and stood at the entrance of each tent and the *Shekhinah* went before him. A *Bat Kol* [divine voice] came out of the tent and said: 'There are so and so many infants in this tent.' That is why it is said: *Upon the word of the Lord.*

The *Bat Kol*, the divine voice, which is One with the *Shekhinah*, is what dispenses the *Shekhinah* from entering the tent and answers for it and through it, thus responding to what is necessary for the census commanded to Moses.

Another biblical context must be examined here, even though its pharisaic-rabbinic interpretation speaks neither of the *Shekhinah* nor of the *Bat Kol*. The verses in Exodus 25:8–9, 20–22 discuss the construction of the Tent of Meeting and the makeup of its furnishings, in particular of the Ark and the Seat of Mercy.[75]

Let us listen to the interpretations given by Rabbi Akiba and his disciple Rabbi Shimeon ben Azzai on Leviticus 1:1: *The Lord called Moses and he spoke to him from the Tent of Meeting and told him . . .*

Sifra on Leviticus 1:1, *4a* (Text 84)

> *From the Tent of Meeting.* Is it possible that this is speaking of the whole house [of the whole Tent]? [No!] The Talmud says (Ex 25:22): *from above the mercy seat.* If it is from above the

75. However, one cannot ignore the resonances that are to be heard in the verses Ex 25:8, 10–22. Ex 25:8 speaks clearly of the Lord's will to reside among them: Let them make me a sanctuary *[mikdash]* and I shall dwell *[ve-shakhanti]* in their midst. To speak of the *Shekhinah* in relation to the verses Ex 25:21–22 would be a redundancy.

> mercy seat, is it possible that it is the whole space above the mercy seat? [No!] The Talmud says (Ex 25:22) *from between the two cherubim*, words of Rabbi Akiba. Rabbi Shimeon ben Azzai says: 'I am not coming as someone who objects to the words of my master, but as the one who completes them [so that they might be understood]. The Glory, of which it is said (Jer 23:24): *do I not fill heaven and earth?*, behold! How far did his love for them [for Israel] lead this Glory?! It made itself narrow, so to speak, so as to speak from above the mercy seat and from between the two cherubim.'

The verses interpreted here follow those by which the Lord declared his intention of dwelling in their midst (Ex 25:8: *ve-shakhanti betokham*), and then to meet (Ex 25:22: *ve-noadati*) with Moses and to speak with him. R Akiba and Rabbi Shimeon ben Azzai mention neither the *Shekhinah* nor the *Bat Kol*. Nevertheless, the text is talking about these divine realities. The divine voice comes out from the Tent where the Presence resides. Here again, a trinitarian resonance can be heard. The Holy One, blessed be He!, who is transcendent, narrows himself out of love into the ever more reduced space of the Tent, from above the mercy seat, from between the two cherubim, from the space whence goes forth his divine Word.[76]

We have seen where, when and how the *Shekhinah* revealed itself to Israel as an immanent manifestation of the transcendent Lord. The *Shekhinah* is one with God, it is God who reveals himself. The Holy Spirit makes the human being capable of seeing God in the *Shekhinah* and causes the human person to say: 'This is my God.'[77]

Once the Tent of Meeting is set up, we saw how the *Shekhinah* is henceforth linked to the sanctuary in which God wants to reside in the midst of the children of Israel, out of love. The biblical accounts point towards the place chosen as God's definitive residence (Ex 15:17–18; Deut 12:5, 11, 18).

---

76. It is to be noted that Saint Paul calls Jesus the atonement (mercy seat) (Rom 3:25). In reality, Christ is **the Place** where God restrains himself and lowers himself in order to be in the midst of humankind, to speak to them in human language, with the weakness of that language and in order to atone for their errors.

77. Ex 15:2. *Cf* the *Mekhilta de-Rabbi Ishmael* on Ex 15:2, pp. 126–127 (text 78b) This experience and its explanation are so clear that it is not necessary to return to it each time the Holy Spirit is not mentioned together with the Shekhinah.

This place was the Temple that Solomon built and inaugurated in Jerusalem (1 Kgs 8 and 9). The *Shekhinah* resided in this Temple until its destruction in the year 587 BCE. The *Shekhinah* returned to Zion when Israel returned from exile in the years 520–515 BCE. It resided in the Second Temple until its destruction in the year 70 CE. The Lord will bring it back to Zion at the end of time.[78]

The Shekhinah *in the First Temple and in the Second Temple*

Scripture speaks in detail of the continuity between the Tent of Meeting and the Temple built by Solomon (1 Kgs 8 and 9). The *Shekhinah* resides in the Temple, and by means of liturgical memory, it remains there throughout the destructions and until the end of time.[79] The Jewish feast of Dedication (*Hanukkah*), to which the New Testament attests (Jn 10:22), manifests even to our day the people's attachment to the memory of the miracle of light, which marked the re-establishment of the divine Presence in the Temple. Founding texts give support to Tradition, which maintains even to our day the direction of liturgical prayer and of return (*teshuvah*) to God, in particular of the return after sin: towards the Land of Israel, towards Jerusalem, towards the Temple. Jerusalem and the Temple, which will be rebuilt, are the door to heaven, the Place where the Temple below communicates with the Temple on high.[80]

It must be affirmed that the *Shekhinah* remained in the Temple until the Temple was destroyed by the Romans in the year 70 CE, even if a certain tradition, often discussed and cited, can give the impression that the *Shekhinah* was not in the Second Temple. In reality, if Tradition teaches that the Second Temple did not have all the elements of the First Temple, one must understand with the Tosaf-

---

78. *Cf* the conclusion to the 17th blessing of the Amidah for ordinary days (5th blessing for Shabbat and feast days): 'Blessed are you, Lord, who causes [will cause] his [sic, your] Presence [*Shekhinah*] to return to Zion.'

79. Here, we cannot go into detail as regards the successive destructions, reconstructions, and dedications of the Temple. The destruction of the First Temple, 587 BCE; reconstruction and dedication, 515 BCE; profanation by Antiochus Epiphanes IV, 169–167 BCE; dedication (*Hanukkah*), 164 BCE; destruction of the Second Temple, 9th of Av, 70 CE.

80. The door to heaven, Gen 28:17. Regarding the Temple on high and the Temple below *cf* the *Mekhilta de-Rabbi Ishmael* on Ex 15:17 pp. 149–150.

ists that these elements, to which the *Shekhinah* must be added, were present in the Second Temple, but in a less effective way than in the First Temple. Above all, it must be seen that the sacrifices, which were indubitably maintained in the Second Temple until its destruction, presuppose that the *Shekhinah* was in the Temple.[81]

The ancient, anonymous Tradition that speaks of the *sacrifices for the Feasts of Pilgrimage* certainly has the lived reality of the Second Temple in mind. It teaches that the fixed time (*moed*) for the pilgrimages is the time of a **reciprocal vision**: God sees Israel, which presents itself before God, and Israel sees God, who is present in the Temple.

The Second Dyad: The Holy Spirit and the *Shekhinah*

Let us listen to the teaching given in the *midrash* on Deuteronomy 16:16. We shall complete it by what is taught on the action of the Holy Spirit during the feasts of pilgrimage. We shall again encounter the Holy Spirit, the divine reality that makes it possible to recognise the *Shekhinah* as God's presence.

Sifre Deuteronomy on 16:16, pp. 195–196 (Text 85)

> Deuteronomy 16:16: *Three times a year your whole male population will be seen.*
> Will be seen [*yera'eh*, but the consonantal text can be read *yr'eh*, will see]: just as he came to be seen, in the same way he came to see.
>
> Deuteronomy 16:16: your male population, to exclude the women.
>
> Deuteronomy 16:16: the whole male population, to include the children. Based on this, they said [*mikhan ameru*]: Who is a child? Every [child] who cannot sit on his father's shoulders and go up from Jerusalem to the Temple mountain; words of the disciples of Shammai. The disciples of Hillel say: Every [child] who cannot hold his father's hand and go up from Jerusalem to the Temple mountain, for it is said (Ex 23:14): Three *regalim* [pilgrimages, legs].

81. *Cf* P Lenhardt, 'La tradition d'Israël sur la Présence Divine (Shekhinah)', *Cahiers Ratisbonne*, 2 (June 1997): 147–148, and note 18, reprinted in *A l'écoute d'Israël*, volume II, 79.

> Deuteronomy 16:16: before [*et penei*] the Lord your God, if you do everything that is said in this context, I shall make myself free [*poneh*] of all my occupations and I shall be occupied only with you.

The consonantal text of Scripture allows two ways of reading it. It is understood that the masoretic scholars suggested the reading: *will be seen*, for no one can see God without dying (*cf* Ex 33:20 *passim*). However, an attentive examination of the different versions of this text makes it possible to believe that the teachers who were responsible for this ancient tradition knew that Scripture could originally have wanted to say *will see*. In any case—and this is important—it is taught that the feast of pilgrimage is the time of reciprocal vision between Israel and God who is present in the Temple. The vision (*reiyyah*) is the specific commandment for each feast of pilgrimage. This commandment included the offering of a holocaust (*olah*). Two other commandments accompanied the vision: the commandment of a festive offering (*hagigah*) and that of joy (*simhah*), which included the offering and the eating of sacrifices of communion (*shelamim*) and the obligation to rejoice while drinking wine, in reference to Scripture (Ps 104:15). It is interesting to note to what extent the spiritual experience of the vision, the sacrifices, joy, is rooted in the concrete reality of the obligation: financing the sacrifices, eating the flesh of the animals offered in sacrifice of communion, drinking wine. Since it is not possible to cite here Tradition's rich exposition on the coherence of the practice of pilgrimages and Scripture,[82] we shall content ourselves with seeing what Rashi says on *the joy* commanded for the feast of Sukkot:

Rashi on B.T. Sukkah 42b, *ve-Ha-Simha* (Text 86)

> *Ve-Ha-Simha* (and the joy) (Mishnah Sukkah 4, 1): [the commandment of joy] has to do with the eating of the flesh of the sacrifices of communion [*shelamim*]. For we have a teaching in [the Babylonian Talmud] *Pesahim* [109a], according to which at the time when the Temple existed, there was no joy except in [the eating of] the flesh [of the

82. *Cf* Maimonides, Positive Commandments 52, 53, 54: *Sefer ha-Hinukh, Livre de l'Education*, translated into French by Robert Samuel with the title *Le livre des 613 commandements* (Paris: C.L.K.H., 1974), Commandments 451–452.

> sacrifices of communion], as it is said (Deut 27:7): *You will immolate sacrifices of communion, you will eat them there, and you will rejoice.* And even though this scriptural passage was not written for the pilgrimages but in the context of Mount Garizim and Mount Ebal [*cf* Deut 27:12–13], joy is mentioned in Scripture in any case for the pilgrimages according to (Deut 16:14): *You will rejoice in your feast.*

Let us look also at what the Talmud says about festive sacrifices and at Rashi's commentary.

B.T. Sukkah 9a (Text 87a)

> What is the School of Shammai's reason? Scripture said (Lev 23:34): *It is the Feast of the Sukkot, seven days, for the Lord*: it is required that a Sukkah be made in view of the feast. And it was taught: R Yehuda ben Bathyra says: Just as the Name of the Heavens falls upon the festive sacrifice, so the Name of the Heavens falls upon the *Sukkah*, for it is said: *It is the Feast of the Sukkot, seven days, for the Lord the Sukkah is for the Lord.*"

Rashi on a Sukkah made in view of the feast (Text 87b)

> Because it is written: *Sukkot . . . for the Lord*, in view of the King's commandment.

Rashi on the festive sacrifice (Text 87c)

> The festive sacrifices of communion, the Name of the Heavens falls upon them in order to forbid them until after the burnt parts have risen up as incense. As for the parts from which they [those who offered the festive sacrifice] benefit after that, they receive them from the table of the Most High, as a servant who receives a present (from his master).

These commentaries by Rashi on the Babylonian Talmud regarding the feast of Sukkot repeat the teaching of Tradition on the joy of the pilgrimages. This joy is connected with the eating of the flesh of the sacrifice that is received from the table of the Most High in a meal of communion with Him and in the Holy Spirit.

The Holy Spirit and the Shekhinah *cannot be separated*

A first text introduces us to the experience of the Holy Spirit and the *Shekhinah* that cannot be separated. The *Mishnah Sukkah* describes the exuberant joy in which is fulfilled the water libation established by Tradition for the night following the first day of the feast of Sukkot.

Mishnah Sukkah 4, 9–10; 5, 1–4 (Text 88)[83]

> 4, 9: 'The Water-libation, seven days'—what was the manner of this? They used to fill a golden flagon holding three *logs* with water from Siloam. When they reached the Water Gate they blew [on the *shofar*] a sustained, a quavering and another sustained blast. [The priest whose turn of duty it was] went up the [Altar-] Ramp and turned to the right where were two silver bowls. R Judah says: they were of plaster, but their appearance was darkened because of the wine. They had each a hole like to a narrow snout, one wide and the other narrow, so that both bowls emptied themselves together. The bowl to the west was for water and that to the east was for wine. But if the flagon of water was emptied into the bowl for wine, or the flagon of wine into the bowl for water, that sufficed. R Judah says: With one *log* they could perform the libations throughout eight days. To the priest who performed the libation they used to say, 'Lift up thine hand!' for once a certain one poured the libation over his feet, and all the people threw their citrons at him.
>
> 4, 10: As was the rite on a weekday so was the rite on a Sabbath save that on the eve of the Sabbath they used to fill with water from Siloam a golden jar that had not been hallowed, and put it in a [special] chamber. If it was upset or uncovered, they refilled it from the laver, for wine or water which has been uncovered is invalid for the Altar.
>
> 5, 1: 'The Flute-playing, sometimes five and sometimes six days'–this is the flute-playing at the Beth ha-She'ubah, which over-rides neither a Sabbath nor a Festival-day. They have said: He that never has seen the joy of the Beth ha-She'ubah has never in his life seen joy.

83. Danby, Herbert, *The Mishnah,* translated from the Hebrew with Introduction and brief Explanatory Notes (Oxford University Press, Kondon: Geoffrey Cumberlege, 1933), 179–180.

> 5, 2: At the close of the first Festival-day of the Feast they went down to the Court of the Women where they had made a great amendment. There were golden candlesticks there with four golden bowls on the top of them and four ladders to each candlestick, and four youths of the priestly stock and in their hands jars of oil holding a hundred and twenty *logs* which they poured into all the bowls.
>
> 5, 3: They made wicks from the worn out drawers and girdles of the priests and with them they set the candlesticks alight, and there was not a courtyard in Jerusalem that did not reflect the light of the Beth ha-She'ubah.
>
> 5, 4: Men of piety and good works used to dance before them with burning torches in their hands, singing songs and praises. And countless levites [played] on harps, lyres, cymbals and trumpets and instruments of music, on the fifteen steps leading down from the Court of the Israelites to the Court of the Women, corresponding to the Fifteen Songs of Ascents in the Psalms; upon them the levites used to stand with instruments of music and make melody. Two priests stood at the upper gate which leads down from the Court of the Israelites to the Court of the Women, with two trumpets in their hands. At cock-crow they blew a sustained, a quavering and another sustained blast. When they reached the tenth step they again blew a sustained, a quavering and another sustained blast. When they reached the Court [of the Women] they again blew a sustained, a quavering and another sustained blast. They went on until they reached the gate that leads out to the east. When they reached the gate that leads out to the east, they turned their faces to the west and said, 'Our fathers when they were in this place *turned with their backs toward the Temple of the Lord and their faces toward the east, and they worshipped the sun toward the east*; but as for us, our eyes are turned toward the Lord'. R Judah says: They used to repeat the words 'We are the Lord's, and our eyes are turned to the Lord'.

The *Jerusalem Talmud* collected a tradition about what one of those who went up to the Temple in pilgrimage experienced. It also gives us the key to this experience.

J.T. Sukkah 5, 1 55a (Text 89)

> Rabbi Yona says: Yona ben Amitai was one of those who went up in pilgrimage. He entered into the joy of the *Beit ha-Sho'eba* [house of water drawing, water libation the night of the second day of the feast of Sukkot] and the Holy Spirit rested upon him. This teaches you that the Holy Spirit only rests upon a joyful heart. What is the [scriptural] reason [for this]? (2 Kgs 3:15): *While the musician played, the Spirit of God was upon him* [on Elisha]. It is not written 'while someone played the instrument', but: *While the musician played, the Spirit of God was upon him.*[84]

> Rabbi Yehoshua ben Levi says: Why was it called *Beit Ha-Shoeba* [house of water drawing]? Because that is where one drew the Holy Spirit, according to (Isa 12:3): *And you will draw water with joy at the springs of salvation.*

It is the Holy Spirit who gives joy. This joy comes from the Saviour God who makes himself present to his people. This experience establishes a significant link between the water and the Holy Spirit, but the water ritual does not limit the gift of the Holy Spirit to the libation. This Spirit is present to the whole pilgrimage reality, and it is the Spirit who makes the vision of which we have spoken possible and real.

Tradition insists on the superabundant joy of the feast of Sukkot, because of which Tradition calls this feast simply 'the Feast' (*ha-hag*) and 'the time of our joy', which in no way means that the Holy Spirit is not given or is less given on the other feasts of pilgrimage, Pesah and Pentecost.[85]

One interpretation that is not very convincing from the point of view of a rigorously historico-critical exegesis leaves no doubt as to the outpouring of the Holy Spirit during the three pilgrimages:

Genesis Rabbah on Genesis 29:2–3, *Par.* 70, § 8 (Text 90)

---

84. The Talmud modifies Scripture, which has 'the hand of the Lord'. For the Jerusalem Talmud or for the scribe, 'the hand of the Lord' becomes 'the Spirit of God'. In the *Babylonian Talmud Pesahim* 117a, quoted above, and in its parallels, 2 Kgs 3:15 is quoted without modification, and 'the hand of the Lord' is understood as meaning the *Shekhinah*. This last meaning confirms that one can see the *Shekhinah* in 'the hand' of Ex 14:31 (*cf* Text 78).

85. According to Acts 2:1–4ff., the Holy Spirit comes upon the group of apostles on the day of the Jewish Pentecost. This is entirely in conformity with the experience of the feasts of pilgrimage at the time of the Second Temple, and if the Holy Spirit comes, it is because the Shekhinah is in the Temple.

> Genesis 29:2: *And behold, he saw a well in the field.* That is Zion [Jerusalem, which is to say the Temple, where is the *Shekhinah*].
>
> *Genesis* 29:2: *near which three flocks of sheep were lying.* These are the three feasts of pilgrimage.
>
> Genesis 29:2: *This was the well where the flocks were watered.* For it is from there [from Zion, the Temple, the *Shekhinah*] that they drew the Holy Spirit.
>
> Genesis 29:2: *and the stone that closed its opening was large.* That is the joy of the water [this alludes to the special ritual of which we spoke above in connection with the feast of Sukkot].
>
> Genesis 29:3: *the livestock was watered there, then the stone was put back in place upon the mouth of the well.* And the well remained closed thus until the following feast of pilgrimage.

The Tradition teaching that the Holy Spirit was drawn, which is to say received, on every feast of pilgrimage is based on Scripture in a way that will not convince everyone. What is most important is to see that in a collection of the third to fourth centuries, the outpouring of the Holy Spirit on each of the feasts of pilgrimage is affirmed. In a collection of the seventh to eighth centuries bringing together in the *Pesikta Rabbati* all the previous expressions, this outpouring is again affirmed.[86]

Pesikta Rabbati, a homiletic anthology of the seventh or eighth century, takes up traditions of the third century, in particular the tradition transmitted by Rabbi Yehoshua ben Levi on the outpouring of the Holy Spirit on the feast of Sukkot. This late anthology has the merit of giving the key to the experience of the three feasts of pilgrimage, which is the link between the Holy Spirit and the *Shekhinah*.

Pesikta Rabbati Pisk. 1, 1a-b – 2a (Text 91)

> Isaiah 66:23: And it will come to pass that from new moon to new moon and from Shabbat to Shabbat all flesh will come to prostrate itself before my face, says the Lord.

86. *Cf* the translation and notes by WG Braude, *Pesiqta Rabbati*, (New Haven and London: Yale University Press, 1968).

But whence do we know that the new moons are in reality just as important as the Sabbaths? We know this from the prophet through whom [the reading of the Torah on the first day of the month, Isa 66:23] is completed: And it will come to pass that from new moon to new moon and from Shabbat to Shabbat all flesh will come to prostrate itself before my face, says the Lord. Thus R Tan'huma opened [*patah*] (Ps 42:3): *My soul thirsts for God, for the God of life; when shall I come and present myself [era'eh] before the face of God?*

Israel says to God: Master of the world! When will You re-establish the glory that was ours when we went up to see the face of your Presence [*Shekhinah*] at the time of the three pilgrimages?

R Isaac says: Just as they came to be seen, in the same way they came to see, for it is said: When shall I come and shall I see? [one can read: *'er'eh*. In the Yalkut it has: 'and shall I see in the Holy Spirit?']

R Yehoshua ben Levi says: Why was the celebration of the second day of the feast of Sukkot called 'joy of the house of water drawing'? Because from there [from the water drawn at Siloam and offered in libation in the Temple] the Holy Spirit was drawn.

Israel says: So when are You going to re-establish our glory? See how much time has passed since the destruction of the house of our life! One week of years ago, already a jubilee, already 777 years—and now that makes already 1151 years![87]

When shall I come and shall I see the face of God? He answered them: My children! In this world, how many times did you go on pilgrimage? Was it not [only] three times a year? When the end comes, I myself will rebuild my House and you will not only go up three times a year, but every month and every Shabbat you will go up there, as it is said (Isa 66:23): *And it will come to pass that from new moon to new moon and from Shabbat to Shabbat all flesh will come to prostrate itself before my face, says the Lord.*

87. These notes by copyists, 777 and 1151 years, are in relation to the destruction of the Second Temple in the year 70 CE. They thus mark the dates 847 and 1221. These references to the destruction of the Second Temple testify to the copyists' conviction that the Shekhinah was in the Second Temple.

The homily, whose aim it is to show the importance of the new moons, concludes that everything is in relation to God who makes himself present to all flesh by his particular Presence at the time of the feasts and of the Sabbath, during the liturgy and in the space of the Temple.

The joy of the feasts of pilgrimage thus comes from a vision of the *Shekhinah*, which is made possible through an outpouring of the Holy Spirit. This joy is experienced in the eating of the flesh of the sacrifices of communion. It is particularly exuberant on the feast of Sukkot, the night of the second day of the feast in the ritual of the water drawing, which is called 'house of water drawing' (*beit ha-shoevah*), 'because from there (from the water drawn at Siloam for the libation) the Holy Spirit was drawn according to Isaiah 12:3: *And you will draw water with joy from the springs of salvation*'.[88]

88. JT Sukkah 5, 5, 55a in the name of Rabbi Yehoshua ben Levi. In the context of the Jerusalem Talmud, another tradition attributes the outpouring of the Holy Spirit to the joy. It shows Yonah ben Amitai at the time of the Second Temple: 'Rabbi Yona says: Yonah ben Amitai was one of those who went up in pilgrimage. He entered into the joy of the house of water drawing and the Holy Spirit rested upon him. This teaches you that the Holy Spirit only rests on a joyful heart.' Another tradition speaks of 'the joy of the water' (*Genesis Rabbah* on Gen 29:2–3, 706). These expressions converge in testifying of an experience that connects the joy, the water, and the Holy Spirit. According to the Gospel of John 7:37–39, Jesus refers to Scripture in the context of the feast of Sukkot saying: From his bosom rivers of living water will flow. He certainly has in mind what Zechariah announces in the chapter that is read on the feast of Sukkot (Zech 14:8): And behold, on that day living waters will come forth from Jerusalem. Jesus identifies himself with Jerusalem, which is Zion, the Temple where the Shekhinah resides. He announces that those who believe in him will receive the Holy Spirit, which is not possible so long as he is not glorified. In resonance, the context of Israel's pilgrimages thus suggests the following teaching: the glorified Jesus who is recognized as Glory (Shekhinah) is the Place (the known Place, Jerusalem, Zion, the Temple) whence the living waters will come forth, which is to say the Holy Spirit. Without the present and recognized Shekhinah, there is no Holy Spirit; but equally, without the Holy Spirit, the Shekhinah is not recognised *cf* (1 Cor 12:3). According to Jn 7:37, this teaching is given on the last day of the feast, which is also the most solemn. One can see it better on the second day of the feast in connection with the water libation (the house of water drawing) of which we have spoken. For it is on the evening and during the night with which the second day begins that the joyful celebration of the water drawing begins, of which Mishnah Sukkah 5, 1 says: 'He who has not seen the joy of the house of water drawing has not seen joy in his life', and the Mishnah describes the songs, the dances and the light that filled the Temple during the entire night, to the extent that 'there was no courtyard in Jerusalem that was not illumined by the light

The superabundance of joy on the feast of Sukkot certainly underlines the greatness of this feast, called simply '*the Feast*', which according to the prophet Zechariah was chosen to unite all peoples with Israel at the end of time in the adoration of the One God.[89] But the eschatological note on this last feast of pilgrimage does not mean that the importance of the other two pilgrimage festivals preceding it is forgotten: Pentecost and Pesah. These two feasts are also *encounters* with God together with a *vision* of God's *Shekhinah* in the Temple, which is made possible by the outpouring of the Holy Spirit.

The reciprocal vision, the joy through eating of the flesh of the sacrifices of small livestock—these experiences come from a founding experience, which is that of the community united by God and in God. Tradition teaches that Israel must attach itself to God (Deut 11:22) and also that it was able to do this (Deut 4:4). However, the masters hesitate to go so far as to speak of Unity.[90] But this could be said in the teaching about Shabbat, which as we have seen, is the great instrument of return to God and of unification.[91]

---

from the house of water drawing' (Mishnah Sukkah 5, 3). These passages from the Mishnah were compiled orally based on testimonies given by witnesses who knew the Temple before its destruction and who experienced the joy of the feast linked with the water and the Holy Spirit (signified sacramentally by the water). Jesus knew this reality, which he applies to himself without wanting to diminish it or even less, to replace it. His reference to Zech 14:8 is made within a broader reference to the lived tradition of the feast. For it is Tradition that establishes the ritual of the house of water drawing without deducing it from Scripture, without even giving it a scriptural basis.

89. Zech 14:1–21 is the prophetic reading established for the first day of the feast of Sukkot. The climax of this reading is Zech 14:9: And the Lord will be king over all the earth; on that day, the Lord will be One and his Name will be One. This verse is quoted in the liturgy of Rosh ha-Shanah in the blessing of the Kingdoms (Malkhiyyot) of the additional prayer and on all days in the summary of that liturgy, the Aleinu prayer at the end of the morning liturgy. It is evoked in the central blessing of the community prayer on the afternoon of Shabbat. This blessing places the verse into the present: 'You are One and your Name is One', because on Shabbat the Lord is already One and his Name is already One.

90. *Cf* G Sholem, *The Messianic Idea in Judaism and other Essays on Jewish Spirituality* (New York: Schocken Books, (1971) 1978), *Devekur or Communion with God,* 203–227.

91. *Cf* Rabbi Meshullam Leib Feibush of Zbarah (died 1795), *Yosher Divrei Emet* § 12 and 46.

The First Temple and then the Second Temple was the privileged place of the *Shekhinah* in the world. This place remains the one towards which prayer and the return to God are oriented. Since the destruction of the Temple, the request for its reconstruction and for the reestablishment of the sacrifices concludes every day with this blessing: '*Blessed are You, Lord, who re-establishes Your* [literally: *His*] *Shekhinah in Zion*.'

All these realities are inseparable: Jerusalem, the Temple, Shabbat, the rest (the place of rest, *menuhah*) of the Lord and of Israel at the end of time: Psalm 95:11; Zechariah 9:1; Psalm 132:14; *Sifre Deuteronomy* on 1:1 7–8; Hebrews 4.

The fact that the *Shekhinah* is no longer in Zion does not prevent it from being with those who, as a group or individually, call upon the Name of the Lord in prayer or in study.

We saw that the *Shekhinah* is in every place, since the all-powerful Creator God constantly upholds the world by his unfathomable immanence which is inaccessible except through faith, through the knowledge that the Holy Spirit gives. As we saw, the *Shekhinah* reveals itself in the burning bush so as to be with Israel in distress. It reveals itself in the night of Egypt, in the passage through the Red Sea, at Mount Sinai.

Over and beyond these manifestations that are linked to times in the past and to places of Israel's passage on its journey towards the future, the *Shekhinah* is and will be with those who are in distress as well as with those who seek God and who find God in prayer and in study.

As regards prayer, it is taught that the *Shekhinah* is with every community that prays, whereby the minimum for constituting a community is determined to be ten persons.[92] It is said clearly that God prefers to meet with a community, but that the *Shekhinah* is also with five, three, two persons, and finally with one single person who calls upon God's Name.[93]

In listening to these traditions, a Christian hears their resonance with what Jesus says about his presence with those who suffer (Mt

92. The minimum is fixed at ten persons, an age-old decision for which it is not impossible to find support in Scripture. As the *halakhah* for the obligation to pray in community stands at present, the quorum of ten is made up of men, thus excluding women.

93. *Mishnah Abot* 2, 3.6; *B.T. Berakhot* 6a; M*t* 18:19–20

25:31–46), with those whom he wants to protect from destruction (Mt 23:37–39), with the two or three who pray or study in his name (Mt 18:19–20). In these New Testament passages, Jesus presents himself as the *Shekhinah*, which confirms that in his time, the feminine gender of the word *Shekhinah* was not taken into consideration. Entering into the people of Israel through conversion is truly *to find shelter under the wings of the Lord*, the God of Israel, referring to the conversion of Ruth (Ruth 2:12), or *under the wings of the Shekhinah*, referring to the proselytes whom Hillel the Elder welcomed and taught at the end of the 1st century BCE (*B.T. Shabbat* 31a). The fact that the *Shekhinah* hastens to save Israel during the night of Egypt signifies that the Beloved, the Lord, the God of Israel hastens to save his Beloved, Israel.

The Unity of the Shekhinah and of the Holy Spirit in the life of personalities present in Israel's memory

The personalities that interest us here are David, Hillel the Elder, and Samuel the Small.

David

King David composed through the inspiration of the Holy Spirit.[94] A tradition on David's inspiration as author of the Psalms enlightens us as regards the freedom of the Spirit.

B.T. Pesahim 117a (Text 92a)

> [The title of the Psalm:] *Of David, Psalm* (Ps 24; 101; 110), in which David is mentioned in first place, signifies that the *Shekhinah* first rested upon him and that he then said the *Psalm*.
>
> [The title:] *Psalm, of David* (Ps 23; 29; 38; 63) signifies that David first said the *Psalm* and that the *Shekhinah* then rested upon him (*cf* Acts 2:38; 8:17; 10:44).
>
> This teaches you that the *Shekhinah* does not rest upon a person who is given to idleness, to sullenness, to frivolity, to

94. *Cf* Acts 4:25.

> thoughtlessness, to vain occupations and words, but it rests upon a person when he experiences joy connected with the fulfillment of a commandment, as it is said (2 Kgs 3:15): *Now bring me someone who plays the lyre! And when the musician played, the hand of the Lord was upon him.*[95]

Rashbam (***R**abbi **Sh**emuel **b**en **M**eir, grandson of Rashi*) *ad locum* (Text 92b)

> *Of David. Psalm.* This lets one hear that the Holy Spirit came first to David and after that the Psalm.
>
> *Psalm, of David.* This lets one hear that based on the Psalm, the divine Presence [*Shekhinah*] came to David.

Rashi on Psalm 23:1 (Text 93)

> Our Masters said: In every place where it is said *Psalm, of David*, he played and after that the *Shekhinah* rested upon him. *Psalm* 'Psalm' in order to bring the Holy Spirit, *of David* 'to David'. And everywhere where it is said *Of David, Psalm*, the *Shekhinah* rested upon him and after that he said the song.

Here, the Holy Spirit and the *Shekhinah* are spoken of as if these realities were interchangeable. In the experience of a person who receives the Holy Spirit and/or the *Shekhinah*, there is the suggestion of an interaction or of a reciprocity. Without doubt God, who gives the gift, precedes the experience of the one who receives the gift, and God can launch the experience by means of the perceptible gift. But God can also wait that the person seeks and finds first in him- or herself the One who wants to give him and her the gift of his Spirit and of his *Shekhinah*. The perceptible gift then confirms the imperceptible gift. In the *Acts of the Apostles*, Luke noted well these two ways in which the Holy Spirit acted upon the first believers. In certain cases, baptism in the name of Jesus precedes the gift of the Spirit (Acts 2:38; 8:15–17; 19:1–6); in other cases, the Holy Spirit comes before baptism (Acts 10:44–47). In all cases, God is present through his *Shekhinah* (Jesus) in the person who has already embraced the faith or who is preparing to embrace it. Jesus is present in the Word given by the apostles

95. Here too 'the hand of the Lord' is understood as the *Shekhinah*

on Pentecost. He is present in the act of baptism given in his Name. The perceptible gift of the Spirit guarantees that God is present in the believer through his *Shekhinah* (Jesus). The gift of the Holy Spirit makes it possible to recognize Jesus as Lord, as *Shekhinah*, as Presence of God, as Son of God, as 'true God from true God'. That is what Paul says clearly: *No one can say 'Jesus is Lord' except through the Holy Spirit* (1 Cor 12:3).

Let us also underline the pertinence of this experience of the Spirit and of the *Shekhinah*, which the Jewish teachers base on David's experience as indicated in the titles of Psalms. It seems that Christian liturgy with the various ways in which it sees and organizes the eucharistic *epiclesis* sheds light on this interaction with inversions and chronological gaps. In the opposite sense, Israel's Tradition sheds light and confirms the diversity of Christian traditions regarding the *epiclesis*.[96]

Is it possible to shed more light on the connection between the Holy Spirit and the *Shekhinah* by means of texts from Israel's Tradition regarding the gift of the Torah at Sinai?

We know that the connection between the Feast of Weeks and the gift of the Torah was not established by rabbinic Tradition before the 3rd century, before the final oral composition and publication of the Mishnah, the *terminus ad quem* of which is the year 219 CE. Neither the Mishnah nor the Jerusalem and Babylonian Talmuds have a treatise on the Feast of Weeks. The destruction of the Temple brought with it the loss of all the agricultural rituals connected with this feast, which was known and implemented as the *Harvest Festival* (Ex 23:16) and the *Day of the First Fruits* (Num 28:26). Moreover, since in contrast to the feasts of Pesah (seven days) and of Sukkot (eight days) this feast has only one day, it became and remained the 'poor relation' among the feasts, and only over the course of the centuries did it receive a specific ritual, which moreover has no liturgical status: *the study and teaching of the Torah throughout the entire night.*

We have to be satisfied with the light shed by the *midrashim* and the *Talmudim* concerning the gift of the Torah without this being seen in relation to the Feast of Weeks. The texts studied above teach the

96. In this study, it is enough to refer to the article 'Epiclèse eucharistique' in the encyclopedia Catholicisme No 13 and in the *Cathechism of the Catholic Church* (New York, London, Toronto, Sydney, Auckland, 1997).

multiplicity of voices and lights given to individual persons within the people; they also legitimise the diversity of languages.

Even though these texts transmit traditions that precede the official recognition of the Feast of Weeks as the feast of the gift of the Torah, they nevertheless also shed light on the universalism of the particular Torah given to Israel and of the message preached by Peter on Pentecost (Acts 2:14–36). This very particular message of Peter, centered on Jesus Christ, is meant for all (Acts 2:39). Its universal bearing is prepared for by the gift of tongues, which in Luke's account is not the gift of glossolalia but rather that of various languages. Let us note that in the rabbinic texts, the point is not the diversity of understanding given to each one according to 'his or her strength' and based on the unheard-of limitation which is imposed on human beings by the strength of the All-Powerful, as in the texts studied above, but on the infinite diversity of interpretations that proceed from the inexhaustible Word of the One, transcendent, Only God. The corresponding point in the account by Luke is the proclamation of God's infinite power, which raises Jesus, which makes him Lord and Messiah, and which gives him the Spirit so that he might pour out this Spirit upon everyone.

One can also say that from the point of view of Christian faith, the gift of the Spirit on Pentecost, the gift of knowing the Lord (*Shekhinah*) Jesus Christ (Jesus Messiah) is attached to the resurrection on Easter, to the liberation from death. Luke's Pentecost, which becomes the **Pentecost of the Church**, is the **conclusion of the Passover of Jesus Christ**, just as the Feast of Weeks, the *Harvest Festival*, becomes the *Feast of the gift of the Torah* and the **conclusion** (*atseret*) of the Jewish Passover. The coherence of the Torah of the One God means that for the Christian, the Traditions of Israel and of the Church, with their gaps in time, reciprocally enrich one another and become united. Listening to Israel as recommended by the Catholic Church since the Second Vatican Council is here again the foundation for seeking the Unity.

Hillel/Samuel the Small: *Tosefta Sotah* 13, 3–4, 231–232[97] (Text 94)

97. We are quoting the *Tosefta* according to the edition by S Lieberman, *The Order of Nashim-Sotah, Gittin, Kiddushin* (New York: The Jewish Theological Seminary of America, 1973). In this edition, we are following the version of the Vienna manuscript as chosen by S Lieberman.

> 3. When the last prophets Haggai, Zechariah and Malachy died, the Holy Spirit ceased [*pasqah*] in Israel; in spite of this, [Israel] was made to hear the heavenly voice [*Bat Kol*]. It came to pass that the Sages entered into the upper room in Guryo's house in Jericho. And a heavenly voice came forth and said to them:[98]
>
> "There is here among you a man who is worthy of the Holy Spirit, but his generation does not merit it." They turned their eyes to Hillel the Elder. When he died, it was said of him: "See, he was humble; see, he was *hassid*; he was the disciple of Ezra."

4. Again another time, they [the Sages] were seated in Yavne. They heard a heavenly voice which said: 'There is here a man who is worthy of the Holy Spirit, but the generation does not merit it.' They turned their eyes to Samuel the Small. What did they say at the hour of his death? 'See, he was humble; see, he was *hassid*; he was the disciple of Hillel the Elder.'

B.T. Sanhedrin 11a[99] (Text 95)

> Since the last prophets Haggai and Malachy died, the Holy Spirit has separated [*nistallekah*] itself from Israel [*Tosefta*: the Holy Spirit has ceased], but in spite of that, the heavenly voice is used [*Tosefta*: the heavenly voice is made to be heard].
>
> Once, they were at table in the upper room of Guriah's house in Jericho [*Tosefta*: an event: the Sages entered into the upper room of the house]. A heavenly voice was given them from the heavens [*Tosefta*: a heavenly voice came forth and said to them]: 'There is here a man [*Tosefta*: among you] who is worthy that the *Shekhinah* rest upon him [like upon Moses our Master] [*Tosefta*: who is worthy of the Holy Spirit], but his generation is not worthy of this.' The Sages turned their eyes to Hillel the Elder. When he died, they said concerning him: 'Alas! *Hassid*, alas! Humble, the disciple of Ezra.'

---

98. The Erfurt manuscript has this variant: 'And they heard a heavenly voice telling them.'

99. Between brackets, we shall indicate the variants in the *Tosefta*. We do not consider it necessary to examine the manuscripts of the Babylonian Talmud in order to note other variants. Finding other expressions that show that *Shekhinah* and Holy Spirit appear in an interchangeable manner would not shed more light on the debate that has already been stated clearly.

> Another time they were at table in the upper room in Yavne. A heavenly voice was given them from the heavens [*Tosefta*: And they heard a heavenly voice that said]: 'There is here a man who is worthy that the *Shekhinah* rest on him, but his generation is not worthy of this.' They turned their eyes to Samuel the Small. When he died, they said concerning him: 'Alas! *Hassid*, alas! Humble, the disciple of Hillel.'

This anonymous tradition, which was received before the destruction of the Temple and was taught in Yavne after its destruction, refers to the three last prophets. The *Tosefta Sotah* version that we have just seen, as also that of the *Jerusalem Talmud Sotah* 9, 14, 24b, speaks only of the Holy Spirit, whereas the *Babylonian Talmud Sanhedrin* goes from the cessation of the Spirit to the non-residing of the *Shekhinah* upon Hillel and Samuel the Small. Its version seems less original, which confirms the anomaly of the expression used for the Spirit: 'the Holy Spirit separated itself [*nistallekah*, literally *detached itself while going up*] from Israel', a current expression for the *Shekhinah* which corresponds with its spatial connotation.[100]

Thus the Talmud tacked onto the beginning of the text the expression which is appropriate for the continuation of the tradition. We shall not enter more into the comparison of the versions. Moreover, such a comparison has not drawn the attention of Jewish scholars who could have pointed out its importance.[101] However, let us note

100. However, *cf* P Schäfer, *Die Vorstellung, 160,* where many references are given for the use of the expression *nistallekah* for the Holy Spirit.

101. S Lieberman, *Tosefta ki-fshutah,* A comprehensive commentary on the *Tosefta (New York: 1973), on Tosefta Sotah* 13, 3–4, 736–737; E Urbach, 'Matai paskah ha-nebuah?' (When does prophecy cease?), in *Tarbiz,* XVII (1946): 1–11. In his article *'Matai',* E Urbach adopts the expression from the *Tosefta,* whereas in his book on the *Sages of Israel,* he quotes the expression from the Talmud and only mentions the expression in the *Tosefta* in the footnote (173, 928). In the two texts as they are available to us, Holy Spirit and *Shekhinah* appear interchangeably; however, this does not make clarification unnecessary, for what is said of the one is not said of the other. A Goldberg, *Untersuchungen,* mentions and discusses the differences between the Palestinian and Babylonian versions without being able to uncover the reasons; he suggests that the undifferentiated use of the terms *Shekhinah* and Holy Spirit is in relation to a connection that unites these two realities, as the outpouring of the Holy Spirit upon *Yonah ben Amitai* during the celebration of the water drawing in the Temple on the Feast of Sukkot would show (*cf J.T. Sukkah* 5, 1, 55a). Since the Temple was the place

for what will follow in our study what this 'automatic' passage from the Holy Spirit to the *Shekhinah* in the *Babylonian Talmud* could signify. The 'automatic passage' means that these two divine realities are inseparable to the point of being interchangeable.

If these two realities are inseparable, the cessation of the Holy Spirit is necessarily accompanied by the absence of the *Shekhinah*, which no longer rests on persons, even on those who would be worthy of it. However, as we saw in the first part, the *Shekhinah* remains present in the world and rests in many ways upon Israel, on the community and on persons. The departure of the *Shekhinah*, like the cessation of the Holy Spirit, must be heard as the absence of intense experiences that are recognised by the people as having authority for its life. This absence is not absolute. There are exceptions that confirm the rule, there are limited experiences that are recognised as authentic and that are authorised for the good of the persons experiencing them and for the good of those who testify to them.

Let us present one of those exceptions, which is especially interesting and which, as we shall see, sheds light on Luke's Pentecost, which is considered to be a Jewish feast of pilgrimage.

B.T. Sukkah 28a[102] (Text 96)

---

of the *Shekhinah*, the experience of *Yonah* would testify to the link between the Spirit and the *Shekhinah* (467–468). Two comments on this suggestion: Is *Yonah ben Amitai* really the prophet by that name? Was the outpouring of the Holy Spirit limited to *Yonah* and to the feast of water drawing?

P Schäfer, *Die Vorstellung*, 94–97 quotes the *Tosefta* and mentions the parallel versions in the Babylonian Talmud Sotah 48b and Sanhedrin 11a, without saying clearly that only the *B.T. Sotah* replaces the Holy Spirit with the *Shekhinah* in this passage. *B.T. Sanhedrin* only passes from the Holy Spirit to the *Shekhinah* when it comes to Hillel. This detail confirms that the version in B.T. is secondary in relation to that in the *Tosefta*. P Schäfer on 94, note 15 mentions the variant in *B.T. Sotah and Sanhedrin: ve-nistallekah* instead of *paskah* without discussing it. *Cf* however his note 59, 160.

102. The parallels in *Talmud Sukkah, B.T. Baba Batra* 134a (identical), *Abot de-Rabbi Nathan* A 14, 29a; B 28, 29a (shorter, in particular without the ending about *Yonathan ben Uzziel*) use the same expression in regard to the *Shekhinah*. None of these versions speaks of the Holy Spirit. It is not impossible that the versions in *Abot de-Rabbi Nathan* have the same origin as the Babylonian *Talmud Sukkah* or *Baba Batra*. MB Lerner however does not mention these passages from *Abot de-Rabbi Nathan* among the Babylonian Talmud's borrowed sources (*cf* MB Lerner, *'Abot de Rabbi Nathan', The Literature of the Sages*, 376–377).

> Our masters taught: Hillel the Elder had eighty disciples. Thirty of them were worthy that the *Shekhinah* rested upon them as it rested upon Moses our Master. Thirty of them were worthy that the sun stop at their command, as was the case with Joshua ben Nun. The twenty others were average men. The greatest of them all was Jonathan ben Uzziel, the least of them all was Rabban Yohanan ben Zakkai. It is said of Rabban Yohanan ben Zakkai that he knew in depth: *Mikra* [Scripture, written Torah] and *Mishnah* [oral Torah], *Gemara* [Talmud, teaching connected with Scripture], *Halakhot* [juridical decisions] and *Aggadot* [non-juridical expositions] . . . All this so as to fulfill what is said (Prov 8:21): *So as to procure goods for those who love me in such a way that I might fill their treasures.*
>
> And if it was thus for the least among them, how much more must it be thus for the greatest! Of Jonathan ben Uzziel it is said that when he was seated and was occupied with the Torah, every bird that passed above him was immediately burnt.

Here, the Holy Spirit is not the subject but rather the *Shekhinah*, which corresponds with the Babylonian version of the Tradition and for which no certain Palestinian parallel exists. One can without difficulty adopt the position of P. Schäfer, who believes it is possible to read here 'Holy Spirit' instead of *Shekhinah*. In any case, the Tradition transmitted by the Talmud makes two points with consummate art and humor: The first concerns the greatness of Rabban Yohanan ben Zakkai, whose immense knowledge is admired while he was the least of the disciples of Hillel.[103] The second point is about the greatness of Yonathan ben Uzziel, who was certainly a disciple of Hillel at the end of the last century of the former era.[104] The account shows that "being occupied with the Torah" is not a pastime limited to pious subjectivity. It is an activity that leads to responsible teaching turned towards

103. Tradition ignores the chronological difficulty: did Hillel and Rabban Yohanan ben Zakkai really live for 120 years so that the one could be the teacher of the other? *Cf Sifre Deuteronomy* on Deut 34:7 pp. 429, which teaches that Hillel, Rabban Yohanan ben Zakkai and Rabbi Akiba lived 120 years like Moses. In reality, Tradition wants to attach Rabban Yohanan ben Zakkai to Hillel and to present him with Hillel as a new Moses.

104. The Targum of the Prophets is attributed to Yonathan ben Uzziel *(cf B.T. Megillah 3a).*

the outside. The unfortunate bird did not know that Jonathan ben Uzziel was a great master; above all, he did not know that a ray of fire linked Jonathan ben Uzziel with the Sinai and with God. Without doubt, God is always present in his Word in a more or less visible manner, as the blessings said before and after the liturgical reading of the Torah (Pentateuch) affirm in their conclusion: "Blessed are You, Lord, who give [in the present] the Torah." But it happens that the fire of Sinai manifests itself with strength in an exceptional manner when a person is occupied with the Torah. That is what witnesses of the death of the poor bird, a victim of Yonathan ben Uzziel's Torah, experienced. The legendary genre corresponds with the concern to show that the fire reveals a real *objective* experience of the community over and beyond the personal piety of the teacher. For the *Tosafot*, the fire that burned the bird is the same as the fire of Sinai, which surrounded Rabbi Eliezer and Rabbi Yehoshua in the circumstances reported in the Jerusalem Talmud regarding the circumcision of Elisha ben Abbuya (text 18).

The fact that the Shekhinah rested neither upon Hillel nor upon Samuel the Small is blamed on the bad generation in which they lived and which hampered their effectiveness. This kind of explanation is known during the New Testament period and Jesus refers to it.[105]

Let us see how the fact that the *Shekhinah* cannot support Israel's activity in its fight against sorcery and demons haunting the cemeteries is deplored.

Lamentation over the absence of the Shekhinah and the inactivity of the Holy Spirit

It is interesting for us to note that there are no more manifestations of the Holy Spirit after the last prophets, neither in the people nor in persons who would be especially worthy. This cessation is general and permanent, but it does not exclude the possibility of an exceptional intervention on the part of the Spirit in a particular person in view of making that person say a word which the people needs to hear.[106] For the time before the destruction of the Temple, such a

105. Mt 12:38–42; 16:1–4; Lk 11:29–32.

106. *Cf* E Urbach, *The Sages,* 576. However, E Urbach says that these visionaries, seers, miracle workers do not appear as prophets or as messengers from God.

possibility is confirmed in the Gospel according to Luke for Zechariah (Lk 1:67ff.), for Simeon (Lk 2:25ff.), and for Anna (Lk 2:36ff.). This possibility is taught regarding all times by Maimonides, based on sources (*Hilkhot Yesodei ha-Torah*, 7). In the same way, the separation of the *Shekhinah* is not to be understood in an absolute way, as we shall see further on.

Let us also note that the Talmud sees the cessation of the Holy Spirit and the separation of the *Shekhinah* from Israel as connected, as if the one did not happen without the other. We have seen and we shall see again other texts that will show that *Shekhinah* and Holy Spirit are inseparable and that by this very fact, they shed light on the manifestation of the Spirit, of which Luke speaks (Acts 2:1–11).

If at the time of the Second Temple the Holy Spirit and the *Shekhinah* are no longer active in the life of Israel and even less in the life of individual persons, this absence is *a fortiori* felt after the destruction of the Temple. Two testimonies concerning two great masters, Rabbi Eliezer and his disciple Rabbi Akiba, bear on this absence as it is felt at the end of the 1st century CE.[107]

Sifre on Deuteronomy 18:12, pp. 220[108] (Text 97)

> Deuteronomy 18:12: *For whoever does these things is an abomination to the Lord your God.*
>
> When Rabbi Eliezer came to this verse, he said: 'Woe to us! Impurity rests upon whoever attaches himself to impurity. *A fortiori*, this must result in the *Shekhinah* resting upon whoever attaches himself to the *Shekhinah*. And what is the cause [of the *Shekhinah* not resting upon us]? Israel's sin, as it is said (Isa 59:2): For it is your faults that have caused the separation between you and your God.'

107. This concerns Rabbi Eliezer and not Rabbi Eleazar ben Sammua, as P Schäfer suggests with some hesitation in *Die Vorstellung*, 103, note 58, based on the edition by M Friedmann, Vienna 1864. L Finkelstein's critical edition suggests R. Eliezer without any variant; and on the other hand, the parallel version of the Talmud, which brings R. Akiba onto the scene, speaks of an experience that is almost identical with that of R Eliezer, R Akiba's main teacher.
108. *Cf* Mt 8:28ff; Mk 5:1ff; Lk 8:28ff; Mt 17:14; Mk 9:14ff; Lk 9:37.

> [L. Finkelstein's eclectic version: Woe to us! The spirit of impurity rests upon whoever attaches himself to impurity. *A fortiori*, this must result in the Holy Spirit resting upon whoever attaches himself to the *Shekhinah*. And what is the cause . . .]

B.T. Sanhedrin 65b on Deuteronomy 18:11 (Text 98a)

> It has been taught (*Deut* 18:11): *Whoever calls upon the dead*, that is he who is starving and who spends the night in the cemetery so that the spirit of impurity might rest upon him. When Rabbi Akiba came to this passage of Scripture, he wept [saying]: 'If when he is starving for the spirit of impurity to rest upon him, the spirit of impurity rests upon him, [how much more should the spirit of purity rest upon] the one who is starving for the spirit of purity to rest upon him! But what should I do? For it is our iniquities that are the cause, as it is said (Isa 59:2): *For it is your faults*.'

Rashi on she-tishreh [*for the spirit of impurity to rest upon him*] (Text 98b)

> [That] the demon [*Shed*] of the cemetery love him and help him in his practice of sorcery.

Rashi on ha-mar'iv [*he who is starving for the spirit of purity to rest upon him*] (Text 98c)

The prophecy of the *Shekhinah*.

Rashi on al ahat [*how much more*] (Text 98d)

> For this is what the rule should give [*Middah*: here the rule is the *a fortiori* reasoning]: which is that through fasting and prayer of petition, the *Shekhinah* rests upon him, for the measure [the attribute] of kindness is more than the measure of chastisement; and we cry for this and we are not heard. *But what should I do . . .*

These two texts and the Talmud's commentaries attributed to Rashi show once again that the Holy Spirit and the *Shekhinah* are inseparable. This goes without saying to such an extent that the masters and the texts that transmit and comment on their experiences and their teaching mention the Holy Spirit and the *Shekhinah* interchangeably. Nevertheless, we must distinguish between them, something which L Finkelstein does perfectly in the eclectic text quoted above.[109] What can be criticized in this text from the scientific point of view is entirely justifiable from the point of view of the spiritual reality it deals with and to which the New Testament testifies when it speaks of Jesus (*Shekhinah*) and of the Holy Spirit.[110]

Thus the *Shekhinah* and the Holy Spirit no longer manifest themselves in a tangible and visible way for the benefit of individual persons. However, if persons act in community and for the community, an experience of the Holy Spirit and of the *Shekhinah* is possible, as we saw for Yonathan ben Uzziel, Jesus, Simeon and Anna (*Lk* 2:20–38), the believers on the day of Luke's Pentecost, Rabbi Eliezer and Rabbi Yehoshua, Ben Azzai, Rabbi Abbahu. More currently and better known, the *Bat Kol* (heavenly voice) makes itself heard from heaven in order to teach the community or to confirm the legitimacy of a teaching or the authority of a person. In so doing, it acts in a manner coherent with the situation described by Tradition: the (relative) cessation of the Holy Spirit and the (relative) absence of the *Shekhinah*, which we have discussed.

All in all, we have heard two messages: that of the **Unity of God and of the *Shekhinah*** (*first dyad*) and that of the **Unity of the *Shekhinah* and of the Holy Spirit** or of the heavenly Voice (*second dyad*). If we join these two dyads, we come by resonance to the **triad: God, *Shekhinah*, Holy Spirit.**[111]

---

109. *Cf* the critiques on the eclectic text suggested by L. Finkelstein in his edition of *Sifre on Deuteronomy*: JN Epstein, *Tarbiz* 8 (1936): 375–392; S Lieberman, *KS* 14, (1937): 323–336.

110. *Cf* Lk 3:21–22 *passim*. *Cf* Basil of Caesarea, *Sur le Saint-Esprit*, Sources Chrétiennes, No 17 *bis*, 387, quoted by R Cantalamessa, *Viens Esprit Créateur*, *Burtin*, edition of the Beatitudes, 2008, 70. In Ephrem's writing and elsewhere in Syria, the Spirit is identified with the Shekhinah. 'It goes without saying that a theology in which no clear distinction is made between Christ, the Spirit, the Name and the Shekhinah, was no longer accepted after a certain moment, in any case no longer after the Council of Chalcedon.' *Cf* G Rouwhorst, Colloque organisé par la Faculté de Théologie de Louvain, 23–25, April 1980, Abbaye du Mont César-Leuven (Louvain), 1981, 37.

111. *Cf* the recapitulation of the triads above in Unity, the 'Jewish trinity'.

3
Trinity

Having reached this point, we must look at how what we have heard resonates with Christian faith in the Trinity. Obviously, this does not mean that we shall pass automatically from each element in the Jewish triad, God, the Torah, Israel, to each of the elements in the Christian triad (*Trinity, trias*), Father, Son, Holy Spirit. Nevertheless, let us see what can be perceived that corresponds with Christian faith when this faith becomes open to the Word of God coming to it from Israel's Tradition.

Christian Faith in the Trinity and the Jewish Triad

The Father in the Trinity

The Father in the Trinity is the *Father who is in the Heavens* in Israel's faith and in that of Jesus, who makes him known as such (Jn 1:18) and who prays to him as God in the prayer of the *Shema Israel* (Mk 12:29). From the Christian point of view, there is no break in passing from the God of the Jewish triad to the Father of the Christian Trinity.

However, there is a *radical newness* in the Christian faith because that faith *makes God known through Jesus who knows the Father*, his Father with whom he is One (Jn 10:30).

The Son in the Trinity

The Son in the Trinity is the Presence of God in the world, the *Shekhinah par excellence*, who highlights all the manifestations of the *Shekhinah* in time and space. To affirm that Jesus Christ is the *Shekhinah par excellence* is without doubt to affirm a radical newness in relation to what Israel's Tradition teaches. This newness can be considered to be like a *hiddush*, an innovation or novation that certainly brings about a break with what preceded it, but which confirms the preceding and fulfils it, while manifesting what was hidden in the preceding. The new is radically new because before its manifestation, it is unheard of, unknown. But it is old because it was contained in what preceded it and held it concealed. The *hiddush* is necessarily produced in a living tradition. There is no house of study that does not produce a *hiddush* every day.[1] The Sage is the good scribe who knows how to draw new and old from his treasure (the Torah) (Mt 13:52). The bad scribe is he for whom the new abolishes the old, for whom the New Covenant abolishes the Old Covenant.

The Holy Spirit in the Trinity

It is difficult to find a correspondence between the third element in the Jewish triad, Israel, and the Holy Spirit of the Trinity. Nevertheless, it is possible to suggest a correspondence based on the similarity of the functions of Israel and of the Holy Spirit in the respective contexts. Israel is the people that witnesses, that makes God known (Isa 43:12), and that proclaims not only God's being the Only, but above all and before all else the mystery of God's Unity (Deut 6:4). In order to make God known, one must know God, which is impossible without the free gift of the Holy Spirit (*fourth blessing of the Amidah for ordinary days*, on which *Rashi* on Exodus 31:2 sheds light; *daat, knowledge. Cf texts 47 and 48*). It is the Holy Spirit who makes God and God's *Shekhinah* known in the life of Israel, in Israel's prayer and study. From the Christian point of view, it is the same Holy Spirit who makes God known, who is present in Jesus Christ (*Shekhinah*), in the life of the Church, in its prayer and study.

This correspondence between Israel and the Holy Spirit could enable one to hear two possible messages that are pertinent to Christian faith in the way the *Filioque* in the Nicene-Constantinopolitan *Creed* is understood:[2]

1. *Cf* what Rabbi Yehoshua says in B.T. *Hagigah* 3a.
2. On the subject of the *Filioque, cf* the Cathechism of the Catholic Church, art. 246–248; 264.

- Because it is the Spirit who, directly or through the *Bat Kol*, makes God and God's *Shekhinah* known to Israel, one can say that in the Creed of the Church, resonating with the Jewish Triad, the "monarchy" of God is strictly respected; this does not justify the *Filioque*.
- On the other hand, the Spirit is never separate from the *Shekhinah*. God first begets God's *Shekhinah*, who in Unity is distinct from God. The gift of the Spirit who makes known the *Shekhinah* is what follows (not chronologically) from the begetting of the *Shekhinah*. The Holy Spirit thus depends on the *Shekhinah*. This would justify the *Filioque*.

It seems to me that it is not possible to go further in bringing closer together the Jewish Triad and the Christian Trinity. This impossibility has the advantage of maintaining a distance to Israel in Christian faith and life. What Israel lives in its relationship with God cannot be absorbed (taken possession of) by Christians. The Christian knowledge of God in Jesus Christ cannot be restricted to what has already been experienced and expressed. This Christian knowledge must leave room for the Jewish refusal to see in Jesus the Son of God, *true God from true God, begotten, not made.*

These reservations regarding the relationship with Israel cannot diminish the legitimacy of the proclamation of the Trinity in Christian life and prayer sustained and orientated by the dogmatic expressions of the Church.

It is known that the Christian Creeds, the Symbol of the Apostles in the Western Churches, the Nicene-Constantinopolitan Creed in all the Churches, teach the Trinity through their structure if not through their explicit formulations.[3]

It is remarkable that the Creeds do not explicitly express the Trinity. This reserve is characteristic of Tradition's prudence when it offers reference points for Christian life and prayer. Scripture does not teach the Trinity explicitly. It does not use the word 'Trinity' (*shillush, trias, trinitas*), nor does it use the concept. Thus, the believer must not be disturbed in his or her prayer by a scriptural recourse that would

3. *Cf* H de Lubac, *La foi chrétienne, essai sur la structure du Symbole des Apôtres* (Paris: Aubier-Montaigne, 1970). On the Nicene-Constantinopolitan Creed, *cf* the Catechism of the Catholic Church.

always remain controversial. In its prudence, the Church's Tradition imitates Israel's Tradition. Prayer is not the place for speculation and discussion.[4]

However, let us note that the Church offers the *Credo Quicumque* of *Pseudo-Athanasius* for its prayer,[5] a creed that is technically highly speculative.

Let us look at the text of this Creed. We shall then suggest what is possible to say about it today.

Credo Quicumque (The Book of Common Prayer, Cambridge University Press (Text 99)

> Whosoever will be saved: before all things it is necessary that he hold the Catholic Faith.
> Which Faith except every one do keep whole and undefiled: without doubt he shall perish everlastingly.
> And the Catholic Faith is this: That we worship one God in Trinity, and Trinity in Unity;
> Neither confounding the Persons: nor dividing the Substance.
> For there is one Person of the Father, another of the Son: and another of the Holy Ghost.
> But the Godhead of the Father, of the Son, and of the Holy Ghost, is all one: the Glory equal, the Majesty co-eternal.
> Such as the Father is, such is the Son: and such is the Holy Ghost.
> The Father uncreate, the Son uncreate: and the Holy Ghost uncreate.
> The Father incomprehensible, the Son incomprehensible: and the Holy Ghost incomprehensible.
> The Father eternal, the Son eternal: and the Holy Ghost eternal.
> And yet they are not three eternals: but one eternal.
> As also there are not three incomprehensibles, nor three uncreated: but one uncreated, and one incomprehensible.
> So likewise the Father is Almighty, the Son Almighty: and the Holy Ghost Almighty.
> And yet they are not three Almighties: but one Almighty.

4. *Cf* the first blessing before the Shema in the morning (text 10) and the concealment of Isa 45:7.
5. *Cf* G Dumeige, *La Foi Catholique* (Paris, Orante editions, 1961), 29–31; *Denzinger* 25; *Roman Breviary*, Office of Prime for the Sunday of the Blessed Trinity (breviary before 1984).

So the Father is God, the Son is God: and the Holy Ghost is God.
And yet they are not three Gods: but one God.
So likewise the Father is Lord, the Son Lord: and the Holy Ghost Lord.
And yet not three Lords: but one Lord.
For like as we are compelled by the Christian verity: to acknowledge every Person by himself to be God and Lord;
So are we forbidden by the Catholic Religion: to say there be three Gods, or three Lords.
The Father is made of none: neither created, nor begotten.
The Son is of the Father alone: not made, nor created, but begotten.
The Holy Ghost is of the Father and of the Son: neither made, nor created, nor begotten, but proceeding.
So there is one Father, not three Fathers; one Son, not three Sons: one Holy Ghost, not three Holy Ghosts.
And in this Trinity none is afore, or after other: none is greater, or less than another;
But the whole three Persons are co-eternal together: and co-equal.
So that in all things, as is aforesaid: the Unity in Trinity, and the Trinity in Unity is to be worshipped.
He therefore that will be saved: must thus think of the Trinity.
Furthermore it is necessary to everlasting salvation: that he also believe rightly the Incarnation of our Lord Jesus Christ.
For the right Faith is that we believe and confess: that our Lord Jesus Christ, the Son of God, is God and Man;
God, of the Substance of the Father, begotten before the worlds: and Man, of the Substance of his Mother, born in the world;
Perfect God, and Perfect Man: of a reasonable soul and human flesh subsisting; Equal to the Father, as touching his Godhead: and inferior to the Father, as touching his Manhood.
Who although he be God and Man: yet he is not two, but one Christ;
One, not by conversion of the Godhead into flesh: but by taking of the Manhood into God;
One altogether, not by confusion of Substance: but by unity of Person.

> For as the reasonable soul and flesh is one man: so God and Man is one Christ. Who suffered for our salvation: descended into hell, rose again the third day from the dead.
> He ascended into heaven, he sitteth on the right hand of the Father, God Almighty: from whence he shall come to judge the quick and the dead.
> At whose coming all men shall rise again with their bodies: and shall give account for their own works.
> And they that have done good shall go into life everlasting: and they that have done evil into everlasting fire.
> This is the Catholic Faith: which except a man believe faithfully, he cannot be saved.[6]

In our day, the threats in the introduction and the conclusion of this Creed are difficult to accept. Could the Church modify them, relativize them or simply suppress them?

But before we criticise this *Creed*, it is right to listen to the Christians who attribute great value to it. Among these Christians, I shall refer to Dorothy Sayers and to Cardinal Newman.

Dorothy Sayers[7] is known by the large public because of several subtle and very humorous mystery stories that put her among the best authors of this genre: GK Chesterton, Conan Doyle, and Agatha Christie.[8] She is above all the author of a masterly introduction to Dante's *Divine Comedy.*[9] her translation of this work in rhymed verse is an amazing feat and a masterpiece in its exactness. D Sayers was a fervent Anglican Christian and close to Catholicism. Another work, *The Mind of the Maker*, attests to her Christian and theological culture. In that book, written as a homage to Saint Athanasius (*in gloriam majorem Sancti Athanasii*), D Sayers finds support in the *Credo Quicumque* of *Pseudo-Athanasius*, which has been preserved by

6. http://www.churchofengland.org/prayer-worship/worship/book-of-common-prayer/the-creed-of-sathanasius.aspx
7. D Sayers (1893–1957), *The Mind of the Maker* (New York: Harcourt, Bruce & Company, 1941, Meridian Books, 1956).
8. *Whose Body?*, 1923, whose detective-hero is Lord Peter Wimsey, was the first in a long series.
9. D Sayers, *The Comedy of Dante Alighieri, Hell* (London: Penguin Books, 1949); *Purgatory* (London, Penguin Books, 1953). D Sayers died before she was able to complete her edition of *Paradise*. Her student, Barbara Reynolds, took up D Sayers' preparatory work and published: *Paradiso* (London, Penguin Books, 1962).

the Anglican Church in *The Book of Common Prayer*. She underlines the need to maintain this Creed in the Church's prayer. As regards its introduction and its threats, D Sayers perhaps did not know that Jewish Tradition, when it goes as far as expressions of anathema, does not want to condemn but to threaten pedagogically the person who through lack of faith can communicate his or her incredulity to others.[10]

Cardinal Newman (1801–1890) is so well known that it is not necessary to introduce him. It will suffice for me to quote his praise of *Credo Quicumque.*

John Henry Cardinal Newman, *An Essay in Aid of a Grammar of Assent, (Notre Dame, Indiana: University of Notre Dame Press 1979), Belief in the Holy Trinity*, 117–118 (Text 100)

> It must be recollected especially that the Athanasian Creed has sometimes been called the 'Psalmus *Quicumque*'. It is not a mere collection of notions, however momentous. It is a psalm or hymn of praise, of confession and of profound, self-prostrating homage, parallel to the canticles of the elect in the *Apocalypse*. It appeals to the imagination quite as much as to the intellect. It is the war-song of faith, with which we warn first ourselves, then each other, and then all those who are within its hearing, and the hearing of the Truth, who our God is, and how we must worship Him, and how vast our responsibility will be if we know what to believe, and yet believe not. It is
>
> The Psalm that gathers in one glorious lay
> All chants that o'er from heaven to earth found way;
> Creed of the Saints, and Anthem of the Blest,
> And calm-breathed warning of the kindest love That ever heaved a wakeful mother's breast.
>
> For myself, I have ever felt it as the most simple and sublime, the most devotional formulary to which Christianity has given birth, more so even than the *Veni Creator* and the *Te Deum*. Even the antithetical form of the sentences, which is a stumbling-block to so many as seeming to force, and to

---

10. *Cf* P Lenhardt, *'A l'origine du mouvement pharisien . . . A l'écoute d'Israël, en Eglise'*, 88–89 and notes 94–95.

> exult in forcing a mystery upon recalcitrating minds, has to my apprehension, even notionally considered, a very different drift. It is intended as a check upon our reasonings, lest they rush on in one direction beyond the limits of the truth, and it turns them back into the opposite direction. Certainly it implies a glorying in the Mystery, but it is not simply a statement of the Mystery for the sake of its mysteriousness.

This praise of the *Quicumque* can serve as a conclusion to this stage of our study. For this Creed can be the enthusiastic prayer of the Christian who has listened to Tradition, has studied the sources and assimilated their vocabulary.

Nevertheless, it remains difficult to think that the *Quicumque* is appropriate for everyone. Other ways must always be offered to Christians who prefer vision to reflection, contemplation to speculation. This occurs in an exemplary manner in the catechism *Dieu est vivant* [God is alive] of France's Orthodox Christians.[11]

I shall quote a few passages from this Orthodox catechism.

Catéchisme pour les familles: Dieu est Vivant (Paris: Cerf (1979), 2005) (Text 101)

The Baptism of Jesus[12]

> John saw the Holy Spirit coming down upon Jesus in the form of a dove and remaining upon him. The word 'to remain' expresses that at all times, the Holy Spirit rests upon Him of whom the voice coming from heaven said: *This is my Beloved Son*. That is why Saint Cyril of Jerusalem tells us that in manifesting Jesus as Christ, the baptism of Jesus at the same time reveals to us the mystery of the divine Trinity: for so that there be a Christ, an Anointed—the Son—there must be someone who anoints him, the Father, and someone who is the anointment—the Holy Spirit who rests upon Him. Thus we cannot think of Christ without thinking of the Father and of the Holy Spirit; without them, the word Christ would have no meaning. We cannot confess Jesus as Christ without confessing the (*One*) and only God as God in three persons

11. *Catéchisme pour les familles: Dieu est Vivant [Family Catechism: God is alive]* (Paris, Cerf (1979), 2005).
12. *Catéchisme pour les familles: Dieu est Vivant*, 76–77.

[. . .]. John the Baptist sees the Christ upon whom the Spirit rests, and he hears the voice of the Father calling Jesus *Beloved Son*: John recognised one single God in three persons. The Trinity manifested itself for the first time at the Jordan. That is what the Church describes for us both through the icon and through the song on the feast of the *Epiphany* (or *Theophany*).

Troparion for the Epiphany

Your baptism in the Jordan, Lord, shows us the adoration owed to the Trinity, the voice of the Father bore witness to you, it called you Beloved Son, and the Spirit in the form of a dove confirmed the unshakable truth of that word. Christ-God, You appeared, You illumined the universe, Glory to You.

The Transfiguration[13]

The Transfiguration is a theophany like the baptism of Christ. Like John, the apostles have the revelation of the (One) and only God in three persons: "The Father speaks, the Son shines forth splendor, the Spirit covers with the luminous cloud" (Sermon on the Transfiguration by Saint Peter the Venerable). Through the Person of the Son, man accedes to the knowledge of God in three Persons. *No one has ever seen God; the only Son who is in the bosom of the Father has shown him to us* (Jn 1:18). Jesus Christ is the radiance of the Father, and through him the Holy Spirit acts in the world. When we pray to Christ, he leads us to his Father through the Holy Spirit.

Canticle for Vespers

Joyous light of the holy glory of the immortal Father, Heavenly, Holy, Blessed Jesus Christ. Having come to the setting of the sun, seeing the light of the evening, let us celebrate God Father, Son and Holy Spirit. You are worthy at all times to be celebrated by holy voices, O Son of God who gives Life, and the world glorifies You.

This prayer invites us to adore the Trinity through Christ, Light of the world, Light who gives perfect joy. We are coming

13. *Catéchisme pour les familles: Dieu est Vivant,* 104–105.

to the setting of the sun, we have come to the end of time; the sun will pass, will cease to shine one day, but the true Light, the divine Light will have no decline . . .

In a letter written to the disciples, Saint Peter remembers the transfigured Christ whom he saw with his own eyes on Mount Tabor. The apostle prepares his brothers and us to receive the Light of the day that has no decline: *Until the day begins to dawn and the morning star rises in our hearts* (2 Pet 1:19).

The icon of the Trinity[14]

André Rublev, an iconographer (painter of icons), Russian monk of the 15th century, represented the Holy Trinity. He did not invent the image of the Trinity; rather, he illustrated the account in the Book of Genesis, in which the mysterious three angels visit Abraham [. . .]. By illustrating this biblical text, Rublev does not risk deforming the divine mystery through his personal imagination, for the painters of icons do not invent the representation of God according to their imagination; rather, they are always faithful to Sacred Scripture.

André Rublev made a classical icon on a theme that is often reproduced in churches, a very great work that is both a masterpiece at the artistic level and a testimony to prayer [. . .]. Before this icon, silence imposes itself, as it does before the mystery of the Trinity. Nevertheless, we shall try to approach it through prayer, because for André Rublev this icon is a prayer, a profession of faith, and adoration. If one puts the texts of the *Creed* next to a reproduction of the Trinity, one cannot help but see that the image is composed with the same structure as the confession of faith: '*I believe in one single God*.'

Rublev expresses the Unity both through the similarity of the three angels and through the one circle in which the three persons appear. In the *Creed*, everything concerning the Father is very brief, for He is the unknowable, the one of whom we know almost nothing. In the icon, three quarters of the first angel, the one on the left, is presented; the color of his garment

14. *Catéchisme pour les familles: Dieu est Vivant*, 79–82.

> is very pale, indefinable, almost transparent. The text unfolds as in the icon, stopping the longest with the Son. The second angel is facing us, manifests himself to us most fully. We know many things about the Son, for He became incarnate, made himself known and let himself be seen. His garment is a clear and distinct colour, blue and brown. This expresses the two natures of Christ. The blue symbolizes heaven, the divinity. The brown is the earth, the humanity. Jesus is both God and man. Behind the central angel, a tree rises up; its roots are planted in the earth and its branches reach toward heaven. This is the wood of the cross, which through Christ becomes the tree of life in Paradise [. . .]. With the Holy Spirit, the Creed is again brief and succinct, for little can be said about the third divine Person, who makes us live concretely and historically; the Spirit's activity is always hidden and mysterious. Three quarters of the third angel can be seen, as was the case with the first, The color of his garments symbolizes the force of life. The dominant green expresses youth, the sap of life that causes all things to grow and to exist.
>
> The circle with the three angels is completed and does not close. This circle seems to open onto the chalice that is on the table. The last part of the Creed is dedicated to the Church: this is where the chalice of the Eucharist dwells, and all are invited through baptism to the banquet of eternal Life; and eternal Life is to enter and to dwell at the very bosom of the Trinity.

Some Further Considerations

Our study has not proven the truth of the Christian dogma of the Trinity. Its task was not to prove, but to let the reader experience that the One and Only God of Israel is Father, Son, and Holy Spirit. Listening to Israel's Tradition, this experience was illumined by the numerous debates, the many questions calling forth answers that are always open to new questions. That is why I am now suggesting some further considerations resulting from this study.

I shall present a few texts that let us hear the necessity of an ever open and renewable commitment on the part of Israel (and of the Church) to a relationship with the One (and Triune) God. I am situating these consequences in the context of the fundamental axiom of the trinitarian doctrine offered by Karl Rahner: 'The Trinity that manifests itself within the economy of salvation is the immanent Trinity, and vice versa.'[15]

I will take the liberty to use this axiom while interpreting it as follows: The Trinity, which manifests itself within the economy of salvation, first revealed itself to Israel as Unity; it then manifested itself to other persons and groups chosen in Jesus Christ (Eph 1:4, 14). Those who have seen, heard, experienced and believed, must witness to their experience and their faith. Without their witness, the immanent Trinity would, so to speak, not exist.

I shall indicate five themes for reflection which will make it possible to see how God is, so to speak, dependent on his creatures.

The role of the angels[16]

The paradox of monotheism

In his book *Le paradoxe du monothéisme*, H. Corbin, a specialist in Islamic philosophy and in the mysticism of Shiite Islam, discusses the divine Unity and Shiite angelology, which testifies to this Unity.

In an interdisciplinary course at the Lyon theological faculty, Pierre Gibert finds support in H Corbin's writing, which he sums up as follows:[17] 'Theophany reveals *the One who places Unity at the center of everything*' (11). According to H Corbin, 'one often loses sight of the fact that without angelology, what one so easily calls monotheism sinks into an illusory triumph.'

In fact, H Corbin's teaching on Shiite angelology shows the necessity of basing one's teaching on the testimony of the angels in order to save monotheism from the double danger of monism and pantheism.

For his part, P Gibert discusses the theophany in Isaiah 6; he does so briefly without drawing any teaching from it that is pertinent to the question of monotheism.[18] While awaiting a teaching by a Christian scholar which is of the same quality as that of H Corbin, we must

15. *K Rahner, Dieu Trinité; Fondement transcendant de l'historie du salut, Paris, Cerf, 1971, p. VIII.*
16. H Corbin, *Le paradoxe du monothéisme* (Paris: Editions de l'Herne, 1981).
17. *Le Monothéisme* (Lyon: Profac, 1983), 18.
18. *Le Monothéisme*, 20–22.

rejoice that the interfaith dialogue practiced in our day already makes it possible to receive lessons in theology from Islam.[19]

Nevertheless, let us say that the Tradition of Israel and of the Church teaches the One God. This teaching, as that of Islam, is considered to be the teaching of monotheism. However, we must criticise the way the term *monotheism* is used. In reality, the monotheism of the three great religions should rather be called *henotheism*. This word is defined in the dictionaries of Littré and Lalande in a way that does not correspond with the teaching of the three religions.[20] For henotheism is the doctrine according to which God is One (*eis, unus*) before being the Only (*monos, unicus*). According to the three religions, God is One not only for those who adore God (Jews, Christians, Muslims), but for all human beings. Henotheism is more fundamental than monotheism, which is its consequence. Moreover, it is obviously in opposition to polytheism. However, we acknowledge that the word *monotheism* is understood in a way which in reality is what is meant by *henotheism*. And we accept that it is not possible to uproot the incorrect use of the term *monotheism*.

Let us also say that *henotheism* should be taught as *panentheism*. Panentheism, which is correctly defined by Littré and Lalande, teaches that all things are in God.[21] Judaism without doubt accepts Ben Sirach's expression (43:37): *He is All*, but it teaches that there is an insurmountable gulf between the transcendent Creator and his immanent creature. The creature is nothing in relation to the Creator, but it has a real, distinct existence of its own that is willed by the Creator. Judaism and following it Christianity are aware of this

19. Christian theology should capitalize on H Corbin's rich presentation on 'to be' and 'being'. His presentation is too speculative for me to be able to find inspiration there. I prefer to remain as far as possible in contact with the expression in Sefer Yetsirah and to highlight its concrete nature: God 'made his being of his nothing.' Being is *mammash*, concrete.

20. Littré: 'Worship of one single god by a people that can have its god in opposition to a monotheism, which says that there is only one single God. Henotheism is the starting point of all religions.' Lalande: 'In opposition to monotheism and to polytheism: a form of religion that consists of worship given to one single God, but without excluding the existence of others.'

21. Littré: 'A word created by the German philosopher Krause to express the doctrine claiming that everything is in God, in opposition to pantheism, which claims that everything is God.' Lalande: 'A doctrine according to which everything is in God.'

nothingness of the creature. The two religions must dissipate 'the cosmic illusion' which Hinduism denounces in its doctrine of the 'non-duality-Advaita'.[22] Thus there is an insurmountable distance between the creature and the Creator. The creature who testifies to the Creator cannot profess *monism*.

It is also necessary to listen to Israel's Tradition on the value of the Land of Israel, the Temple and Jerusalem. God who reveals himself to Isaiah in the Temple, by that revelation manifests to Israel that God remains forever holy, transcendent, unknown.

As we have seen, God presents himself as "the Place of the world", and the world is not God's place.[23] This teaching does away with pantheism by affirming the transcendence from on high, so to speak.

Moreover, Tradition teaches that God's presence in the world, in the Land of Israel and more particularly in the Temple occurs by means of a restriction, through a narrowing of God's glory that is the result of God's "love which destroys the established order". Through such an excess of immanence, God makes pantheism so to say impossible from below.

Finally, let us remember that the *Kedushot* we looked at in our study, and very especially the *Great Kedushah*, teach that God is transcendent, unknown, of ineffable Unity, which is proclaimed by Israel (text 38) and by Jesus (text 1). Without these testimonies, henotheism and thus monotheism 'sink into an illusory triumph', to return to H Corbin's expression.

The Holiness of God depends so to speak on the Holiness of Israel

We know *Sifra*, the *midrash halakhah* on the *Book of Leviticus*, which is also called *Torat Kohanim*. Its dialectic highlights the essential: God is holy, separate; the Pharisees, like all Jews, must be holy, imitating God. They must be those who teach the Jews that they are separate. 'God needs human beings.'

Sifra on Leviticus 19:1–2, pp. 86c (Text 102)

---

22. Regarding the Hindu non-duality and the Christian way of referring to it, *cf Un moine d'Occident, Doctrine de la Non-Dualité (advaita-vâda) et Christianisme* (Paris: Dervy Livres, 1982).
23. *Cf Genesis Rabbah* on 28:11, Par. 68 § 9, 777–778. Cf the study of text 30, cf. text 10, the *Yotser blessing*.

> Leviticus 19:1–2: *The Lord spoke to Moses and said: Speak to the whole community of the children of Israel. You will tell them: You shall be holy, for I am holy, I, the Lord your God.*
>
> This teaches that this pericope was said in the *Hakhel* [assembly of the whole people established according to Deut 31:10–13]. And why was it said in the *Hakhel*? Because most of the principles in the Torah depend on it. *You shall be holy.* You shall be separate [*perushim*; Pharisees]. *You shall be holy, for I am holy, I, the Lord your God.* This means: if you sanctify yourselves, I will ascribe it to you as if you had sanctified me; and if you do not sanctify yourselves, I will ascribe it to you as if you had not sanctified me. Or else this means precisely: If you sanctify me, then behold, I am sanctified, and if not, then am I not sanctified? The Talmud says: "For I am holy": I am in my holiness, either when you sanctify me, or when you do not sanctify me. Abba Shaul says: [This is like] the entourage of a king. Just as it is incumbent upon this entourage to imitate the king [so it is with Israel].

The dialectic shows that God is holy in God's own self, independently of Israel. Nevertheless, God needs Israel in order to be known as holy, as unknown.

Abba Shaul's saying was not notated in its entirety. This is characteristic of an oral tradition that does not need to write everything down. In addition, the incomplete notation has the advantage of inviting the person to study, to search for the message's complete and deep meaning. It is certain that the King of kings must be imitated, but he must not be imitated like people imitate a king of the earth, who is imitated out of fear or out of conformism to the point of imitating his vices and of facilitating them. There is here an invitation to reason in an *a fortiori* manner that speaks in contrasts: not to imitate like the world imitates what is evil and for evil. If unfortunately this is done in the world out of servility, how much more must one imitate God and serve God for the good!

God must be imitated to the point of *sanctifying the Name*. This sanctification leads to Unity, as we have seen.

The Unity of God depends, so to speak, on the Unity of Israel

The *Midrash Tannaim*, which David Hoffmann (1843–1921) restored, constitutes a parallel to *Sifre Deuteronomy*. It transmits an ancient anonymous tradition of the Tannaim.

Midrash Tannaim on Deuteronomy 14:1, D Hoffmann edition, 72 (Text 103)

> Deuteronomy 14:1: *Do not cut yourselves* (*hitgodedu*] . . . Do not be of the groups [*agudot*] and the groups [cut off from one another], but all be one single group [*agudah ahat*], as it is said (Am 9:6): *He who constructs his upper chambers in the heavens and who founded his group* [*agudato*] *on the earth.* When Israel as a group does the will of the Place [God], its upper chambers are in the heavens. But if Israel is not as a group and does not do the will of the Place, then if it is possible to say . . . in an analogous way you say (Ps 123:1): *To You I lift up my eyes who are seated in the heavens.* For because of me, You are seated in the heavens. But if I wasn't there, then if it is possible to say . . .

This text invites its listener to complete with fear, trembling and enthusiasm what is not said: If Israel is divided, God is so to speak divided; if Israel did not exist with its eyes turned to God, God would not, so to speak, be King in the Heavens!

The text points to Israel's identification with God. God's Unity depends, so to speak, on Israel and on the Church. The Trinity depends so to speak on the Church.

There is no king without a people

Rabbi Shneur Zalman of Liady, Shaar ha-Yihud, *chapter 7 81b* (Text 104)

> The cause of and the reason for *tsimtsum* [restriction] and for that concealment by which the Holy One, blessed be He!, concealed and hid the vitality [*hiyyut*] of the world is so that the world appear as a separate, autonomous entity; now everyone knows that the goal of the creation of the world is that the royalty of God, blessed be He!, be revealed, for 'there is no king without a people' [*cf Pirkei de-Rabbi Eliezer*, chapter 3].

Commentary by A Steinsaltz, 90:

> 'There is no king without a people': This is a significant definition. There is no king who is king in himself. All that concerns the king is his domination over the people. Royalty is the relationship of the king with the people, and in the absence of the people, there is no way at all for royalty to exist. And thus the revelation of the divine royalty is only [possible] through the existence of the people. The *tsimtsum* is the *restriction* that God imposes on himself, which was understood in two ways:

- *during the ancient period*: God restricts himself, limits himself so as to make himself present in a limited place: the burning bush, the Tent of Meeting, the praying and studying community . . .
- *in the Middle Ages*: from the beginning of the Kabbalah, the restriction is the withdrawal that God imposes on himself within his omnipresence so as to leave space for the creation of the world, for the freedom of the human person . . .

These two understandings are pertinent to our study.

- God restricts himself in order to reveal to Israel (and to the Church) the mystery of Unity (and of the Trinity) in human language.
- God restricts himself so that Israel and the Church might witness freely to the One (and Triune) God through their word and their deeds.

Through his restriction, God hid the vitality of the world. This vitality (*hiyyut*) is the vital force, the life that God is and that God gives to the world in 'ongoing and continuing creation', which Tradition teaches in the established and obligatory morning prayer (*cf* the *Yotser blessing*, text 10).

Israel (and the Church) must witness to the Savior God, savior because God is concealed (Isa 45:15), because God entrusts to Israel (and to the Church) the manifestation of his royalty.

The Lord (*YHWH*), Savior of Israel (and of the Church), is the redeemer of Israel (and of the Church, Ps 19:15) through the ongoing and final redemption that he brings about with the collaboration of Israel (and of the Church).

The Lord (YHWH), Israel's Redeemer, so to speak redeems himself

Mekhilta de-Rabbi Ishmael on Exodus 12:41, 51–52 (Text 105)

> *Exodus* 12:41: *And it came to pass that at the end of the four hundred and thirty years.* [Scripture] declares [*maggid*, teaches] that as soon as the end came, the Place did not delay them for one single instant [bat of an eye]. On the 15th of Nisan, the Place had spoken with Abraham our Father between the divided animals (cf. Genesis 17–18). On the 15th of Nisan, the angels of service came to Abraham our Father to announce good news to him [the birth of Isaac, *cf* Gen 18]. On the 15th of Nisan, Isaac was born (cf Gen 21). And whence do we know that it was the 15th of Nisan when the decree between the divided animals was decreed (*cf* Gen 15:13–14)? Because it is said: *And it came to pass that at the end.* There was an end to all [these events]. And this is what Scripture says (Ex 12:41): *And it came to pass that on that very day all the armies of the Lord went forth from Egypt*; this is talking about the angels of service. Thus you find that every time that Israel is in servitude, the *Shekhinah* so to speak is in servitude with them, as it is said: (Ex 24:10): *They saw the God of Israel and under his feet there was something like a sapphire pavement.* And when they were redeemed, what does Scripture say? (Ex 24:10): *as pure as heaven itself,* and it is said (Isa 63:9): *In their distress, the distress is his.* All I have is the distress of the community; as regards the distress of the individual, whence [do I know it]: The Talmud says (Ps 91:15): *He calls me and I answer him; I am with him in distress.* Scripture says furthermore (Gen 39:20): *Joseph's master seized him* and said (Gen 39:21): *And the Lord was with Joseph.* Scripture says furthermore (2 Sam 7:23): *Is there any like your people Israel, One people on earth* [a people that passes] *before your people whom you have redeemed* [*padita*] *for you, the people* [the *midrash* says: *goy*, people in the singular; the masoretic text has *goyyim* in the plural] *and its God.* Rabbi Eliezer says: "An idol crossed the sea with Israel, as it is said (Zech 10:11): *A rival* [*tsarah*] *crossed the sea and struck into the sea* [giving rise to waves]. What was that idol? The image of Micah (*cf* Judg 17). Rabbi Akiba says (2 Sam 7:23): *Is there any people like your people Israel, a people on earth whom a God went to redeem for himself* [in order to make it] *his people, in order to make it famous and in order to work great and terrible things in*

its favor [before your people whom you redeemed, you, from Egypt]. If it were not written, it would be impossible to say: Israel, if it is possible to say, said before the Holy One, blessed be He: "You redeemed yourself!" And you certainly find that in every place where Israel was exiled, the divine presence [*Shekhinah*], if it is possible to say, was exiled with them. They were in exile in Egypt, the *Shekhinah* was with them, as it is said (1 Sam 2:27): *Thus I revealed myself to the house of your father when they were in Egypt.* They were in exile in Babylon, the *Shekhinah* was with them, as it is said (Isa 43:14): *Because of you I was sent* [the *midrash* says: *shulla'hti* in the passive. The masoretic text has: *shilla'hti*, I sent] *to Babylon.* They were in exile in Elam, the *Shekhinah* was with them, as it is said (Jer 49:38): *I shall establish my throne in Elam.* They were in exile in Edom, the *Shekhinah* was with them, as it is said (Isa 63:1): *Who is this coming from Edom, from Botsra, in brilliant garments?* And when they return in the future, the *Shekhinah* will so to speak return with them, as it is said (Deut 30:3): *And the Lord will return with* [*et*] *your captivity*: Scripture does not say 'will cause to return' [*ve-heshiv*], but 'will return' [*shav*]. And Scripture says furthermore (Song 4:8): *With me* [*itti*] *from Lebanon, my spouse.* But did she really come from Lebanon? Is she not rather in the process of going up to Lebanon? What does the Talmud mean, 'with me from Lebanon, my spouse'? So to speak: 'I and you, we were exiled from Lebanon, I and you will go up to Lebanon.'

Rashi on Deuteronomy 30:3 (Text 106)

The Lord your God will return [*va-shav*] *with your captives.* It should have been written '*ve-heshiv*' [*He will cause to return*]. Our rabbis deduced from this that the divine presence (*Shekhinah*) dwells with Israel in the midst of the distress of exile, if it is allowed to say thus. And when they are redeemed, God makes his own redemption to be mentioned in Scripture through the fact that he returns with them [from exile]. One must say furthermore that the day of the gathering together of the exiles is so great and surrounded by such difficulties that everything will happen as if God himself had truly to seize each person by the hand in order to tear him to his place, as it is said (Isa 27:12): *And you, you will be gathered together one by one, children of Israel.* We also find this concerning the

> gathering together of the exiles from the other nations (Jer 48:47): I will bring back the exiles from Moab [it is written *ve-shavti, I shall return . . .*].

Rashi on Exodus 17:16 (Text 107)

> Exodus 17:16: *the house is on the throne* [kes] *of Yah, the Lord's war against Amalek from generation to generation.* The hand of the Holy One, blessed be He, was lifted in order to swear by his throne that there would be for him eternally war and enmity with Amalek. And why *kes* [throne] and not *kise*? Moreover, why is the Name divided in half [*YH* and not *YHWH*]? The Holy One, blessed be He, swore that his Name would not be complete and that his throne would not be complete until the name of Amalek would be completely obliterated. And when his name is obliterated, the Name will be complete and the Throne complete, as it is said (Ps 9:7): *the enemy is finished, ruins without end*, and this means Amalek, of whom it is written (Am 1:11): *He keeps his anger forever.* (Ps 9:7): *You have turned over cities and their memory has disappeared.* What does [Scripture] say after that? (Ps 9:8): *The Lord* [*YHWH*] *is seated forever*: here the Name is complete. *He makes his throne* [*kise-v*] *firm for judgment*; here, his throne is complete.

Israel must fight against evil. Amalek would not have come if Israel had not sinned. That is what Rabbi Yehoshua and Rabbi Eleazar Hisma taught at Yavne: 'Israel cannot exist without the Torah. Because they had separated themselves from the Torah, the enemy cut them down, for the enemy comes only because of sin and transgression.'[24]

Thus it is necessary to fight against the external enemy and against the internal enemy. God is on the side of the human person in this battle. God wanted the human person to be committed freely at God's side in the battle against evil and in the fulfillment of redemption. God makes himself dependent on the human being's consent.[25]

---

24. *Mekhilta de-Rabbi Ishmael* on Ex 17:8, 176. The masters probably find support for this in the *et* of 'et Amalek arose'. The *et*, which translations suppress, suggests that Amalek arose for reasons that Scripture does not say precisely and does not have to say precisely. It is Tradition's task to give the message through one or several interpretations.

25. God wants to obtain the consent of Moses for the first redemption, for the exodus from Egypt (*cf the Mekhilta de-Rabbi Shimeon ben Yohai* on Ex 3:2ff., text 41), for

God too is concerned by the evil that God let enter into the world by restricting himself in order to leave space for the freedom of the human being. God, together with the human being, submits to suffering (and in Jesus Christ to death) in order to overcome evil and death. The highest witness to the Unity (and to the Trinity) occurs through martyrdom.

At the end of this sketch, I want to say clearly that I shall not discuss the possible consequences of faith in the Trinity in attempts to apply this mystery to the activity of the Church and of Christians. I know some of these attempts, and I respect those people who risk suggesting them. I cannot help thinking that they fall short of what it is possible to express.

In her great book, Dorothy Sayers speaks of the Scalene Trinities, which is to say, 'rickety trinities', which she detects in the literary creations of certain English writers in whom she would like to find a trace of the divine trinitarian resemblance. The theological attempts to implement the trinitarian faith do not go beyond this criticism. These attempts are not 'rickety', but they risk being incomplete, insufficient and not really convincing.

To conclude this sketch, I suggest that its readers unite with Israel in the following prayer:

We beg you, All-Powerful God, protect as the apple [of your eye] those who seek your Unity

[*dorshei yihudkha*].[26]

---

the gift of the Torah (*Sifra* on Lev 26:46; *Leviticus Rabbah* on Lev 1:1, text 42). For the Incarnation, God 'needs' the consent of Mary (Lk 1:38). God waits for Jesus to consent to die (Mt 26:39; Mk 14:36; Lk 22:42).

26. *Anna Be-koah* (Prayer attributed to Rabbi Nehunia ben-Ha-Kana), *Kabbalat Shabbat.*

APPENDICES
Appendix I
To Complete the Study of the Paradox of Creation

'Ongoing creation':
Matthew 19:16–17: (One (only, single) is the Good.
Psalm 119:68: You are good [tov] and doing good [u-metiv], teach me your precepts.

1. First blessing (*yotser*) before the Reading of the Shema in the morning (text 10).
2. Yalkut Shimeoni on Psalm 119:68.
3. Blessings after meals (*Birkat ha-Mazon*)
   Zemirat Leil ha-Shabbat, 'The Rock, of Him we have eaten'.

Job 1:20–22; 2:9–10: [God] must be blessed for evil as for good.

4. *Mishnah Berakhot 9, 5.*
5. The blessing 'The good and the one who does good' The blessing "The Judge (in) truth'. B.T. *Berakhot* 59b-60a:

This too is for the good (Nahum Ish Gam-zo, 2 Chron 28:18-19)

6. B.T. *Taanit* 21a.

Through God's Presence (immanence), God makes known his Absence (transcendence).

7. First blessing *(yotser)* before the Reading of the Shema in the morning (text 10)
8. H de Lubac *on Dei Verbum 3,* in *La révélation Divine* (Paris: Cerf, 1983), 16, 63–65.

God's glory fills the earth. God's glory points to the unknown Place.
From God's (unknown) Place,
God turns his mercy towards the world.

9. Third blessing of the Amidah for the additional prayer (*mussaf*) for Shabbat and feasts (*Kedushah rabbah*) (text 38)

God is present in his creation.
Deuteronomy 4:39: Know today and meditate in your heart: It is the Lord *[YHWH]* who is God *[ha- Elohim]* above in the heavens and below on the earth. There is no other.

No place in the world is void of the Presence (*Shekhinah*).

10. *Pesikta de-Rav Kahana,* Pisk. 1, § 2, 4

There is no place devoid of Him.

11. *Tikkunei Zohar* 57

God is the Place of the world and the world is not God's place.

12. *Genesis Rabbah* on Genesis 28:11, Par. 68 § 9, 777–778
13. Rabbi Hayyim of Volozhyn (1759–1821), *L'âme de la vie* (*Nefesh Hahayyim*) [*The Soul of Life*], Translation into French by Benjamin Gross, Verdier, (Paris:Verdier, 1986), III, 3, 122–123.

The absence and silence of the Creator God.
Deuteronomy 32:52; 1 Sam 2:6: I cause to die and I cause to live.

14. *Sifre Deuteronomy* on 32:39, pp. 379.

Suffering is kind.

15. B.T. *Berakhot* 5a (A Steinsaltz, M Sussmann, A Néher)
16. B.T. Sanhedrin 101a–b.

Appendix II
To Complete the Study of the Paradox of Redemption

The delay of the end and awaiting the end.
The delay of the end.

1. The *Pesah Haggadah* on Genesis 15:13–14, Bloch, 27
2. *Mekhilta de Rabbi Ishmael* on Exodus 12:41, 51;
   Rashi on Exodus 12:41
3. *Genesis Rabbah* on 22:4, Par. 56, § 1, 595.

The prayer of the righteous is not granted immediately (J.T. *Taanit* 3, 4 66c)

4. B.T. *Taanit* 21a
5. Rabbi Moshe Hayyim Ephraim of Sudlikov (died 1800)
   Degel Mahaneh Ephraim
   Li-parashat Ki tetze of Sudlikov

Awaiting the end (Acts 1:6–8)

6. B.T. *Sanhedrin* 97b
7. Maimonides:
   12th principle (Chapter *Helek*)
   Yigdal Elohim
   Creed of Maimonides, the Thirteen Articles of Faith

Appendix III
The Tension in Awaiting the Final Redemption (*Geullah*) and Salvation (*Yeshuah*)

The blessings in the established and obligatory prayer

Abraham's shield (Gen 15:1)

The sending of a redeemer and a savior (*Eucharistic Prayer* II)

1. *The first blessing in the* Amidah *for ordinary days.*

The beginning of redemption (*athalta di-ge'ullah*)

2. *The seventh blessing in the* Amidah *for ordinary days*
3. *B.T. Megillah* 17b;

Rashi on athalta di-ge'ullah.

The prosperity of the Land, a "sign of the end" (Ezek 36:8)

4. *The ninth blessing in the* Amidah *for ordinary days*
5. *B.T. Megillah* 17b
6. *B.T. Sanhedrin* 98a.

The messianic blessings

7. *The blessing for redemption*: the Pesah Seder, Bloch p. 53
8. *The blessings 10, 11, 12, 13, 14, 15 of the* Amidah *for ordinary days.*

The Lord, King who loves justice and right (Ps 33:5)

9. *The eleventh blessing for ordinary days.*

Lk 1:6–8: *The Lord, the God of Israel,* [. . .] *who causes the horn [strength] of salvation to grow in the house of his servant David*

10. *The fifteenth blessing for ordinary days*
11. *the sixteenth blessing for ordinary days*
12. *the seventeenth blessing for ordinary days*

The prayer for the peace of the State of Israel

13. *The evening prayer (the beginning of redemption)*
14. *The morning prayer (the beginning of the growth of our redemption)*
15. *Rashi on B.T. Megillah 17b, athalta di-geullah.*

Appendix IV
To Complete the Teaching on the Return (*Apokatastasis*) of all things to their origin, Which Includes the Repentance (*Teshuvah*) Required after Sin

---

The return to the original Unity

Creation's return to its Creator

The fulfillment of the One and Only Covenant

You remember the act of creating the world . . .

1. Zikhronot (*Remembrances*) *blessing in the additional prayer* (mussaf) *for* Rosh ha-Shanah (Text 29)

God creates the world

- in the literal sense – *pashut* (chronologically): 'in the beginning'
- in the midrashic sense – *midrash* (ontologically): 'by means of a beginning (principle), in view of a beginning'

2. *Rashi* on Genesis 1:1 (Col 1:15–20) (Text 53)

Return [*teshuvah*] to God (Hos 14:2) includes more than repentance after sin.

Teshuvah is created before the creation of the world.

3. *Genesis Rabbah* on Genesis 1:1, Par. 1 § 4, 6 (*cf* Rav Steinsaltz, *L'homme debout* [Paris: Albin Michel, 1999], 69–90).
4. Rav Kook (1865–1935), *Les lumières du retour*, B Gross (Paris: Albin Michel, 1999), 36–41.

The Incarnation precedes (ontologically, not chronologically) reparation for sin.

5. St. Irenaeus, *Ad Haer.* 3, 10, 2; 3, 19, 1
6. Rupert of Deutz (died 1135), *Dictionary of Spirituality*

7. St. Francis de Sales, *Treatise on the Love of God* 2, 4
8. Serge Boulgakov (1871–1944), *Du Verbe Incarné; L'Agneau de Dieu*, (Editeurs réunis (in Russian—YMCA, Paris, 1933) Paris, 1982), *L'Incarnation*, 94–101.

God's love is enveloped in God's mercy (Deut 6:4)

9. *Rashi* on Genesis 1:1 and Genesis 2:4.

The sinful human being's return [*teshuvah*] to God

God, the merciful Father, calls the sinners to return to him through repentance (*teshuvah*).

> **Through the Holy Spirit, God gives Knowledge (*da'at*).**
> **God has pleasure in repentance.**
> **God multiplies forgiveness.**

10. *Fourth blessing in the Amidah for ordinary days*
11. *Rashi* on Exodus 31:3
12. *Fourth blessing in the Amidah in the evening of Motsaei Shabbat*
13. *Fifth blessing in the Amidah for ordinary days*
14. *Sixth blessing in the Amidah for ordinary days.*

Israel's repentance and the redemption of the world

15. B.T. *Sanhedrin 97b-98a*

The joy of heaven and of the repentant sinner (Ps 97:1; Lk 15:16)

16. *Pesikta Rabbati* on Hosea 14:2, *Pisk.* 44 184b–185a
17. Maimonides (1135–1204), Norms for Repentance (*Hilkhot Teshuvah*) 7, 4–8
18. Felix Culpa, Catholic Easter Vigil liturgy.

Appendix V
Excursus on Miracles, Based on Nahmanides (Hidden Miracles and Visible Miracles)[1]

Nahmanides' teaching on miracles, both visible and hidden, seems to me to be essential because I believe it shows the coherence of the Torah, of the Tradition of Israel (and of the Church) regarding an essential reality of faith: God acts invisibly, in a hidden way, and by means of hidden miracles God gives good things to this world that are already over and beyond this world: for Jews the joy of the Torah (*simhah shel torah*) that is experienced in contact with God's Unity and with the Unity of God's Word, the delight of Shabbat (*oneg shabbat*); for Christians, the joy of the Torah, the joy of the resurrection, the joy of attaining the Union with the Father through the Son in the Spirit.

In saying this, I am perhaps only stating the obvious. For already Saint Augustine wrote that the biblical miracles were in no way more

1. Nahmanides' teaching, the importance he continues to have in the present-day life of Israel, and the meaning that visible and hidden miracles have for Jews today need to be better understood. For example, is not the existence of the State of Israel a miracle (visible and/or hidden) for some? The way in which a person prays on the Independence Day of the State of Israel depends on the answer given to this question (*cf* P Lenhardt, 'La fin du sionisme?', in *Sens* [2004]: 134–136).
   The following works should be consulted:
   Rabbi C.B. Chavel, *Rabbi Moshe Ben Nahman* (Jerusalem: Mossad Harav Kook, 1967) (in Hebrew).
   Haviva Pedaya, Nahmanides Cyclical Time and Holy Text (Tel Aviv: Am Oved, 2003) (in Hebrew).
   Moshe Halbertal, *By Way of Truth, Nahmanides and the Creation of Tradition.* Shalom Hartman Institute, 2006 (in Hebrew). *Moshe Idel and Mauro Perani, Nahmanide, exegeta e cabalista,* Firenze, Giuntina, 1998.

marvelous than the miracles that are constantly wrought by nature.[2] However, what is new or what can be new in the perspective of this study is to receive from the Jews, in this case from Nahmanides, the conviction that rain falls in its time; the fact that it falls on the day of Shabbat in the Land of Israel is worked directly by God for his people. Similarly, when a righteous person is healed of an illness, it is a miracle worked directly by God. What appears to be a purely natural phenomenon is in reality supernatural for the believer who benefits from it. The hidden miracle is the reward of faith in God who creates the world and for the practice of the commandments which God stipulates. What is specific to Jews, the practice of the commandments of the Torah, sheds light on the Christian experience of hidden miracles. These miracles are worked for those who believe in Jesus Christ and who keep his commandments (Jn 15:10–12; 17:1–3). Let us say clearly that the Tradition of Israel, like that of the Church, teaches that God works miracles either directly or through the deeds of human persons to whom God has given the ability to work them.

This appendix, which presents the teaching of Nahmanides and his criticism of Maimonides, sets out in an authorized way the Jewish faith in God who works miracles.

I do not think I need to discuss the Tradition of the Church. It shall suffice for me to indicate in a note the documents and works to consult regarding miracles in the understanding of Christian faith.[3]

Many questions arise concerning the nature of miracles, the degree of their authenticity and of the reality that should be attributed to them, concerning the relationship with God that they presuppose, the link they have with the faith and the life of those who benefit from them or who witness them.

---

2. *Huitième homélie s/Jn 2, Isq. Oeuvres de saint Augustin,* 71 (Institut des Etudes Augustiniennes, 1993), 464–473.
3. Regarding miracles in the understanding of Christian faith, the following works can be consulted:
   Xavier Léon-Dufour (ed) *Les miracles de Jésus selon le Nouveau Testament* (Paris: Seuil, Coll. Parole de Dieu, 1977). *Gerd Theissen, The Miracle Stories of the Early Christian Tradition* (Edinburgh: T&T Clark, 1983). And above all John P Meier, *Un certain Juif, Jésus. Les données de l'histoire. II. La parole et les gestes* (Paris: Cerf, Coll Lectio Divina 2005), 475–754 and 1069–1250.

Two main questions arise:

- *The first question* is to know whether an extraordinary event that is inexplicable by means of a verifiable cause, is the result of the activity of a creator God or the product of a magical operation worked by a human being or by some other instance.
- *The second question* is to know whether a miracle worked by God is always of an extraordinary, exceptional nature, by reason of which it is considered to be a miracle. This second question is the more interesting one for our study.

First question

E Urbach expresses it as follows: 'The problem is how to distinguish between miracles, which break nature's barrier and laws and accentuate the absolute power of God, and acts of magic, which likewise appear as wondrous deeds.'[4] E Urbach and G Vermès discussed miracles worked by certain Jewish *healers* or *charismatics*.[5]E Urbach especially underlined the difference that he sees between the miracles of Jesus and those of certain Jewish *healers*.[6] In essence, I shall base what I say on his teaching.

Second question

The basis for what I shall say is *Nahmanides* and *his criticism of Maimonides*. The conflict between these two teachers is situated in the extension of the *debate between Rabbi Ishmael and Rabbi Akiba* on the relationship between Tradition and Scripture.[7] Abraham J Heschel showed how the points of view of Rabbi Ishmael and Rabbi Akiba on miracles are coherent with their interpretations of the Torah.[8]

4. Urbach, *The Sages*, 102.
5. Urbach, *The Sages*, 103–104; G Vermès, *Jésus le Juif* (Paris: Desclée, 1977), chapter 3, Jésus et le judaïsme charismatique, *'Les charismatiques juifs'*, 90–108.
6. Urbach, *The Sages*, 116–118.
7. Nahmanides, *Hassagot on Maimonides' Book of the Commandments. Cf* P Lenhardt, *'L'exégèse (Midrash) de la Tradition d'Israël'; A l'Ecoute d'Israël*, volume 1, 137.
8. AJ Heschel, *Heavenly Torah* (New York, Continuum, 2006), 'Miracles', 65–70.

Rabbi Ishmael and **Rabbi Akiba** at the end of the 1st century CE are known for their disagreement on how to understand the relationship between Tradition and Scripture. Both of them follow their respective teachers. They confirm and complete their teaching, which was given and known before the destruction of the Temple in the year 70 CE.[9]

They agree that "the Torah comes from Heaven" (*torah min ha-shamayim*, Ex 20:22), which is to say that by its origin it is divine, and that "the Torah spoke *in* the language of human beings (*dibberah torah* bi-*leshon bnei adam*)".

For Rabbi Ishmael, by descending from Heaven onto the earth, the Torah not only spoke in the language of human beings; 'it spoke *according to* the language of human beings (*dibberah torah* ki-*leshon bnei adam*)'; it limited itself to the weakness of the human language which it adopted. Thus one must avoid giving too much importance to the details, especially when one wants to find support in Scripture in order to determine the norms of conduct (*halakhah*). Human reason is there in order to fill the gaps, to relativise the repetitions, to explain the anomalies.

For Rabbi Akiba, in descending from heaven, the Torah reached the earth without losing contact with Heaven. The Torah that was written and heard in the fire of Sinai (*cf* Deut 4:36) must be given importance in all its details: apparently superfluous letters and strokes, repetitions, gaps, anomalies, etc.

The two views are assumed by Israel's Tradition. They are considered to be equally legitimate, with a preference given to matters concerning *halakhah*, however, for the rules of interpretation attributed to Rabbi Ishmael.[10]

Maimonides and Nahmanides extend the teaching of their ancient masters, Maimonides along the lines of Rabbi Ishmael, Nahmanides along the lines of Rabbi Akiba.

---

9. Rabbi Akiba, disciple of Nahum Ish Gamzo, retained the essential of the latter's view of the Torah: at Sinai, the written Torah received a significant literalness in all its details. In the Gospel according to Matthew (5:17–21), Jesus shares this view.
10. *Rabbi Ishmael's Thirteen Rules,* which develop those attributed to Hillel, are offered for study in the prayer ritual before the morning liturgy.

These positions taken by Maimonides and Nahmanides are shown by Nahmanides in his criticism of the *Book of the Commandments* by Maimonides.[11]

According to Maimonides, the interpretation of Scripture (*midrash*) uses Scripture as a *support* (*asmakhta*), unless Tradition says clearly for a particular case that the words of Scripture must be heard according to their written literalness (*debarim khi-khetabam*).[12]

In contrast, *according to Nahmanides*, the literalness of Scripture is to be taken as the source and to be interpreted as source and not as support, unless Tradition says clearly for a particular case that it is to be otherwise.

As is the case in the controversy between Rabbi Ishmael and Rabbi Akiba regarding the relationship between Tradition and Scripture, the disagreement between Nahmanides and Maimonides on this relationship conditions their disagreement on how miracles are to be understood.

As is the case for the relationship between Tradition and Scripture, Nahmanides presents the position of Maimonides and criticises it before expressing his own position in his treatise *The Torah of the Lord is perfect.*

Nahmanides, The Torah of the Lord is perfect.

Let us first see what Nahmanides writes in *The Torah of the Lord is perfect* (Ps 19:8). His criticism of Maimonides is stated explicitly in a passage of this text. We shall then complete the study of Nahmanides' position based on other passages in this book and in his commentary on the Pentateuch.

I am translating the text of *The Torah of the Lord is perfect* (into French, and from the French into English) from the Hebrew of Nahmanides, which is concise and elliptical. I will then give a brief explanation.

> The *Rambam* (Rabbi Moshe ben Maimon, Maimonides), may his memory be blessed!, surprises us, for he diminishes the

11. Nahmandies, *Hassagot on Maimonides' Book of the Commandments*, *cf* P Lenhardt, 137.
12. Tradition requires that Scripture be taken literally in certain cases. This in no way implies fundamentalism. *Cf* W Bacher, *Die exegetische Terminologie der jüdischen Traditionsliteratur*, (Leipzig: Erster Teil, 1899), 89.

> miracles [*nissim*] and increases nature [*teba*]. And he says that the miracles [*nissim*] are not permanent, but are only temporary. However, all the marvels [*moptim*] are permanent and persistent. And he himself, may his memory be blessed!, recognised this in his *Letter on the Resurrection of the Dead.*

Maimonides decreases the number of miracles that are recognized as such, those that cannot be explained by natural causes, and increases the number of marvels that can be explained by natural causes or that are only prophetic exaggerations, such as those announced by Isaiah (11:6–7): *The lion and the ox will eat straw . . . the young child will put his hand on the hole of the viper.*

Maimonides

In fact, in his *Letter on the Resurrection of the Dead* Maimonides writes:

> This is what is said about it: 'to do repentance in such a way as to eat straw'!
>
> And here is accomplished what is said (Isa 29:11): *And all the visions have become for you like words in a sealed book.*

After making ironic comments against those who take literally certain expressions in the prophetic announcements and who deserve that the verse in Isaiah (29:11) be applied to them, Maimonides then refers back to his book *Guide to the Perplexed* (2, 29), where he discussed the question of miracles.

Here the main passages from what he says in *the Guide* (2, 29):

> Here is what is said [in *Genesis Rabbah*, Par 5, 5]: Rabbi Jonathan [this must read Rabbi Yohanan] says: God had made a pact with the sea so that it would divide before the Israelites. That is what is written (Ex 14:27): *And the sea returned to its level* [*le-etano*], to its pact [*li-te nao*, to the pact that was concluded] with it. Rabbi Yirmeyah ben Eleazar says: The Holy One blessed be He!, did not only conclude a pact with the sea, but with all that was created during the six days of the beginning. That is what is written (Isa 45:12): *It is I who with*

> *my hands spread out the heavens and who gave orders to their whole army.* I ordered the heavens and the earth to be silent before Moses, as it is said (Deut 32:1): *Heavens, give ear and I shall speak; earth, listen to the words of my mouth.* I ordered the sun and the moon to stand still before Joshua, as it is said (Josh 10:12): *Sun, stop on Gabaon, and you, moon, over the valley of Ayalon.* And in an analogous way the other [miracles] must be explained.
>
> [. . .] We believe that this universe will always exist and perpetually with this nature that God wanted to put there, and that nothing will be changed in it in any way unless in some particularity and through a miracle, even though God has the power to change it totally or to reduce it to nothing, or to bring to an end whatever physical arrangements he wishes; however, there was a beginning, and first there was nothing that existed except God. His wisdom demanded that he produce creation at the moment when he created it, that what he would have produced would not be reduced to nothing, and that its nature not be changed in anything except in some particularities that it would please God [to change], some of which we already know in part, but which in part are still unknown to us and belong to the future. That is our opinion and that is the fundamental principle of our Torah.

Thus, according to Maimonides, God originally wanted to create everything from nothing, including the particular arrangements that God wanted to establish in creation, which is to say the miracles, some of which are already known (the separation of the Red Sea, the sun's standstill), and others remain unknown and belong to the future (the resurrection of the dead).

Other marvels announced by the prophets are not to be considered as miracles, but as emphases that celebrate the newness of the times to come. Thus with the lion who will eat straw and the child who will put its hand on the viper's hole (Isa 11:7–8). Those who take these announcements literally deserve to be told (Isa 29:11): *And all the visions have become for you like the words of a sealed book.*

Returning to Nahmanides, we understand how according to him, Maimonides 'decreases the miracles' and 'increases nature':

On Genesis 17:1: *I am El Shaddai*. The reason why this Name is mentioned now is that the hidden miracles are worked for the righteous by this Name, *to preserve their soul from death and to let them live at the time of famine* (Ps 33:19), as also to deliver them in war from the power of the sword (*cf* Job 5:20), as in the miracles that were done for Abraham and for the Fathers, and according to all [the words] mentioned in the pericope *be-hukkotai* (Lev 26:3–46) and in the pericope *va-yehi ki tabo* (Deut 28:1–69), words of blessings and of curses that all speak of miracles, for it is not according to nature that the rains come for us in their time when we serve God (*cf* Lev 26:4) [. . .], and thus it is for all the promises that are in the Torah. But [let us say that] all these phenomena are miracles, because in all of them the system of the stars [that govern nature] is vanquished, but there is no change in them in the 'custom of the world', as was the case in the miracles done by Moses our Master in the ten plagues, in dividing the sea, in the mannah, in the well, and in other cases, for all these phenomena were marvels that changed nature in a manifest way, and [manifest] miracles were done by the Proper Name [*YHWH*] that He told him.

On Exodus 6:2–3: *God spoke to Moses and said to him: 'I am YHWH. I appeared to Abraham, to Isaac and to Jacob as El Shaddai, but my name YHWH I did not let them know.'* The intention of Scripture [which says that] He appeared with this Name (*El Shaddai*), is that he is victorious over the armies of heaven, doing great miracles for them, except that no change in relation to the order of the world could be observed [in contrast to the miracles worked by Moses our Master]. In famine, he delivered them from death, in war [he saved them] from the attack of the sword (Job 5:20), and he gave them wealth, honor and all good things, exactly according to the assurances given in the Torah [in the passage that speaks] of the blessings and the curses (Lev 26:3–46; Deut 28:1–69).

On Exodus 13:16: Starting with the great manifest miracles, the human being recognizes the existence of the hidden miracles that are the foundation of the whole Torah, for the human being has no part in the Torah of Moses our Master unless he believes that in all that concerns us and in all that happens to us, everything is miracle and nothing is nature and custom of the world, whether it be a matter of the public domain or of the private domain. But [contrary to the opinion that attributes things and events to nature, that he believes that] if he does the commandments, He will let him benefit by his rewards, and if he transgresses them, He will inflict his punishment upon him, all that by the decision of the Most High, as I have already mentioned. The hidden miracles will become manifest to the eyes of the public when one comes to the announcements in the Torah in the context of the blessings and the curses, as Scripture said (Deut 29:23–24): *And all the nations will say: Why did the Lord treat this land in this way?* [. . .] *And one will say: Because they abandoned the covenant of the Lord, the God of their fathers.* In such a way that the matter be manifest to all the nations, that this comes to them from the Lord as punishment. As for the fulfillment of the commandments, Scripture said (Deut 28:10): *All the peoples of the earth will see that you bear the Name of the Lord and they will fear you.* And that again I will explain with the help of the Name.

On Leviticus 26:11: *And I will establish my abode in your midst and my soul will not be disgusted with you.* And now these blessings in their literal sense, these blessings that are numerous and general [that are addressed to the people as a whole], that concern rain, abundance, peace, fertility, are not like the blessings with which He blessed before in summary (Ex 23:25): *And He will bless your bread and your water, and I shall remove sickness from you.* For there He promised that food and drink would be a blessing in such a way that no sickness would affect your bodies, and that consequently the reproductive organs would be whole and healthy, and that we would beget as is appropriate, and that we would live full years, as he said (Ex 23:20): *There will be no woman in your land who aborts nor a sterile woman; I will fill the number of your days.* And that is what He said in the beginning (Ex 15:26): *I am the Lord who heals you.* And the reason why it is thus [the reason why the blessings are divided into two sections] is that [all] the blessings [mentioned in the Torah], even though they be miracles, are hidden miracles of which the whole Torah is full, as I have explained. These miracles even apply to the individual who serves [God]; for when the pious person [*hassid*] observes all the commandments of the Lord his God,

> God [*El*] keeps him from sickness, from sterility, from the loss of a child, and fills his days with good. But these blessings that are in that pericope are general and apply to the people as a whole, and they become effective when all our people will be [made up of] righteous people [*tsaddikim*, *cf* Isa 60:21]. That is why it always mentions the land here, *and the land will give its produce* (Lev 26:4), *and you will dwell in security in your land* (Lev 26:5), *and I shall give peace in the land* (Lev 27:6), *and I shall cause the harmful animals to disappear from the land, and the sword will not go through your country* (Lev 26:6).

Now we have already explained that all these blessings are miracles; for there is nothing in nature that makes the rains arrive [in their time], that makes peace from our enemies come to us, that makes fear of you enter their heart, and that makes a hundred [of them] flee before five [of you], [that all that happens] because of our observance of the decrees and commandments, and that all the opposite [the curses are fulfilled] because we have planted during the seventh year. And although these [blessings and curses in Lev 26] are hidden miracles, because the custom of the world is realized in them, they are manifest [miracles] because they are produced constantly in the whole land. For if there is one [*ehad*] righteous individual who lives and from whom the Lord removes sickness and whose days He fills, that also happens to some bad people; but that the entire land be One and that the people be One, with the rain that always falls in its time, with abundance, security, peace, valor and the defeat of the enemies in a way that has no like in the whole world, this will be known by all that *this came from the Lord* (Ps 118:23). And it is about this that Scripture said (Deut 28:10): *And all the peoples of the earth will see that you bear the Name of the Lord and they will fear you.* And the opposite of that will happen through the curses when the punishments will fall upon [all] the land, for he said (Deut 28:23): *and I will make your heavens to be like bronze*; and punishments of sickness, as he said (Deut 28:59): *bad and persistent diseases*, spoiled and pernicious food.

And the miracle will be manifest because it will constantly be maintained in all. That is why it is written (Deut 29:21): *The future generation, that of your children who will rise up after you, and also the stranger who has come from a faraway land will see the scourges that strike this land and its diseases.* For they will not be surprised about this person upon whom all these evils fall (*cf* Deut 29:19), for it is often thus in the custom of the world among all the nations that these misfortunes happen to one particular person [*ehad*]. They will only be astonished about this land (*cf* Deut 29:21) and that all the nations will ask (*Deut* 29:23): *Why did the Lord treat this land in this way?* For all will see and will know (Isa 41:20) *that the hand of the Lord did this,* and they will say (Deut 29:24): *Because they abandoned the covenant of the Lord, the God of their fathers.*

In short [*ve-ha-khelal*], when Israel is in complete [agreement with God] and when a large number of their affairs are not at all done according to nature, neither for themselves, nor for their land, nor for them as a whole, nor for one individual among them, because the Name blesses their bread and their water, and He removes sickness from their midst in such a way that they do not need a doctor nor to observe any of the ways of medicine, as He said (Ex 15:26): *For I am the Lord who heals you.* (*Nahmanides* [1195–1270] on Gen 17:1; 46:15; Ex 6:2; 13:16).

Bibliography

Aboth de Rabbi Nathan, S SCHCHTER, Vienne-Francfort: Kauffmann, 1887.

Aggadoth du Talmud de Babylone (Ein Yaakov), trad. francaise de Arlette ELKAIM-SARTRE: Editions Verdier, 1982.

ALBECK, Hanoch (ed.), *The Mishna (Shishah sidrei Mishna)*, Jérusalem-Tel Aviv: The Bialik Institute et Dvir, 1988.

ARTHUR GREEN, *Tormented Master. A life of Rabbi Nahman of Bratslav*, The University of Alabama Press, 1981.

BENOIT, P. et BOISMARD, ME, *Synopse des quatre évangiles en français*, tomes I et II, Paris: Cerf, 1965 et 1980.
Synopsis Graeca Quattuor Evangeliorum, Peeters, 1986.

BLACKMAN, Philip (éd.), *Mishnayoth*, New York: The Judaica Press, 1963.

BROWN, F., DRIVER, S. R., BRIGGS, CA, GESENIUS, *A Hebrew and English Lexicon of the Old Testament*, Massachusetts: Hendrickson, 1979.

CARREZ, M and MOREL, F, *Dictionnaire grec-français du Nouveau Testament*, Genève: Labor et Fides, 1992.

COHN, MM, *Nouveau dictionnaire hébreu-français*, Tel-Aviv: Achiasaf, Paris: Larousse, 1994.

Concordance de la Bible, Nouveau Testament, par Jeanne d'ARC, Paris: Cerf, 1983.

Concordance de la Traduction Œcuménique de la BIBLE (TOB), Paris: Cerf, 1993.

ELLIGER, K, and RUDOLPH, W, *Biblia Hebraica Stuttgartensia*, Stuttgart: Deutsche Bibelgesellschaft, 1990.

ELMAN, Yaakov, *Autority and Tradition: Toseftan Baraitot in Talmudic Babylonia*, New York- New Jersey: Yeshiva University Press and Ktav, 1994, 328 p.

EVEN-SHOSHAN, A, *Hamilon hehadash*, 4 volumes, Jérusalem: Qiriat-Sefer, 1985.

HATCH, E, and REDPATH, H, *A concordance to The Septuagint*, Graz: Akademische Druck, 1954.

HEINEMANN, Joseph, *Prayer in the Period of the Tanna'im and the Amora'im: Its Nature and Its Patterns.*(héb.), Jérusalem: Magnes Press, 1964. Trad. inglesa: *Prayer in the Talmud. forms and Patterns,* (Studia Judaica IX), Berlin-New York: Walter de Gruyter, 1977.

HUCK, Albert, *Synopse der drei ersten Evangelien mit Beigabe der johanneischen Parallelstellen*, Tübingen: Mohr, 1981.

HYMAN, A, *Torah haketubah vehamessurah (héb.). A Reference Book of the Scriptural Passages quoted in Talmudic, Midrashic and Early Rabbinic Literature,* Jerusalem: Dvir, 1998, 3 vol.

JASTROW, M, *A Dictionnary of the Targumim, the Talmud Babli and Yerushalmi, and the midrashic litterature,* New York: The Judaica Press, 1992.

KITTEL, Gerhard (ed), *Theological Dictionary of the New Testament (TDNT),* 9 volume, (English translation of GW BROMILEY), Michigan: Eerdmans, Grand Rapids.

KOSOVSKY, Moshe, *Concordance to the Talmud Yerushalmi (Palestinian Talmud)*, Jerusalém: Keter Press, 1982.

LIEBERMAN, S., *Tosefta Ki-Fshutah:A comprehensive Commentary on the Tosefta, Order Mo'ed,* New York: The Jewish Theological Seminary of America, 1962.

MANDELKERN, Solomon, *Concordantiae Hebraicae Atque Chaldaicae* (2 vol.), Graz, Verlagsanstalt, 1975.

MARTINEZ, F G, (ed.), *The Dead Sea Scrolls, Study Edition*, Leiden, New York, Köln: Brill, 1997 (Vol I), 1998 (Vol II).

MELAMED, Ezra Tsion, *Dictionnaire Araméen-Hébreu-Français* (trad. française par Jean-Jacques GUGENHEIM), Paris: Fondation Samuel et Odette Levy, 1996.

Mechilta d'Rabbi Ishmael cum variis lectionibus et adnotationibus editit H. S. HOROVITZ. Defuncti editoris opus exornavit et absolvit I. A. RABIN,(héb), Jerusalém: Shalem Books, 1997.

Midrash Rabbah, ed MIRKIN (hebraico), Tel Aviv: 1977, 9 volumes; Trad. inglesa de FREDMAN and MAURICE SIMON, London: Soncino Press, 1951, 9 volumes.

MUNK, Elie, *Le monde des prères,* Paris: Keren hasefer ve-halimoud, 1993.

NESTLE-ALAND, *Novum Testamentum Graece,* Stuttgart: Deutsche Bibelgesellschaft, 1993.

Pesikta de-Rab Kahana (hébreu), of Bernard MANDELBAUM, New York: 1962; English translation of William G BRAUDE and Israel KAPSTEIN, Philadelphia: 1975.

Pesikta Rabbati (hebraico), of M FRIEDMANN, Wien: 1880; English translation of William BRAUDE, Yale University Press, 1968, vol I et II.

Pirqé Avot et Avot de Rabbi Nathan, of Eric SMILÉVITCH, Paris: Editions Verdier, 1983.

RATNER, Ber, *Midrash Seder Olam*. (héb.) A photostatic Reproduction of Ber Ratner's Edition of the Text, Notes and Introduction. Samuel K. MIRSKY, New York: The Talmudical Research Institute, 1966.

SAMELI, Alexander, *Rabbinic Interpretation of Scripture in The Mishnah*, Oxford: University Press, 2002.

SCHÄFER, Peter (Ed.), *The Talmud Yerushalmi and Graeco-Roman Culture* (TSAJ 71), Tübingen: Mohr Siebeck, 1998, Vol I, 690.

SCHÄFER, Peter et HEZSER, Catherine (Eds.), *The Talmud Yerushalmi and Graeco-Roman Culture* (TSAJ 79), Tübingen: Mohr Siebeck,, 2000, Vol II, 291.

Sefat Emet (hebraico.), Yehuda Aryeh Leib Alter DE GUZ/GER, New York, 1953, 3 volumes; English translation ARTHUR GREEN, *The Language of Truth. The Torah Commentary of the Sefat Emet,* Philadelphia: The Jewish Publication Society, 1998.

Sifre. A tannaitic Commentary on the Book of Deuteronomy, HAMMER, Reuven, Yale University Press, 1986.

Siphre zu Deuteronomium (heb), HOROVITZ and FINKELSTEIN, Breslau: 1935.

Siphre ad Numeros adjecto Siphre Zutta (heb), HOROVITZ, Jerusalem: Shalem books, 1992.

STRACK, HL, STEMBERGER, G, *Introduction au Talmud et au Midrash,* Paris: Cerf, 1986.

STRACK, Hermann L, BILLERBECK, Paul, *Kommentar zum Neuen Testament aus Talmud und Midrasch,* volume 1: Das Evangelium nach Matthäus, München: Beck, 1922.

Talmud Babli, Vilna 1880, 20 volumes, réimpression, Tora la'am, Jerusalem: 1968.

Talmud Yerushalmi, Shiloh, Jerusalem: 1969.

Talmud Yerushalmi, (heb) According to Ms Or. 4720 (Scal.3) of Leiden University Library with Restorations and Corrections, Introduction by Yaakov SUSSMANN, Jerusalem: the Academy of Hebrew Language, 2001.

The Tosefta according to Codex Vienna, with variants from Codex Erfurt, Geniza MSS and Editio Princeps (héb.), S. LIEBERMAN, 5 volumes, New York: The Jewish theological seminary of America, 1962.

Traduction œcuménique de la Bible, édition intégrale, Cerf, Paris, 2000.

WIGODER, G, *Dictionnaire encyclopédique du Judaïsme*, Paris: Cerf, 1993.

Yalkut Shimoni, Salonique 1521–1526, reimpressão por Lewin-Epstein, Jerusalém: 1968–1973.

Index of Jewish Sources

C

D

E

G

H

J

K

L

M

N

P

R

S

T

Y

Z

CPSIA information can be obtained
at www.ICGtesting.com
Printed in the USA
BVHW080318061219
565801BV00001B/97/P

9 781925 612844